MARTIN LUTHER'S Catechisms

The First Article of the Creed, on Creation: Genesis 1 (God Creating the World)

MARTIN
LUTHER'S
Catechisms
Forming • the • Faith

Timothy J. Wengert

Fortress Press
Minneapolis

MARTIN LUTHER'S CATECHISMS
Forming the Faith

Scripture quotations from the New Revised Standard Version of the Bible are copyright © 1989 by the Division of Christian Education of the National Council of Churches of Christ in the United States of America and are used by permission.

Cover image: Photo © Elena Milevska / iStockphoto. Used by Permission
Cover design: John Goodman
Book design: James Korsmo

Library of Congress Cataloging-in-Publication Data

Wengert, Timothy J.
   Martin Luther's catechisms : forming the faith / Timothy J. Wengert.
     p. cm.
   Includes bibliographical references and index.
   ISBN 978-0-8006-2131-5 (alk. paper)
   1. Luther, Martin, 1483–1546. Kleine Katechismus. 2. Luther, Martin, 1483–1546. Grosse Katechismus. 3. Lutheran Church—Catechisms—History and criticism. I. Title.
   BX8070.L8W46 2009
   238'.41—dc22

                                    2008043291

The paper used in this publication meets the minimum requirements of American National Standard for Information Sciences—Permanence of Paper for Printed Library Materials, ANSI Z329.48-1984.
Manufactured in the U.S.A.

13   12   11   10   09   2   3   4   5   6   7   8   9   10

CONTENTS

Images follow page 100

PREFACE

In 1962, I entered seventh grade and began catechetical instruction in the Lutheran Church, which in those days included the memorization of Martin Luther's Small Catechism. Worse yet, I got a double dose, not only having classes on Saturdays at Gracious Savior Lutheran Church in Detroit from my own pastor, Gerald Labuhn, but also during the week receiving instruction at the Lutheran school I attended from Pastor Paul Faust. As much as the sophistication of Luther's explanations were lost on me, the memorization did me good, especially when in 1972, in the midst of a crisis of faith, I recalled the words (without immediately being able to remember where they came from), "I believe that Jesus Christ, true God, begotten of the Father from eternity, and also true Man, born of the virgin Mary, is my Lord." Jesus is my Lord; what a concept!

Beginning in 1974 I taught portions of the Small Catechism to seventh and eighth graders ("Do unto others, as someone has already done to you") until leaving parish ministry in 1989 for the seminary. Yet, as I will argue in the first chapter of this book, I did not really grasp completely the possibilities of Luther's catechisms, especially the Small Catechism, until I held a sixteenth-century copy in my hands. Suddenly, a book, whose use over the centuries had degenerated into a spiritual medicine for young Lutheran teens, took on an entirely new meaning. The Small Catechism is a handbook for the Christian household or a teacher's guide for beleaguered Christian parents, helping them answer the deepest questions and explain the central texts and activities of the Christian assembly. The Large Catechism, that remarkable summary of Luther's own catechetical preaching to his people, serves simple clergy as a guide for all of their teaching and preaching.

It turns out that Luther's Small Catechism does not only help with children's questions. This I learned from my brother, Eugene Wengert, now a retired professor of forestry from the University of Wisconsin. Just before he retired, he sent me an e-mail in which he described how a colleague had asked him about prayer. Does God only answer our prayers if we are good or if we pray with fervent faith? What did my brother do? He remembered a phrase from Luther: "God gives daily bread to all people, even the wicked." From that point he was able to break the back of the legalistic approach to prayer that had plagued the questioner. Our prayers do not earn God's favor!

Despite this precious resource, I am surprised how seldom pastors and Christian educators use either catechism to inform their instruction of adults in sermons and classroom experiences. Several years ago while attending an impressive gathering of folks involved with confirmation instruction, the one thing that troubled me was that no one—outside a few seminary types who are paid to do it—actually used the content of the Small or Large Catechism to inform their faith, their approach to children, or their understanding of Christian education. The Small Catechism is not just the Lutheran equivalent of a political slogan: sounds nice but means nothing. It actually reveals the heart of the Christian life: revealing one's sickness through the commandments, the Great Physician in the Creed, the desperate call to the pharmacy for medicine in the Lord's Prayer, and some of the medicine itself in Baptism, Confession, and the Lord's Supper. There is nothing more to the Christian life! So why is it that so many Lutherans think they have graduated from the catechism given how little they use it?

Indeed, Luther's catechisms are locked in mortal combat with the religion of the old creature—a religion that dominates the American religious scene and makes Luther's approach to Christian instruction look out of date and silly. Lutherans have often fallen off Luther's catechetical horse on one side or the other: Either disturbing the order so that they can make the law and its fulfillment into the real project for the Christian or downplaying Luther's little book to such a degree that students are forced to create their own creeds, engage in service projects, lead worship, and *do* a thousand other things that, whether the catechists intend it or not, obscure God's grace and mercy in Christ and force the students to rely on themselves.

So this book is an invitation, as the old Kellogg's commercial put it, to "taste the catechism again for the first time." It arises out of a

lifetime of experience with the catechisms: as one who learned the
Small Catechism as a youth, rediscovered it as a young adult, taught
it and preached on it as a pastor, and finally ended up teaching it as
a separate seminar at the Lutheran Theological Seminary at Philadelphia, thanks to a suggestion in 1990 by the director of admissions,
Rev. George Keck, and the dean, Dr. Faith Rohrbaugh. A few years
later, as I worked on a translation of the Small Catechism for the edition of *The Book of Concord*, published in 2000, I was approached by
Rebecca Grothe of Augsburg Fortress to provide catechetical material for a new curriculum. When I heard that they were including
a new printing of the catechism, I offered my translation for this
project, but with all of the "extras" that more "modern" versions left
out: Luther's own preface, his prayers, the chart of Bible passages for
the household, and the services of marriage and baptism, as well as
pictures for each part. The result, intended simply for this one curriculum, was the best-selling title in 1994 from Augsburg Fortress
and has come to be used throughout the church. Since then, the
translation has appeared in a variety of places, including in *Evangelical Lutheran Worship*.

As a result of the serendipitous success of this translation, I have
lectured on the catechisms all over the Evangelical Lutheran Church
in America, beginning with the Virginia Synod a decade ago. This
present work is the distillation and expansion of those presentations,
classroom lectures, and several scholarly articles. In somewhat different forms and with permission, the following articles form the basis
of several chapters in this book. Chapter 1 first appeared as "Forming the Faith through Catechisms: Moving to Luther and Today,"
in: *Formation in the Faith: Catechesis for Tomorrow*, Concordia Seminary Publications, Symposium Papers, no. 7 (St. Louis, Mo.: Concordia Seminary, 1997), 25–48; chapter 2 as "Luther and the Ten
Commandments in the Large Catechism," *Currents in Theology and
Mission* 31 (2004): 104–14; chapter 4 as "Luther on Prayer in the
Large Catechism," *Lutheran Quarterly* 18 (2004): 249–74; chapter 5
as "Luther on Children: Baptism and the Fourth Commandment,"
Dialog 37 (1998): 185–89; chapter 7 as "Luther's Catechisms and
the Lord's Supper," *Word and World* 17 (1997): 54–60. The illustrations used throughout this book come from the first authorized edition of the Latin version of *The Book of Concord*, published in 1584,

the only version that contained copies of the woodcuts also used in printings of Luther's Small and Large Catechisms beginning in 1529.[1] I thank Prof. Karl Krueger of the Krauth Memorial Library of the Lutheran Theological Seminary for providing the scans of these pictures.

I owe special thanks to the Lutheran Theological Seminary and its board for the generous sabbatical policy that allowed me time to write this labor of love during the fall of 2007. I acknowledge a great debt to two writers on the catechisms who have paved the way for me: Albrecht Peters, whose five-volume *Kommentar zu Luthers Katechismen*, edited posthumously by Gottfried Seebaß (Göttingen: Vandenhoeck & Ruprecht, 1990–1994), is an inexhaustible resource, and Charles P. Arand, *That I May Be His Own: An Overview of Luther's Catechisms* (St. Louis: Concordia, 2000). The latter gives a far more complete history of the development of the catechisms than the reader will find here. I am indebted to these two authors more than the footnotes can possibly show. I must also thank those candidates awarded the Doctor of Ministry degree from the seminary, whose programs I directed and who wrote projects centering on the use of the catechisms in the parish and thus kept my own interest in uses for the catechisms alive, Pastors William Hurst, Jeffrey Elliott, and Kenneth Ruppar. Thanks are also due to another Lutheran pastor and Ph.D. candidate at the seminary, Christian McMullan, for his work on the index.

If it is true that one learns more about a subject by teaching it than by sitting in a classroom, then this book is rightly dedicated not just to those who catechized me but to all of my fellow students of the catechisms throughout the years, in the parish, in my home, in my classroom, and in gatherings throughout the ELCA.

Timothy J. Wengert
Riverton, New Jersey
21 November 2007

ABBREVIATIONS

BC   *The Book of Concord.* Edited by Robert Kolb and Timothy J. Wengert. Minneapolis: Fortress Press, 2000.

LC   Large Catechism. Translated by James Schaaf, in BC.

LW   *Luther's Works* [American edition]. 55 vols. Philadelphia: Fortress; St. Louis, Mo.: Concordia, 1955–86.

SC   Small Catechism. Translated by Timothy J. Wengert, in BC.

WA   *Luthers Werke: Kritische Gesamtausgabe [Schriften].* 65+ vols. Weimar: H. Böhlau, 1883–.

The Second Article of the Creed, on Redemption: Matthew 27, John 21 [18-19], Luke 23, and Mark 15 (the Crucifixion)

CHAPTER 1

Martin Luther's Contributions to Christian Catechesis[1]

Do we know what Martin Luther's Small Catechism is? I have to confess that I had barely a glimmer of its true significance and potential until 1990, when I first taught a course on Luther's catechisms at the Lutheran Theological Seminary at Philadelphia. As a parish pastor, I acted as if the only, or at least the most important, use for the catechism was with the "hormonally challenged"—that is, with eighth graders in confirmation. That's the way it had been used on me, when I was taught the catechism in seventh and eighth grade by Pastor Paul Faust—imagine having Faust as a teacher for confirmation instruction! Some of us who are old enough remember those days: "Wengert! The second commandment!" "Thou shalt not take the name . . ." "What does this mean?" "We are to fear and love . . ." The trick was to say it in one breath.

Since 1990, I have taken it upon myself to prove to folks throughout North America that Luther's catechisms are more than just strong medicine for young teens. That is *not* to say they should not be used in confirmation instruction. If properly understood, the Small Catechism could revolutionize such teaching. But that is not its only use. My challenge over the years has been to open the curtain of history just a smidgen so that people can rediscover Martin Luther's precious gift to the whole church.

Already among eighteenth-century Lutherans, and certainly on occasion today, there have been grumblings that this book is simply outmoded. The friendly local Christian bookstore in the mall has much more exciting things to offer than a pamphlet that is over 475 years old. Thus, it would do well to consider some testimonials.

In 1993, my daughter was confirmed. Among the presents we
gave her was a ninety-year-old hymnbook belonging to her great-
grandmother, who received it on her confirmation day in 1903. In
the 1970s, as my grandmother's mind was wasting away from the
ravages of Alzheimer's disease, my father would visit her in the nursing home in Milwaukee. There were times when she wouldn't even
recognize him. "Who are you again?" she would ask. He would read
to her from that hymnbook, especially from the Small Catechism
included there. The small type and his rusty German made it difficult. But whenever he made a mistake, she would correct him on
the spot. What will we remember in our dotage? Nursery rhymes?
Advertising jingles? The golden oldies? My grandma remembered
her catechism. "I believe God made me. . . . I believe . . . Jesus is my
Lord. . . . I believe . . . I cannot believe but the Holy Spirit has called
me. . . ." Is there any better confession to have on our lips in the last
hours of our lives? Years later, when my father was suffering from the
same illness, I took his English-language catechism off the shelf, and
as I began to read it, he chimed in immediately.

Or consider a man who had walked five hours in the blazing
African sun. A friend of mind, a German pastor, was for a while in
the 1980s a missionary in Tanzania. In one of his circular letters, he
described how he had flown with some medical missionaries into the
bush for a day. In a God-forsaken area of the country, the plane set
down, and while the medical staff prepared their clinic, my friend set
up his books and pamphlets for sale in the shade of an old, gnarled
tree. Slowly, people emerged from the bush to take advantage of the
free medical treatment. But one man, a Lutheran catechist in a rural
area, had gotten up at the crack of dawn and walked five hours, all in
order to buy a copy of Luther's Small Catechism in his own language.
This book has more to offer than meets the eye because it crosses
boundaries of culture and time to meet the heart. It confesses the
Christian faith in clear, simple language.

Consider, finally, the stirring testimony attributed to Justus
Jonas, one of Luther's colleagues at the University of Wittenberg:
"The Catechism is a little book. It can be bought for less than six
bucks, but six thousand worlds could not pay for it. If the Lutheran
Church had brought no other benefit into the world than that it
made this Catechism known to the people, it would have done

more than all the universities and seminaries on earth."[2] It is all that and more.

What led me to get so interested in the Small Catechism was discovering what a revolutionary thing it was in Martin Luther's own day. In 1990, when for the first time in my life I held a sixteenth-century copy of the catechism in my own hands, I began to redis-cover what that little book could be in our own day. It was not the blue book I had used with Pastor Faust, packed with Bible verses and organized with an eye toward Melanchthon's theological loci, so that it was a full ten times longer than Luther's catechism itself. It was not the small orange booklet, shorn of many of Luther's insightful texts, that I had used with children and adults in parish ministry. It was, instead, a book so different in content, presentation, form, and intent that even today I am not sure I fully comprehend its import. So this chapter is an introduction to the Small Catechism—not so much the one we are familiar with in our congregations or our own experience as eighth graders, but the one Luther produced for "his own dear Germans," those "dear cattle and irrational pigs" for whom he wrote it.

Martin Luther did not invent the catechism. The word, to cate-chize, is a Greek verb (κατηχέω) that described a form of instruction used in ancient schools: *kata* and *echo,* to sound over or repeat again. It denoted a form of oral instruction. The teacher said something, and the children responded: learning by repetition. Paul used the word in Gal. 6:6 to refer to Christian instruction, so that it seemed to become almost a technical word among Christians for how they instructed believers.[3] In 2 Clement 17:1, the word already designated prebaptismal instruction. Indeed, the word passed straight into ecclesiastical Latin (as *catechizo*) and was also associated with instructing catechumens: people preparing for baptism. Augustine, in the fifth century, seems to have coined a noun, *catechismus* (something the Greeks never thought to do), to denote the basic instruction itself, which was given to beginners in the faith.[4] By the Middle Ages, those basics had come to mean learning three things in particular: the Ten Commandments, the Apostles' Creed, and the Lord's Prayer (with other prayers, such as the Ave Maria, often included as well). The medieval equivalent of synod assemblies passed resolutions requir-ing priests to preach on the catechism four times a year and to quiz people in the confessional to determine whether they knew these basics.

This is the catechetical tradition Luther inherited. As an assistant pastor at St. Mary's Church in Wittenberg, Luther preached on the various parts of the catechism both before and after the Reformation began. He assumed that people ought to know the Ten Commandments, the Apostles' Creed, and the Lord's Prayer. In fact, in his writings, when he uses the term *catechism* he is referring not to what we call the Small Catechism but to the three chief parts: the Ten Commandments, the Creed, and the Lord's Prayer. But Luther did more than simply preserve cherished catechetical traditions—he re-formed them, making them evangelical in the process. That reformation reflected in the catechisms constitutes a remarkable gift to the church.

Changing the Catechism's Order

By the late Middle Ages, catechetical instruction was connected to the Sacrament of Penance for two reasons. First, there the priest could determine what the penitent knew of Christian teaching. Second, and more important, the catechetical material itself was geared toward this sacrament and its view of the Christian life moving from contrition (sorrow for sin out of love of God) to confession (of all one's known sins) and finally to works of satisfaction (doing meritorious works to reduce the temporal punishment—*poena*, hence *poenitentia*, penance—that remained for sin after its guilt had been removed). One of the most popular of the late-medieval catechisms was *A Fruitful Mirror or Small Handbook for Christians*, written in 1470 by Dietrich Kolde, an observant Augustinian turned Franciscan. It was printed at least nineteen times before 1500 and another twenty-eight times thereafter.[5]

The structure of Kolde's work demonstrates the power of penance to define Christian life and teaching in the late Middle Ages. Kolde began with a discussion of what must be believed (twenty-two sections) and moved to an explanation of how one must live (twenty-one sections). A shorter part on how to die (three sections) concluded the book. What Kolde stated in this final section goes for the whole catechism: "Every person who holds to [these lessons] can hope to reach heaven." It was a theology of "musts" and laws and merit.

The first part commenced with faith because medieval theology held that one could in a state of sin, through the exercise of the free will, muster up an "acquired faith," that is, an acknowledgment that the church's teachings were true. Kolde moved immediately to the commandments because with such faith comes anxiety over God's judgment. His goal was to bring the individual to contrition. "Keep each commandment, every word, if you would come to see the Lord."[6] As if not content with his lengthy explanation of the Ten Commandments, he added descriptions of the Five Commandments of Holy Church, the seven deadly sins, the nine alien sins, the six sins against the Holy Spirit, and the like, ending with instruction in how to tell whether one is in a state of grace or not and how to confess. Thus, the first part of Kolde's catechism dealt with contrition and confession.

With the first two parts of penance out of the way, the second part of Kolde's work dealt with living the Christian life, that is, doing works of satisfaction. The penance given by the priest was not sufficient; "therefore it is necessary for us to do even more penance."[7] In this part, exhortations to consider Christ's suffering and hear the Mass were coupled with suggestions for prayer at the monastic hours, during meals, and in the morning and evening, as well as the Lord's Prayer and Ave Maria (neither of which Kolde explained) and a prayer of St. Gregory and one to Mary. After prayers came a recitation of good works, under such titles as "seven works of mercy" or "seven gifts of the Holy Spirit." Kolde described the proper Christian behavior for childbearing and child rearing. He even showed how the cloak of Mary, by which she protects the faithful from the wrath of the Son, was woven by good works, such as undergoing conversion, fasting, hearing mass, praying the rosary, feeding the poor, or reciting the Psalter.

We know from Luther's own experience what the effect of such catechesis was. It left people wondering. Have I done enough? Do I really think that what the church teaches is true? Have I confessed all of my sins, or have I held some back? And have I confessed with true sorrow out of love of God or only with a watered-down sorrow out of fear of punishment? Am I leading a Christian life and satisfying God's demands with the proper prayers, fasting, and almsgiving? Christian instruction had become the recipe for spiritual uncertainty.

It is not much different in our day. When I first became a pastor, I had learned my Reformation history well enough. I knew all about Luther's search for a gracious God, about the medieval church's support for uncertainty. But I thought it was old hat. I had yet to realize that what the Reformation tried to confront in the sixteenth century was nothing less than the religion of the Old Adam and the Old Eve in each of us. All of that changed when I went to the hospital to visit a dying woman. The "real" pastor was on vacation, so I, the youth pastor, had to make all the calls that week. As I entered the room of this lifelong Lutheran, I saw her sitting on the edge of the bed in a flannel robe. As her story unfolded, it became clear, although she never said it, that she knew she was dying, and that I knew, and that she knew I knew. Finally, after an awkward pause, she suddenly blurted out: "Pastor, I've tried to live a good life, but I just don't know if I've done enough."

Have I done enough? It is precisely that religion that Martin Luther set out to break in the catechisms. And he did it in one simple stroke. He changed the order. The old order was the order of *musts*—from creed to commandments to prayer. Here is what you must believe; now that you believe, here's what you must do; now that you feel guilty, here are the right words to pray. The new order was the order of baptism: from death to resurrection, from terror to faith and comfort; from commandments to creed, that is, from law to gospel. Here, I wish to call gently into question one of the most cherished parts of present-day catechetical instruction: the service project. We have managed in the church to mix law and gospel by making good works appear to be at the center of our teaching. This kind of thing has led to the widespread notion—I think more than 50 percent in the latest Lutheran poll—that our relation to Christ depends on what we do. It does not. It depends on Christ alone. At least that is Luther's confession.

This shift is already clear in one of the very first pieces of catechetical instruction Luther produced, his *Betbüchlein* (*Personal Prayer Book*) of 1522.[8] That work, more a devotional book than a catechism,[9] was a collection of some of Luther's earlier writings on various parts of the catechism and still shows a strong medieval influence, especially with mention of such things as the seven deadly sins, sins against the Holy Spirit, and so forth, and with an explanation of the Hail Mary. However, Luther knew that he was up to something new and said as much in his preface.

> Three things people must know in order to be saved. First, they must know what to do and what to leave undone. Second, when they realize that they cannot measure up to what they should do or leave undone, they need to know where to go to find the strength they require. Third, they must know how to seek and obtain that strength. It is just like a sick person who first has to determine the nature of his sickness, then find out what to do or to leave undone. After that he has to know where to get the medicine which will help him do or leave undone what is right for a healthy person. Third, he has to desire to search for this medicine and to obtain it or have it brought to him. Thus the commandments teach human beings to recognize their sickness. . . . The Creed will teach and show them where to find the medicine—grace—which will help them to become devout and keep the commandments. The Creed points them to God and his mercy, given and made plain to them in Christ. Finally, the Lord's Prayer teaches all this, namely, through the fulfillment of God's commandments [by faith] everything will be given them.[10]

This insight into the catechism's order, from law to gospel, remained with Luther throughout his life. It matched his insight into baptism and is reflected in the fourth question of baptism. The Christian life itself is marked by the daily drowning of the old creature and raising up of the new by faith alone. The movement from death to life is the movement from law to gospel. As soon as we disturb that order in our teaching, preaching, or parish life, we abandon the gospel itself and leave people on the edge of their beds wondering if they have done enough. That Luther connected the movement from death to life in baptism with the commandments and the Creed comes to full expression in the section of the Small Catechism on confession, added in 1531. There, Luther mentioned the Ten Commandments when instructing the people how to determine what sins to confess. Then, in the final comments on absolution, addressed to the pastor, he noted that "a confessor, by using additional passages of Scripture, will in fact be able to comfort and encourage to faith those whose consciences are heavily burdened or who are distressed and under attack."[11] This gospel, or absolution, was at the heart of Luther's explanation of the Creed.

The movement from law to gospel to prayer using the Ten Commandments, the Creed, and the Lord's Prayer in that order was not the only option considered by Luther to organize catechetical instruction. In the preface to the *Deutsche Messe* (German Mass), published in 1526, Luther not only mentioned the traditional content of the catechism (Ten Commandments, Creed, Our Father) but also proposed an alternative.

> The German service needs a plain and simple, fair and square catechism. . . . This instruction or catechization I cannot put better or more plainly than has been done from the beginning of Christendom and retained until now, i.e., in these three parts, the Ten Commandments, the Creed, and the Our Father. These three plainly and briefly contain exactly everything that a Christian needs to know.[12]

After giving examples of this kind of instruction, Luther then added:

> One may take these questions from our *Betbüchlein* [*Personal Prayer Book*] where these three parts are briefly explained, or make others, until the heart may grasp the whole sum of Christian truth under two headings or, as it were, in two pouches, namely, faith and love. Faith's pouch may have two pockets. Into one pocket we put the part that believes that through the sin of Adam we are all corrupt, sinners, and under condemnation. . . . Into the other we put the part that through Jesus Christ we all are redeemed from this corruption, sin, and condemnation. . . . Love's pouch may also have two pockets. Into the one put this piece, that we should serve and do good to everyone, even as Christ has done for us. . . . Into the other put this piece, that we should gladly endure and suffer all kinds of evil.[13]

Luther then suggested that a child could be encouraged to take Bible verses from the Sunday sermon, memorize them for the parents, and be prepared to put them into one pouch or another.

This second way to organize Christian instruction was used by a wide variety of Christian reformers in the sixteenth century, including by John Brenz in Schwäbisch Hall and later in Württemberg and by Ambrose Moibanus of Breslau.[14] The results were not always successful, since such an approach concentrated on the learning of correct answers and moral behavior—precisely the focus of late-medieval catechesis with its "what must be believed" and "what must be done."[15]

Why, in a preface to a reformed liturgy, did Luther discuss catechisms at all? Aside from the obvious connection between the evangelical reformation of parish worship and instruction in evangelical doctrine, Luther was driven to make the connection in part by a parish pastor, Nicholas Hausmann of Zwickau, from whom the original request for a catechism came. In 1525, Hausmann had appealed to Luther and the elector of Saxony for a visitation of parishes, a worship service in the vernacular, and a catechism for the simple folk.[16] In response, Luther mentioned that Justus Jonas, his colleague, and John Agricola, his student, were working on that very thing. Unfortunately, the death of the elector Frederick and the move of Agricola to Eisleben, where he became rector of the Latin school, intervened to upset Luther's plans. Although Luther then promised to write his own catechism, in 1526 he was content to describe the evangelical options and point to his own *Betbüchlein* as a possible resource.

Into the breach stepped the anonymous compiler of the first "Luther" catechism published in Wittenberg, initially printed in late 1525 and very often thereafter. Entitled *Buchlyn für die Laien und Kinder*, it began with a "lay Bible," that is, the texts of the commandments, the Creed, the Lord's Prayer, the description of baptism in Mark 16, and the Words of Institution.[17] The rest consisted of excerpts from Luther's *Betbüchlein* and other sources from Luther's writings. It concluded with the only section not from Luther, a description of repentance and confession.

Expanding the Catechisms' Scope

The compiler of this little booklet, perhaps Stephan Roth, then student and catechist in Wittenberg and later city clerk in Zwickau, influenced the final shape of Luther's own catechisms in several ways. First, he retained the order of the *Betbüchlein* and excerpted the very section cited above that described the relation of commands, promises, and prayer. Second, he provided texts for baptism and the Lord's Supper. The juxtaposition of Word and Sacrament, crucial for understanding Luther's own work, came from this source. (The *Buchlyn* itself, however, provided explanations from Luther only for the Creed and the Lord's Prayer.) Third, Roth provided a collection of prayers for morning and evening and for mealtimes, some of which passed directly into the Small Catechism.

Thus, to the traditional three parts (Ten Commandments, Apostles' Creed, Lord's Prayer), which constituted a summary of God's word, Luther and his fellow catechists in Wittenberg added the two evangelical sacraments: Holy Baptism and the Lord's Supper. There again, Luther broke new ground or, rather, recultivated some old ground. In his day, the sacraments of baptism and the Lord's Supper were strangely separated from the life of faith, where penance took center stage. In the minds of the people, these other sacraments were, at best, powerful pieces of religious magic, effective in their mere performance. Whether a person understood what was going on—to say nothing of believed it—was not directly relevant to the sacraments' effectiveness. In reaction to what they viewed as a superstitious use of the sacraments, others later made the sacraments empty signs of the people's commitment to God. But Luther rejected both extremes by uniting Word and Sacrament and focusing on the powerful promises in the center of the sacraments and the faith that rests on those promises.

Luther's catechisms give us both the Word and the sacraments: Christ's visible word of promise in water and in bread and wine. By so doing, Luther defined for his readers the essence of the church. Church for Luther was an event, the gathering of believers who hear the Word and participate in the sacraments of baptism and the Lord's Supper. As Philip Melanchthon later formulated in the Augsburg Confession, where the gospel is proclaimed and the sacraments celebrated in an evangelical, gospel-centered manner, there church breaks out.[18] We live in a world where the sacraments and the Word are again being torn apart. Some imagine that only a certain form of church or clergy can confect a proper sacrament— as if the Word of God possessed some guarantee outside its being proclaimed. Others would run the sacraments out of the public worship in favor of seeker services—as if the sacraments were too arcane for Generation X. Luther's catechisms glued the Word and Sacrament together as the heart and soul of the Christian assembly and, thus, of Christian life.

Framing the Catechetical Question

In American Lutheran circles, if someone says, "What does this mean?" those in the know will smile, because that's the question from Luther's catechism that Pastor Faust asked when demanding memory work. There is even a book about Lutherans with that title. Imagine my surprise when, as I paged through a sixteenth-century printing of Luther's Small Catechism, I discovered that this was not Luther's question at all. To ask, "What does this mean?" implies that something is unclear, that there is some deeper, hidden meaning behind the words. Luther's question was simpler by far: "Was ist das?" What is this? Luther's question did not give meaning to the obscure; his question was an invitation to paraphrase. So even though my mother, who probably bought more copies of my translation of the catechism than anyone else, complained about it, I translated the question literally, "What is this?" If I had had the courage, I would have translated it simply "That is to say" or "In other words."

To understand in part why Luther did this, one has to be good at arithmetic. Martin Luther was married in 1525. Because in marriage one plus one often equals three, little Hans was born in 1526. And as Martin Luther was writing the Small Catechism in 1529 (1529 – 1526 = 3), Hans was in his third year of life. Dietrich Kolde's catechisms had more than 50 different questions. The most popular Reformation catechism before Luther's (see below) consisted of 130 questions! Luther's Small Catechism had basically one question—although for a few of the sections he added other questions—six different questions in all. Incidentally, the only place where he asked, "What does this mean?" was for daily bread ("Wie heißt tägliches Brot?"—that is, "How do you define the phrase 'daily bread'?") and for the fourth question in baptism ("Was bedeutet solches Wassertaufen?"—that is, "What does baptizing with water signify?"). In both cases, either some words (daily bread) or an action (using water—which in Luther's day meant dunking a child in a large vat of water) were obscure and required definition.

Martin Luther was the first theologian in one thousand years in the church who witnessed the development of his own children. Little Hans, running around that old monastery turned house and dormitory, asked, "Vatti, was ist das?" "Das ist ein Stuhl." "Was ist das?" "Das ist der Tisch." "Und was ist das?" "Bitte, Hans las' mich in Ruhe. Frag' deine Mutti." "Daddy, what's this?" "A chair." "What's this?" "A table." "What's this?" "Leave me alone; go ask your mother." "Was ist das?" is Hans's simple question. And ours. We forever want to graduate from the simple things to think complicated thoughts and ask complicated questions. Why do we imagine that we are any better or more sophisticated than our simplest children?

Now, as I said, the question "Was ist das?" invites not explanation and meaning but paraphrase. That is why we sometimes find it hard to teach out of the Small Catechism. It does not furnish explanation but simply states the same thing using other words. What is going on here? Let us examine Hans's question and Martin's simple paraphrase. Do you realize what this means? It means that for the most part we have gotten our catechetical dialogue backward in the church. Usually, the pastor asks, "What does this mean? What is this?" and the hapless student provides an answer. But that is not the way it began. It was Hans's question and Martin's answer. And is that not the way it really happens? Talk to any pastor or catechist, and each will tell you that some of the best times in class occurred when the students suddenly became interested in the topic. "Pastor, who made God?" "What is adultery?" "If Jesus is 100 percent human and 100 percent divine, doesn't that make 200 percent?" "Pastor, why did my favorite grandma die?"

When the students ask the questions, the teacher or pastor is forced to confess his or her faith. Pat answers and deft dismissals of serious questions will not wash. And that is what Luther's Small Catechism was. It was not simply an instruction book; it was Luther's personal, direct confession to the Hanses and Magdalenas of his congregation and to today's readers. That is why there's a shift in pronouns in some of the explanations. In the commandments, if Luther simply were paraphrasing, he would have written, "You shall not take the name of God in vain," or "You are to fear and love God." But what did he write? *We! We* are to fear and love God. Luther did not stand over his people shouting at them. "Learn this, believe this, do this . . . or else!" Instead, he stood alongside them and cried: "We, *we* are to fear, love, and trust in God above everything else." And in the Creed where, for example, he could have said, "We believe that Jesus is *our* Lord," according to the pronoun in that phrase of the Apostles' Creed, what did he say? He made it personal: "God created me; Jesus is my Lord; I believe . . . that I cannot believe, but the Holy Spirit has called, enlightened, and made me holy." The catechism contains Luther's true confessions—because here Luther himself is caught in the act of confessing his faith to his own children and fellow believers in Wittenberg.[19]

Measuring the Context:
Why Luther Wrote His Catechisms

Given the plethora of printings for both the *Betbüchlein* and the *Buchlyn fur die Laien und Kinder*, one must seriously ask why Luther bothered to write his own catechism at all. Here three events intervened that are crucial for our understanding the shape of Luther's catechisms from 1529. One event Luther himself referred to in the preface to the Small Catechism: the Visitation of the Saxon Church, begun in 1527. Poor health and the fact that, at Luther's urging, Philip Melanchthon had been elected by Wittenberg's theological faculty as one of the four official visitors (the law professor Jerome Schurff and two officials from the court being the others) meant that Luther was not initially involved in the visitation at all. His brief experience in 1528, however, led him to remark in the preface of the Small Catechism:

> The deplorable, wretched deprivation that I recently encountered while I was a visitor has constrained and compelled me to prepare this catechism, or Christian instruction, in such a brief, plain and simple version. Dear God, what misery I beheld! The ordinary person, especially in the villages, knows absolutely nothing about the Christian faith, and unfortunately many pastors are completely unskilled and

incompetent teachers. Yet they all supposedly bear the name Christian, are baptized, and receive the holy Sacrament, even though they do not know the Lord's Prayer, the Creed, or the Ten Commandments! As a result they live like simple cattle or irrational pigs and, despite the fact that the gospel has returned, have mastered the fine art of misusing all their freedom.[20]

The second event, one that many assistant pastors like Luther have had to endure, was the rather lengthy absence from Wittenberg of St. Mary's head pastor, John Bugenhagen, who was off reforming the city of Braunschweig. As a result, in 1528 all of the preaching duties at the town church fell to Luther, including weekday preaching four times a year on the catechism (the five parts to the lay Bible published in the *Buchlyn*).

The third event, which one can only infer from the sources, had the most profound impact of all on the content of Luther's catechisms. This event arose from the first dispute among students of Luther: the 1527 fight over the meaning of *poenitentia* (translated either "penance" or "repentance") between Philip Melanchthon and John Agricola.[21] Their fight was triggered by the Saxon Visitation. In the summer of 1527, Melanchthon formulated a set of theological articles in Latin to be used by the visitors to train the pastors whom they encountered. After an initial skirmish over the inclusion in the articles of the threefold division of *poenitentia* into contrition, confession, and satisfaction (where satisfaction was made by Christ, not by us), Agricola focused his later attack on Melanchthon's notion that sorrow for sin arises from the law and terror. Agricola insisted that the law leads only to despair and that sorrow for sin must come from the love of God and the gospel. As proof, he cited the stories of Judas and Peter. Judas was condemned by the law and finally despaired and killed himself. Peter, buoyed by the promise given to him in the Upper Room (Luke 22:32), was moved by his love of Christ to repent after his denial.

The dispute came to a peaceful settlement in meetings of all the parties at Torgau Castle in late November 1527. Luther, treading lightly, proposed the compromise that became a part of the German translation of the Visitation Articles published in 1528, the

Instruction by the Visitors for the Parish Pastors in Saxony.[22] Earlier, in a letter to Melanchthon, Luther noted that sinners cannot easily tell what the motivation is for repenting—sometimes it is fear of punishment; sometimes it is love of God. At Torgau, he admitted that one might say that some "general gospel" precedes the preaching of the law, so that a person comes to believe God exists, but such an approach only confuses the common folk. More important, he insisted that preaching of law without gospel led to despair and that preaching of gospel without law led to a false sense of security and abuse of Christian freedom.

All this would not necessarily have led to Luther's publication of his catechisms were it not for the fact that, earlier in November, Agricola published his third, and by far most successful, catechism, *130 Questions and Answers for the Girls' School in Eisleben.*[23] In it, his theory that repentance arose from the gospel and his disdain for the law came to full expression. He wrote:

> Of what does godliness consist? Answer: Of two parts. . . . What are they called? Answer: Word and Faith. . . . There are two sermons: one is of the law and the other is of grace. There have been two preachers: Moses and Christ. . . . What do Moses and the Law preach? Answer: The Law forces and compels people through punishment and torture, that they should love God above all else or else they must die an eternal death. . . . How are Law and Gospel divided? Answer: The Law says, "You are to love God above all things or else you must die." The Gospel says, "I [God] am too high for you, and I simply want everyone to know how much I love you, how favorable I am toward you. But if people want to do what pleases me, they love the brother [and sister], whom they can see, and take care of their needs."[24]

The Ten Commandments were then reduced to an appendix, a list of possible actions for the Christian. Agricola's catechism moved from faith to repentance to good works, much like the medieval catechetical works it was designed to replace. There is some indication that Melanchthon himself had been urged by Georg Spalatin and Stephan Roth to respond. However, he broke off his own work on the commandments once Luther began writing the Large Catechism.

Thus, it was in part Agricola's nascent antinomianism (a charge that Luther himself would make against him ten years later, in 1537) that led Luther to emphasize the centrality of the commandments in the Large Catechism, where 50 percent of the book deals with the Decalogue. It is no accident that he wrote in the preface to the Small Catechism about the way the laity was prone to abuse its Christian freedom. Moreover, the Small Catechism also echoed Luther's compromise in its juxtaposition of the fear and love in the explanations of the Ten Commandments.

Finally, Luther was pedagogically light-years ahead of Agricola when he reduced Agricola's verbose and often aimless 130 questions to a single one: "Was ist das?" (What is this?). Only four times in the Lord's Prayer did he add a second question: "Wie geschieht das?" (How does this happen?) for the first three petitions and "Was heisst das?" (What does this mean?) for the fourth. Only the sacraments contain more questions—four parallel ones, beginning, of course, with "Was ist das?" It was no accident when he stated in the Large Catechism that "because we preach to children we must talk baby talk to them."[25] That included, as we have seen, using simple questions.

Changing the Small Catechism's Function

The clear distinction between law and gospel and the combination of explanations for the Word and sacraments distinguished Luther's catechisms from the others. Then, too, the immediate context out of which the catechisms arose also shaped Luther's work in a unique way: the concern for educating commoners in the basics; a homiletic, paraphrastic style arising out of Luther's own experience; and the rejection of Agricola's antinomianism. However, there was one more factor that contributed greatly to the clarity and longevity of Luther's work. When Luther first began to publish the Small Catechism in January 1529, each section appeared on large, single sheets of paper, to be sold like newspapers and hung up in churches, schools, and homes. Each sheet bore the title "How the head of the household is to present the Ten Commandments [or Creed etc.] to the members of the household."[26]

This orientation toward the household—one might even say the house church, given Luther's comments in the preface to the *Deutsche Messe*—marked Luther's entire catechetical enterprise. Up until Luther, the catechism was most often the business of the priest in the confessional, demanding whether people knew it. Luther had a different approach, as reflected in the titles of the broadsides. These headings were preserved in the booklet form as well. Thus, the Small Catechism actually began its public life as a teacher's guide for confused or beleaguered parents.

To this day, at baptisms we ask parents and sponsors to teach their children the catechism: the Lord's Prayer, the Apostles' Creed, and the Ten Commandments. Now, the hospitals give parents little booklets on hygiene; the doctors' offices give them books on health; and someone is bound to give them some guide to parenting. Then why does the church, in demanding such an awesome responsibility of parents, who at this stage hardly know how to change a diaper, not give them a copy of the Small Catechism—especially one that even has the baptismal service in it—so that the parents can discover what the catechism is so that they might teach their children?

As mentioned above, Luther, as the assistant pastor at St. Mary's, was forced once again in 1528 to deliver the sermons on the catechism during the weekday services, because of the prolonged absence of the head pastor. These sermons became the basis for both the Large and Small Catechisms. In introducing them to his congregation, Luther admonished the parents of Wittenberg's children this way: "Every father of a family is a bishop in his house and the wife a bishopess. Therefore remember that you in your homes are to help us carry on the ministry as we do in the church."[27] Luther proclaimed his Wittenberg bishops in the household as apostolically successful as pastors in their parishes or as bishop in their synods. But then, having called them bishops of house churches, he expected them to do what a bishop is called on to do: preach the gospel to the children. That is, teach them the basics of the faith, namely, the Ten Commandments, the Apostles' Creed, the Lord's Prayer, Holy Baptism, and the Lord's Supper. If they had questions about the meaning of these basics (or if their children asked them questions they could not answer), they could run to Luther's catechism for help.

This appeal, however, was grounded not so much in the priesthood of all believers as in Luther's profound understanding of the
Christian callings in this world. Fathers and mothers were precisely
those called and ordained by God to train their children or to see
that others did it for them. It is no accident that each time Luther
discussed the fourth commandment at length, which after all literally demands something only of children, he insisted on recounting
parental and princely responsibilities, emphasizing in particular their
duty and call to educate their children.[28]

Luther's people were emerging from a religious world where
there had always been two distinctly different kinds of Christians:
the secular ones, destined to follow just the Ten Commandments,
and the *perfecti*, those under a vow and hence in a state of perfection, whose works (by virtue of the vow of chastity, poverty, and
obedience) were always works of supererogation. Luther overturned
that entire scheme by centering the Christian life in baptism and in
everyday affairs.

> If this could be impressed on the poor people, a servant girl would
> dance for joy and praise and thank God; and with her careful work,
> for which she receives sustenance and wages, she would obtain a trea-
> sure such as all who pass for the greatest saints do not have. Is it not
> a tremendous honor to know this and to say, "If you do your daily
> household chores, that is better than the holiness and austere life of all
> the monks"? . . . In God's sight it is actually faith that makes a person
> holy; it alone serves God, while our works serve people.[29]

Nowhere was this new orientation more succinctly expressed than
in Luther's title to what has often misleadingly been called the "Table
of Duties." In fact, Luther called it "The Household Chart [*Haus-
tafeln*] of Some Bible Passages for all kinds of holy orders and walks
of life, through which they may be admonished, as through lessons
particularly pertinent to their office and duty."[30] Even in German,
the language is somewhat stilted. The point, however, was unmistak-
able. Luther took the term used to designate monks and nuns, "holy
orders," and applied it instead to the walks of life of the ordinary
Christian: government, church, and especially the household. Husbands, wives, parents, children, bosses, workers, young people, and

even widows now had standing in God's sight. Luther's sanctification of daily life convicts all societies, even our own, when they utterly fail to appreciate domestic life, workers, and the widowed.

To underscore the point that the Small Catechism was meant first and foremost for the house church, Luther provided other "extras" that are often ignored or misunderstood. To some extent, his approach echoed the earlier work in the *Booklet for the Laity and Children*, which included daily prayers and the like. The Small Catechism provided the basic liturgy (simple prayers for the morning and evening and for mealtimes) and the services of marriage and baptism.[31] To be sure, in the first instance these services were included for the sake of the "ordinary pastors and preachers" who are addressed in the preface and who are, in the booklet form, the other chief recipient of the Small Catechism. However, these two services in fact defined the house church itself, created by God's left hand through marriage and by God's right hand through Holy Baptism. Moreover, Luther's pithy prefaces provided ordinary Christians with pointed admonitions concerning the importance of both liturgies in the light of the gospel and faith. Only the rejection of the exorcism in the baptismal service by some Calvinist-leaning Lutherans in 1580 led to the exclusion of these sections from some, though not all, official versions of *The Book of Concord* and, hence, from later printings of the Small Catechism.

But Luther included still more. Perhaps the greatest surprise in those original catechisms was that they contained pictures. Pictures! To each commandment, article of the Creed, petition, and sacrament the printers attached a picture from the Bible with (starting in 1536) a reference of where to look each up. This meant that a person could use this book—to use the name given to it in the 1580 *Book of Concord*—as the "Laity's Bible." And even if a person were too young to read, he or she could look at the pictures. The link between pictures and the Small Catechism was so strong that the official Latin version of *The Book of Concord* from 1584 contained the standard pictures, used throughout this book. Each portion in the catechism was thus connected to easy-to-remember stories of the Bible. They also provided visual aids for all members of the household. For example, Luther connected hallowing God's name to the preaching of the word of God, which may not seem self-evident.

However, in Luther's catechism, the reader, even the child or adult unable to read, would have seen on the facing page a picture of people in contemporary dress listening to a preacher delivering a sermon. "Hallowed be your name"—that is, "Let the preacher get the gospel right!" What the illustrations demonstrated was that, at least in the minds of Luther's printers (who continued to supply woodcuts throughout Luther's lifetime and beyond), the Small Catechism was much more closely related to that genre of prayer books than most modern versions suggest.

The Small Catechism functioned as a family book, a book for the household. Luther even named it not "Small Catechism" but *Enchiridion*, a Greek word that means handbook. Would that modern translations could be titled *A Handbook for the Christian Household*, because Luther was making the claim that everything a Christian needs for salvation and for everyday life was contained in this book.

Reclaiming Luther's Catechisms for Today's Church

This is what Luther's Small Catechism is—something far richer and more complex than anything many of us had ever imagined. Moreover, what the Small Catechism is convicts our shabby use of it and opens the door to an entirely new way of viewing this little book. First, when our instruction upsets the order of the catechism by moving from "what must be believed" to "what must be done," we will invariably have abandoned justification by faith alone for a mess of late-medieval or antinomian pottage. Recent catechetical material published by an important midwestern Lutheran book concern began with baptism and the Creed ("This is what we believe") and concluded with the commandments ("Now that we believe, this is what we must do"). By this means, the Small Catechism is reduced to a moralism typical of catechetical aids produced since the ages of German Pietism and the Enlightenment but totally destructive of the gospel.

The antinomian approach, also popular today, which Luther later realized was simply another form of legalism, is also roundly rejected by the shape and content of Luther's catechisms. Luther treated the law as law: God's way of ordering our lives and restraining evil and God's way of revealing our sin and driving us to Christ. The pious egotism that searches for correct motives and emotions—"Am I doing this out of fear or love?"—is replaced by a brutally honest assessment of the commandments' demands and a brilliant confession of Christ's victory over sin.

Luther's order—moving from law to gospel to prayer for help—rejects penitential approaches of all stripes. Moreover, it reinforces what in many ways is the center of his catechism: the fourth question on Holy Baptism—what does baptizing with water signify? "It signifies that the old person in us with all sins and evil desires is to be drowned through daily contrition and repentance, and on the other hand that daily a new person is to come forth and rise up to live before God in righteousness and purity forever."[32]

Second, Luther's catechism grounds instruction in the Word and sacraments. There are shocking movements afoot in our own day and age to sever once again the preaching of God's word from the sacraments, opting for liturgies of entertainment, a kind of Christianity Lite. An old pietist heresy, reinforced by the "enlightened" Christianity that has influenced all American forms of Christianity, has obscured both the gathering of the Christian community and the centrality of the Lord's Supper and Holy Baptism in the Christian life. The "Lay Bible" of the *Booklet for the Laity and Children* and Luther's profound explanations of the sacraments counteract this trend. Moreover, it is no accident that the one pastoral problem Luther singled out in both the Large and Small Catechisms was the failure of his people to commune. In the preface to the Small Catechism, he reminds his people and us that Jesus said not, "Neglect this in remembrance of me," but "Do this!"

Third, the catechisms arose out of a serious pastoral crisis revealed in the Saxon Visitation of churches. "Dear God, what ignorance I beheld!" We, too, live in that age. This means that Luther's catechisms, far from being obsolete, provide the very basics that our underinstructed and biblically ignorant people need today. The catechisms have not merely a pedagogical edge but an evangelical, "missional" one as well. At the same time, they were written by a pastor directly involved in the process of evangelizing and catechizing his own people. The continued usefulness of Luther's catechisms stems in part from their origins in his own work at St. Mary's.

Fourth, the catechisms define daily life as the locus of the Christian life. Luther wrote a handbook for the Christian household, not bitter medicine for the hormonally challenged (that is, eighth graders). What Luther's Small Catechism meant for adult Christians can expand the horizons of our modern use. Hans's simple question reveals Martin's profound answers in this teacher's guide for parents. What if our goal were to bring adults to realize that the catechisms were written for them? Then we would use it in premarital counseling, especially with Luther's straight talk on marriage in his preface to the marriage service, and in prebaptismal instruction—perhaps even handing parents a copy of the Small Catechism at the appropriate moment in the service of Holy Baptism. ("Now that we have promised to teach them the Lord's Prayer, the Creed, and the Ten Commandments, here is how Brother Martin can help us.")

Near the end of his life, Luther took a trip to Eisleben to try to solve a dispute between two of his princes, the counts of Mansfeld. After his wife fretted in a letter over his health and safety—and her worries were not unfounded, for he died in Eisleben a few weeks later—Luther tried to allay her fears. He wrote back, "You, dear Katie, read the Gospel of John and the Small Catechism, about which you once said, 'Everything in this book has been said about me.'"[33] What about us? Everything in this book has been said about us, too: the order, from law to gospel; the scope, uniting Word and Sacrament; the question, forcing Luther to confess his faith to us; the context and function, as a handbook of the Christian household. This is not just medicine for eighth graders; it is a simple paraphrase and confession of the basics of the Christian faith.

In his preface to the Large Catechism, Luther challenged the church leaders of his day this way:

> Many regard the catechism as a simple, trifling teaching which they can absorb and master at one reading and then toss the book into a corner as if they are ashamed to read it again. . . . But this I say for myself: I am also a doctor and a preacher, just as learned and experienced as all of them who are so high and mighty. Nevertheless, each morning, and whenever else I have time, I do as a child who is being taught the

catechism and I read and recite word for word the Lord's Prayer, the Ten Commandments, the Creed, the Psalms, etc. I must still read and study the catechism daily, and yet I cannot master it as I wish, but must remain a child and pupil of the catechism—and I also do so gladly.[34]

May God fill our hearts with this same gladness!

The First Commandment: Exodus 32 (the Golden Calf)

CHAPTER 2

Diagnosing with the
Ten Commandments

American Christianity, despite its veneer of conservatism, has suc-
ceeded in reducing Jesus to the Enlightenment's moral teacher,
epitomized in the ubiquitous saw "What would Jesus do?" Lutherans may well be tempted to reduce Martin Luther to a similarly useless role as defender of the ethical status quo. Consider, for example,
the contemporary question of Martin Luther's understanding of the
sixth commandment, especially as it pertains to modern questions
about homosexual relations. What would Luther say? On the one
hand, it is very simple. Luther said little or next to nothing about
such behavior, except to condemn it in the most general terms. Like
others of his age, he was extremely reticent to talk about any sexual
sins, even while he seemed to delight in scatological expressions that
leave modern folks longing for censorship. On the other hand, if
one inquires after Luther's approach to the Ten Commandments
in more general terms, the answer suddenly becomes more complicated and far more interesting for historians and theologians. It is
these complex underpinnings for Luther's comments on the commandments, which resist all attempts at moralization, that are the
subject of this chapter.

It is important to remember that in this chapter we will be
examining only one small piece of Luther's wide-ranging comments
on the Ten Commandments throughout his career, namely, his catechisms, in the hopes of gaining more clarity on Luther's interpretation of the law and the role it played in his overall theology.[1] The
Small and Large Catechisms, standing between expositions in the
Personal Prayer Book of 1522 and *A Simple Way to Pray* of 1535,
have the additional advantage of having been included in *The Book*

of Concord of 1580. Thus, they provide an important confessional voice for Luther's view of the commandments.

The Heart of the Matter Is the Heart

Luther viewed all of God's commandments in the light of the first commandment. It is "to illuminate and impart its splendor to all the others. In order that this may be constantly repeated and never forgotten, you must let these concluding words run through all the commandments, like the clasp or hoop of a wreath that binds the end to the beginning and holds everything together."[2] The recurring "we are to fear and love God" of the Small Catechism sounds the same theme.

However, to say that this commandment is the heart of the matter is not to have said everything, unless one makes clear what this commandment means. In this case, Luther's explanation is one of the most famous in all of his theology: "It is the trust and faith of the heart alone that make both God and idol."[3] Faith, then, is the heart of the matter for all the commandments. Fearing God's wrath and loving God's mercy are simply more traditional expressions that Luther uses to make the same point. To paraphrase an American political campaign slogan, "It's about faith, stupid"; that is, it is about trusting God above all things!

Luther so concentrated on this aspect of all the commandments that he never missed an opportunity to make the same point over and over again. Faith drives us to call upon God, to listen to God's word, to obey God's representatives, to love and care for our neighbor—whether in the person of our children, our parents, our spouse, or the poor. In this regard, Luther—who was only too happy to obey any command of God, no matter how stupid ("If Christ commanded me to eat dung, I would do it," he once said during the debates over the Lord's Supper)—always tied the Ten Commandments to God's purpose and goal for humanity. The Ten Commandments were not given for the same purpose that my second-grade teacher handed out mimeographed "seat work": to keep us busy! Instead, they serve God and the neighbor always by serving faith.

In this regard, one remarkable thing about biblical statements regarding almost any commandment, including the much-debated sixth commandment, is how closely biblical texts links disobedience to unbelief and obedience to faith. The real issue is always faith in God. Indeed, when Luther arrives at the sixth commandment in the Small Catechism, he simply assumes that faith alone is the fulfillment of the commandments: "We are to fear and love God so that we live chaste and decent lives."[4] For Luther, then, the fulfillment of this commandment, like the others, is not simply a matter of external obedience to the letter of the law. Instead, it arises only out of a faith that refuses to worship pleasure or power (in sexual relations or anywhere else) and that worships only the God who gives all good things and protects from all evil. Wherever else the present discussion about sexuality may lead us, it dare not lead us away from faith in the triune God, who creates, redeems, and makes holy.

The Inapplicable Ten Commandments

Luther's creative, open approach to the Ten Commandments has always managed to amaze his heirs. Imagine, if you will, Henry Eyster Jacobs's surprise when he discovered that Luther did not believe Christians had to keep the Sabbath the way late-nineteenth-century American Protestants were insisting. Jacobs, a professor first at Gettysburg College and later at the seminary in Philadelphia and a translator and editor of *The Book of Concord*, had been asked to assemble Luther's comments on the third commandment by his church, the Pennsylvania Ministerium, and by the General Council to which it belonged. The expectation had been that German Lutherans could once again prove how American they had become. The result was the one document for which Jacobs (much to his chagrin) was most well known.[5] Luther did not much care for the fanatical Sabbath-keeping that so preoccupied nineteenth-century American Protestants.

The fact remains: Luther was no biblicist and no fundamentalist. He insisted that Moses' rendition of the Ten Commandments was simply his meditation on the natural law of God written on all human hearts. Those parts that belonged to the specific situation of the Israelites, such as the prologue ("I am the LORD your God who brought you out of the land of Egypt"), had nothing to do directly with Christians. Just because the Bible says it does not mean it applies willy-nilly to us! There are two striking examples of this refreshing attitude toward the commandments in the Large Catechism.[6] The third commandment is the most obvious case. This commandment, Luther wrote, does not apply to Christians literally. We do not keep the Sabbath holy. In Luther's day, everyone worked on Saturday, which is literally the Sabbath. Moreover, Luther did not think much of the notion that Christians had simply transferred Saturday observances to Sunday. Not only did he have Jesus' own behavior to back him up, but he also introduced here the concept of an "external matter" (related to the term *adiaphora*). The important thing for Luther was that this law did not apply to Christians in a literal sense at all![7] God's word makes every day of the week holy for a Christian, Luther stated, so what is all the fuss about Saturday or Sunday?[8]

Of course, this does not mean to say that, for Luther, this commandment had no use at all. He had far too much respect for Scripture as God's word to say that! What he noted in his explanation, however, should give all obsessive-compulsive legalists pause. First, he underscored just how important it is to give people a day off, especially laborers, a piece of good news for workers in every generation.[9] Second, he insisted that the way to apply this commandment to the Christian is to concentrate on its original purpose—not only to provide real rest for tired bodies but also to give people an opportunity to rest in God's word.[10]

On this second point, his treatise *On Good Works*, from 1520 (actually an extended commentary on the Ten Commandments), is particularly insightful.[11] Faith itself frees a person from works and provides the proper way to keep the Sabbath not only externally but also in the heart. Thus, God wants people to come together precisely to hear this word that frees us from work. Of course, this means that the biggest Sabbath breakers, in the Large Catechism's view, may be found not simply among those who lie dead drunk in taverns on Sunday morning (or not so drunk at sporting events, in fishing boats, or God knows where else), but precisely among those preachers whose sermons are paeans to the law and legalism and among those hearers who listen to a year's worth of good sermons with no appreciable effect![12]

The other place where Luther (cavalierly!) dismisses one of the Ten Commandments comes with the ninth and tenth and applies more directly to the current discussion of sexuality. Luther notes at the outset that God gave these two commandments, which forbid coveting, to Moses precisely because otherwise the Israelites would have conceived of the commandments as applying only to externals and not to the heart, that is, to faith.[13] Christians have the advantage that they understand this from sermons on the commandments delivered by Jesus (in the Sermon on the Mount) and by Paul (in Romans 7).

However, there is another reason the tenth commandment in particular did not apply directly to Luther and his readers: Germany had no slaves and did not treat women like chattel—both things this commandment clearly assumes by lumping wives and servants in with the cattle.[14] What a remarkable turn of a text! Here Luther, who more than anyone focuses theology on the Word alone (*solo verbo*), dismisses a clear word of God as inapplicable for social reasons. We have no slaves, and women are not property! Now, unlike some of the Bible's modern readers, who read everything in the light of their own desires and dreams, Luther did not gloat at this point. "So many lands, so many customs," he happily proclaimed in his preface to the Marriage Booklet, citing an adage familiar to his readers.[15] When it comes to questions of social behavior, Luther glorified neither the social relations of the Bible nor those of his own time. Instead, he took both into consideration as he attempted to find his way as a Christian preacher in this world. We are still not to covet, but we dare not mistake the social situation reflected in the commandment for our own and thereby glorify one or the other.

The Expanding Commandments

If Luther was capable of showing how commandments did not apply literally to his situation, he was equally willing to expand the commandments far beyond their original scope so that they did apply to his own age. This was the work not of a literalist or a legalist but of a believer, who assumed that the clearest statement of God's law written on each human heart came in the Ten Commandments.

This approach of expanding the commandments, to some extent already present in the exegetical tradition,[16] began as a reaction to what Luther viewed as a particularly pernicious way to interpret the biblical text—one that infected the late-medieval church. Already, church fathers had distinguished between commandments of God, which were required of all people, and counsels, which a Christian could freely follow. In Thomas Aquinas's *Summa*, the three chief counsels became poverty, chastity, and obedience, and they were best followed by bishops or those under a vow—monks and friars. Such people, by virtue of their vows, were in a status of perfection, and because they fulfilled the counsels, their "works of supererogation" produced more merit than those who simply followed the Ten Commandments.[17]

When Luther challenged this myth in the 1520 *Treatise on Good Works*, he delighted in repeating for each commandment that there were enough works in each to keep a person busy for a lifetime.[18] There was no need to look for better things to do; the Christian believer simply did not have the time.[19] This same theme ran throughout the Large Catechism as well. The first commandment revealed all kinds of idols—not simply graven images but common "gods," such as money or fame, and more complicated ones, such as works righteousness. In the latter case, Luther even warned readers (simple parish pastors) that this might be too complicated for the children to understand.[20] The second commandment, which Luther rightly assumed was meant for the law court, also included every other case where God's name is used for nothing.[21] The third commandment included not simply taking a day off or refraining from work on Saturday but also showing respect for God's word and preaching—something that many congregations in conflict (and sometimes their pastors) fail to do. The fourth commandment included not only parents but also all their helpers (schoolteachers, pastors, employers, and the government).[22]

Explanations of the other commandments showed a similar generosity. Following Jesus' lead in the Sermon on the Mount, Luther was quick to point out all the other ways human beings have invented for killing people that do not involve physical death. The sixth commandment included decency and love and forbade lust. The seventh included not just pickpockets but bigwigs and other "arm-chair robbers."[23] The eighth again went far beyond Moses' concern for the law courts and included simple lying, gossip, and a host of other sins found especially, but not exclusively, in parish life today, too. As will become clear below, Luther also included the positive aspects of these commandments: caring for the neighbor, the spouse, the neighbor's property, and the neighbor's reputation.

"But Instead"

One always must make remarkably important decisions when translating from one language to another. Most translations of the Small Catechism take Luther's little word *sondern*, which occurs in eight of the explanations to the Ten Commandments, to mean "but." Thus, the explanation to the second commandment that I had to memorize as a child ran like this: "We are to fear and love God, so that we do not curse, swear, use witchcraft, lie, or deceive by his name, *but* call upon him in every trouble, pray, praise, and give thanks." However, the word *sondern* is a much more powerful word in Luther's thought, nearly the German equivalent of *immo*, one of Luther's favorite Latin adversatives.[24] It is etymologically related to the English *sunder* (as in "What God has joined together let no man put asunder"), and it still has that meaning as a verb in German. Thus, the current translation renders this powerful word "but instead."

In fact, the *sondern* in Luther's explanations points to a second important way in which he expanded the commandments: by including both "shalt nots" and "shalts." Every word of God—whether a command or a promise—always implied for Luther its opposite. In the case of the commandments, every prohibition ("Do not use my name in vain!") implied that God wants us to put that name to good use ("in every need" we are to call on God in prayer, praise, and

thanksgiving).[25] Commandments were not busywork; they revealed
the best God intends for humanity.

At the same time, every positive command implied that there
was something God did not want human beings to do. Thus, for
Luther, the third and the fourth commandments (which are positive:
"Keep the sabbath" and "Honor your parents") implied prohibitions
("Do not despise the Word or preaching" and "Do not despise parents or superiors"). We often forget what Luther did not: that failure
to honor God's word or other people in their God-given offices is not
neutral; it always implies despising.

This same juxtaposition of positives and negatives in the explanations of the Small Catechism also arise in the Large Catechism.
Thus, again on the second commandment, he wrote (par. 63): "God
at the same time gives us to understand that we are to use his name
properly, for it has been revealed and given to us precisely for our
use and benefit." To paraphrase Philip Melanchthon (and not at all
out of line with the one thing he learned most fully from Luther):
"To know the commandments is to know their benefits."[26] Luther
could not imagine giving commandments for any other reason than
to benefit humankind. It is, after all, an enormous benefit to learn
how God uses the law. God uses all the commandments to promote
the life of the creation and to restrain evil (the first way God uses
the law). Thus, in comments on the first commandment, Luther
noted that God, "who overflows with pure goodness," uses creatures
who "are only the hands, channels, and means through which God
bestows all blessings."[27] But God also forces humanity to come face-
to-face with its sin (the second way God uses the law). In all of this,
however, Luther's point was that God uses the law on humanity, not
the other way around, and uses it to benefit life on earth and life
with God.

Moses' Good Order

Many people read the Ten Commandments like a phone book,
where each entry has equal value. Luther did not. Not only did he
see the first commandment as the most important and as expressed
throughout all the commandments, but he also argued that there

was a distinction to be made among the remaining commandments as well.[28] They were given in descending order of importance. Thus, honoring one's parents or others in authority had an automatic limit: the first three commandments. When parents or other authorities command things that contradict faith in God, prayer, worship, or God's word, Christians must not obey.

In a similar fashion and by virtue of their office, parents and other authorities may "break" the commandments that follow the fourth. Thus, governments wield coercive power (breaking the fifth commandment either literally in capital punishment or in more general ways through imprisonment). They (or the church) can pronounce a couple divorced (breaking the sixth commandment and the dominical command in Matt. 19:6). They can expropriate property through taxes or the right of eminent domain (breaking the seventh commandment). And they can even speak evil of persons, as when a judge pronounces a sentence (breaking the eighth commandment). This last example was a particularly sensitive one for Luther, who took the time to explain to his congregation why he could speak evil of the pope and not break this commandment—he did it by virtue of his office as teacher of the church![29]

Before jumping to the conclusion that such an approach to the commandments would foster tyranny, it should be noted that such lawbreaking was allowed only to the office of good governing (or good parenting, where even moderate discipline also "breaks" the commandments). Luther described such governance not only in his appeals for good schools but also in his explanation to the fourth petition of the Lord's Prayer. Those in authority were to see to it that bread got placed on their subjects' tables. The special place of the fourth commandment could never (in Luther's theology anyway) excuse selfishness or tyranny.[30] However, the office of parent or magistrate or pastor did wield authority. Otherwise, there would be the tyranny of anarchy. Against those who thought that taxation was evil or that no judge could be a Christian, for example, Luther's discovery of the Mosaic ordering of the commandments spoke a firm "No!"

Moreover, in a reverse of this process but consistent with it, Luther also realized that the poor and the oppressed had a special place in the commandments. This became especially clear in his explanation to the seventh commandment. There, Luther (interpreting the commandment positively) insisted that we are to see to our neighbors' bodily needs. What if we or the government do not do it? The poor will cry to God (the only authority higher than neighbor or prince in Luther's world), and God will assuredly hear their cry. Then look out! There will be hell to pay.[31] In the explanation of the Lord's Prayer in the Large Catechism, Luther wrote that the poor also cry to God for daily bread, and he expected that their exploitation would be punished: "How much trouble there is now in the world . . . on account of daily exploitation and usury . . . on the part of those who wantonly oppress the poor and deprive them of their daily bread! This we must put up with, of course; but let those who do these things . . . take care lest this petition of the Lord's Prayer be turned against them."[32]

Moses' Silence and Luther's Loquacity

In one interesting case involving the fourth commandment, Luther had expressly more to say than Moses.[33] Moses, after all, simply commanded obedience to parents, with no questions asked. In our own day, no one could in good conscience simply tell children to obey their parents no matter what. So, too, Luther made two important exceptions. First, as we stated above, he realized what many teachers of the commandments forget: that Moses gave the commandments in order of importance. This meant that Luther expressly excluded the first three commandments, which have to do directly with one's relation to God, from any discussion of obedience to parents or others in authority. For someone who had to defy pope and emperor and whose fellow Christians had even perished for confessing the gospel, this was no small matter. Luther wrote, "If God's Word and will are placed first and are observed, nothing ought to be considered more important than the will and word of our parents, provided that these, too, are subordinated to God and are not set in opposition to the preceding commandments."[34]

Second, Luther realized that—despite Moses' silence—he had to say something about parental responsibilities for children (and governmental responsibilities for their subjects). Even though his brief paraphrase of the fourth commandment in the Small Cate- chism omitted such material, his preface to that work mentioned such responsibilities expressly, as did the Large Catechism.[35] Luther had good authority to go on; Paul himself had done the same thing in Ephesians. Moreover, every chance he got to talk about such mat- ters, Luther urged all authorities to support the education of chil- dren—something one could easily apply directly to today, where the importance of schools and learning is still under attack. Thus, he closed his comments on the fourth commandment in the Large Catechism with these words: "Everyone acts as if God gave us chil- dren for our pleasure and amusement, gave us servants merely to put them to work like cows or donkeys, and gave us subjects to treat as we please, as if it were not concern of ours what they learn or how they live."[36] He concluded, "We really must spare no effort, time, and expense in teaching and educating our children to serve God and the world."[37]

Moses' Loquacity and Luther's Silence

Luther did not always say as much as his text does about certain sins. In the Small Catechism, his explanations of both the first and the sixth commandment break the normal paraphrastic nature of the work. Here, two negative commandments ("No other gods!" and "No adultery!") received only positive explanations: "We are to fear, love, and trust in God above all things," and "We are to fear and love God so that we lead chaste and decent lives, and each love and honor his or her spouse."[38]

The Large Catechism makes clear that Luther had plenty to say about the breaking of the first commandment. However, the explanation of the sixth commandment contained very few specif- ics. Luther first generalized the command to mean (explicitly) the dishonoring of another person's marriage partner. He pointed out that Moses particularly mentioned adultery because the Jewish peo- ple married young, virginity was commended, and prostitution and lewdness were not tolerated. After complaining about the "shameless mess and cesspool of all sorts of immorality and indecency," Luther pointed out that this commandment forbade not only outward acts but "every kind of cause, provocation, and means."[39] He immediately mentioned that sins against this commandment included not helping one's neighbor in preventing unchastity. What he did not do was provide descriptions of such activity. For Christians in a society bombarded with implicit and explicit talk about sex, Luther's reserve may come as a breath of fresh air. Luther was interested not so much in titillating the reader with a salacious list of sexual sins as in getting to the heart of the matter. "You shall not commit adultery" demanded faith in God ("we are to fear and love") and love of neighbor ("leading chaste and decent lives . . . love and honor one's spouse"). Our addiction to casuistry finds a refreshing reversal here, replacing lists of the "works of the flesh" with the fruits of the Spirit, against which there are no laws.

The Commandments and "Self-Chosen Spirituality"

For Luther, the commandments were important not only for what they said but also for what they did not say. When he translated Paul's strictures against certain kinds of pious (and misguided) behavior in the congregation at Colossae, Luther rendered their problem in Colossians 2:23 as "self-chosen spirituality," an expression particularly pertinent for any society infected by "new-age" religion. Against such stuff (Luther had in mind especially the monks), Luther placed the Ten Commandments and other portions of Scripture that give a much better idea of what God has in mind for humanity.[40]

In contrast to modern attempts to bless or condemn the status quo, Luther described as good works those things that have good biblical precedent. Otherwise, without a word of God, as in the case of how one receives communion or other such matters, the conscience would remain uncertain. Luther was properly suspicious of folks who thought they could soothe people's consciences by their own authority. When their last day comes, the devil will laugh at them if they say, "Well, Dr. Luther told me this was all right."[41] Of course, the devil is also not impressed if someone says, "They did it this way in Moses' day."[42] Certainty comes from the sure encounter

with God's word in the real world, where all the hard decisions arise
out of God's word for the sake of the conscience.

In nearly every explanation of the Ten Commandments in the
Large Catechism, we hear echoes of such strictures against "self-
chosen spirituality," especially on the first three commandments
and nowhere better than in the first commandment.

> There is, moreover, another false worship. This is the greatest idola-
> try that we have practiced up until now, and it is still rampant in the
> world. All the religious orders are founded upon it. It involves only that
> conscience that seeks help, comfort, and salvation in its own works and
> presumes to wrest heaven from God. It keeps track of how often it has
> made endowments, fasted, celebrated Mass, etc. It relies on such things
> and boasts of them, unwilling to receive anything as a gift of God, but
> desiring to earn everything by itself or to merit everything by works of
> supererogation, just as if God were in our service or debt and we were
> his liege lords.[43]

On the second commandment, Luther insisted that "the greatest
abuse [of God's name] . . . is in spiritual matters, which affect the
conscience, when false preachers arise and present their lying non-
sense as God's Word."[44] On the third, he railed against "the whole
swarm of clerics in our time who stand day after day in the church,
singing and ringing bells, but without keeping a single day holy,
because they neither preach nor practice God's Word, but rather
teach and live contrary to it." One only wonders what Luther might
say about the self-chosen spirituality filling "Christian" airwaves and
bookstores in our day!

Bucking Social Convention

Luther not only criticized his age's spiritual pretensions, but occa-
sionally criticized social conventions as well. We have already heard
him criticize the wanton abuse of the poor and the failure of parents and rulers alike to education their children properly. Although
Luther was a child of his times and often could not see sins that seem
so plain to us today or, alternatively, could propose solutions that

seem far-fetched or even draconian 475 years later, he was an astute observer of social trends (as every pastor must be) and often allowed the commandments to lead him into new areas of social critique. Taking just one example: one of the most surprising things about Luther's explanation of the sixth commandment is the equality that Luther implied throughout. Despite his use of texts from Genesis 2 and 3 and Ephesians 5 in his marriage service (where even there he toned them down through his use of the promises in Genesis 1 and 2) and his use of Colossians 3 and 1 Peter in the Household Chart, where his point was to prevent women from being fearful,[45] Luther never mentioned any inequality in his exposition of this commandment.[46] Even his paraphrastic explanation in the Small Catechism seems to imply (for both the 1959 and the 2000 editions of English translations of *The Book of Concord*) that Luther had men and women equally in mind.

This outspoken equality was no small feat for a thinker whose entire social life was marked by inequalities. However, for Luther, such social inequalities had little or nothing to do with the marriage bed or the household. Here, the man and woman could fulfill God's blessing of the first couple. Rather than read inequality into the text (and thereby interpret Moses using [deutero-]Paul), Luther followed the lead of Paul in 1 Corinthians 7 (a passage he had interpreted at length in 1523)[47] and viewed the partners in a marriage as equals. Whatever else sexual relations were to him, they were not an invitation to exploitation.

> Thus God wants to guard and protect every husband or wife through this commandment against anyone who would violate them. However, because this commandment is directed specifically toward marriage as a walk of life and gives occasion to speak of it, you should carefully note, first, how highly God honors and praises this walk of life, endorsing and protecting it by his commandment. . . . [God] has established [marriage] before all others as the first of all institutions, and he created man and woman differently (as is evident) not for indecency but to be true to each other, to be fruitful, to beget children, and to nurture and bring them up to the glory of God. God has therefore blessed this walk of life most richly, above all others, and, in addition, has supplied and

endowed it with everything in the world in order that this walk of life might be richly provided for. Married life is no matter for jest or idle curiosity, but it is a glorious institution and an object of God's serious concern.[48]

In the same vein, Luther concluded his remarks on this commandment by stressing mutual cherishing and love in marriage.

This commandment requires all people not only to live chastely in deed, word, and thought in their particular situation (that is, especially in marriage as a walk of life), but also to love and cherish the spouse whom God has given them. Wherever marital chastity is to be maintained, above all it is essential that husband and wife live together in love and harmony, cherishing each other wholeheartedly and with perfect fidelity. . . . Under such conditions chastity always follows spontaneously without any command.[49]

In between this positive assessment, Luther took direct aim at the "self-chosen spirituality" of monastic and clerical celibacy. Men and women of all walks of life, who have been created for it, should be found in marriage. While allowing for some God-given exceptions (unsuitability or the gift of chastity outside marriage), Luther insisted that the rest could not resist these "natural inclinations and stimulations" of their own flesh and blood.[50] This he contrasted, in no uncertain terms, to the "papal crowd" of monks, priests, and nuns who, while abstaining from acts of fornication, had hearts filled with unchaste thoughts and evil desires: "In this regard, even if the monastic life were godly, still it is not in their power to maintain chastity."[51] His reason for giving such warnings, Luther stated, was to foster a desire for marriage among the young and thereby lessen the "filthy, dissolute, disorderly conduct that is now so rampant everywhere."

This attitude had direct consequences for his pastoral and personal life. On a pastoral level, he fought for a woman's right to divorce an abusive husband, despite the Wittenberg City Council's fear that if that became grounds for divorce, no one would be left married in Wittenberg.[52] On a personal level, he fought tooth and nail against the lawyers of his day by attempting (without success, it turned out) to bequeath his estate to Katie Luther. Despite the best efforts of his colleagues, Justus Jonas and Philip Melanchthon, Luther's will was not followed.[53]

An "Ought" Never Implies a "Can"

Why did Luther spend half the text of the Large Catechism talking about the commandments? Part of the reason may have had to do with the proto-antinomian talk of his former student John Agricola.[54] However, Luther also provided an even more important answer to that question in the rest of the Large Catechism. The chief function of the law is not to show us an easy way to heaven, which (with a little hard work) we can reach, but to show us our sin—how infinitely far we are from heaven, God, and our neighbor (who is Christ in our midst!).

The Christian life, like baptism, goes from drowning to rising, from death to resurrection, from confession of sin to forgiveness. Thus, Luther wrote against those who thought that the commandments were easy and who therefore imagined that they had time to fulfill God's counsels: "They fail to see, these miserable, blind fools, that no one is able to keep even one of the Ten Commandments as it ought to be kept. Both the Creed and the Lord's Prayer must come to our aid, as we shall hear later. Through them we must seek and pray for help and receive it continually."[55]

Whatever else we do with the Ten Commandments, we can do nothing worse than to ignore their main function: to put the old creature in us to death by showing our sin and driving us to the one place where there is help—the gospel. It is in Jesus Christ alone, who is the mirror of the Father's heart and whom the Holy Spirit reveals to us by faith alone, that we have our hope. This is not a matter of declaring a wrong right or of telling others to buck up and try harder. This is a matter of the gospel alone, that good news of forgiveness, life, and salvation that comes to us freely, as God's gracious word in Christ.

This brings us back to the beginning, to the heart. Luther began and concluded the commandments with their clear demand for faith. He found the commandments' fulfillment only in the work of the Holy Spirit, who through the Word gives faith in Christ and thus, in him, fulfills all the commandments. The commandments—all of them—keep their rightful place in Christian theology only when they are in first place—that is, as the word of death that drives us inexorably to our crucified and risen Lord Jesus. Whatever else we may want to say about morality, perhaps we need most of all to remind one another of this.

The Third Article of the Creed, On Being Made Holy: Acts 2 (the Coming of the Holy Spirit at Pentecost)

CHAPTER 3

Luther's Down-to-Earth Confession of Faith

Jaroslav Vajda, an English-speaking, Lutheran hymn writer of the 1960s and 1970s, described how, as he worked on one of his most famous eucharistic hymns, "Now the Silence," it occurred to him that in the Lord's Supper Christians experience the Trinity in the reverse order from the baptismal formula (Father, Son, and Holy Spirit). From this insight arose the last lines of the hymn, "Now the Spirit's visitation, now the Son's epiphany, now the Father's blessing, now, now, now." Whether Vajda, whose life and faith were steeped in solid Lutheran teaching and preaching, realized it or not, his inspiration may well have come in part from Martin Luther, who wrote these words in the Large Catechism.

Luther's "Reversed" Trinity

Martin Luther concluded the section on the Creed in the Large Catechism with these words:

> For in all three articles God himself has revealed and opened to us the most profound depths of his fatherly heart and his pure, unutterable love. For this very purpose he created us, so that he might redeem us and make us holy, and, moreover, having granted and bestowed upon us everything in heaven and on earth, he has also given us his Son and his Holy Spirit, through whom he brings us to himself. For, as explained above, we could never come to recognize the Father's favor and grace were it not for the LORD Christ, who is a mirror of the Father's heart. Apart from him we see nothing but an angry and terrible judge. But neither could we know anything of Christ, had it not been revealed by the Holy Spirit.[1]

So we have the Trinity in reverse: the Holy Spirit makes known the Son, whom we could not know and who is in turn the mirror of the Father's heart.[2]

It is not that Luther had something against the order "Father, Son, and Holy Spirit," but in the Large Catechism he did something quite unexpected. In fact, a quick comparison to the three sets of sermons on the catechism preached by him in 1528 shows that he never mentioned this reversal to his Wittenberg congregation. Nevertheless, perhaps not unlike our poet, something must have occurred to Luther as he looked back at his exposition of the Creed in the Large Catechism and tried to summarize his main points. Already, in a 1528 sermon, he had mentioned that whereas the Father's work of creation and the Son's work of redemption were completed, the Holy Spirit's work would continue to the last day, according to his reading of the Creed, since the Holy Spirit makes us holy now in the church by forgiving sin and will in the end raise us and give us eternal life. Indeed, in one series of sermons, he even described the Holy Spirit's work not as making us holy (another insight that came to him while writing the catechisms) but as giving eternal life, which begins with forgiveness here and now (as he wrote in the Small Catechism on the Lord's Supper, "Where there is forgiveness of sins, there is also life and salvation").

This means that, in part, the reversal in Luther's description of the Trinity grew out of his understanding of the Holy Spirit's work. Despite its relative neglect among Lutherans (and Luther scholars!),[3] Luther's doctrine of the Holy Spirit holds the key to his Trinitarian theology. This does not, however, mean (as some might imagine) that Luther would be more at home in a Pentecostal or Charismatic prayer meeting than in a Lutheran worship service. Indeed, Luther's understanding of the Holy Spirit, as we shall see below, unmasks the very *un*spiritual approach of those who, to use Luther's description of Andreas Karlstadt, have swallowed the Holy Spirit, feathers and all. Moreover, Luther's pneumatology is so radically contrary to all that American religion holds dear that it is a wonder that contemporary Lutherans still allow children to read—to say nothing of memorize—the Small Catechism's explanation for the third article of the Creed. It is the Holy Spirit who turned Luther's (and turns our) understanding of the Trinity on its head. Luther already captured this reversal when he wrote for the Small Catechism the shocking first words for his paraphrase of the third article: "I believe that I cannot believe."

In some ways, too, Luther's highlighting of the third article of the Creed arose from his close association with the Gospel of John, where Jesus promises the *paraclete*, a Greek word for "advocate" (as in a court of law), which Luther and Philip Melanchthon (somewhat mistakenly) translated as "comforter." At the very time he was preaching on the catechism in 1528, he was also delivering Saturday sermons on John, beginning with chapter 16. Thus, on June 27, 1528, Luther reached John 16:12-15 and Jesus' promise of the Holy Spirit.[4] Because the Holy Spirit makes us believers, it stands to reason that we experience the Trinity backward—that is, only when we believe in Christ (the work of the Holy Spirit, who does not indulge in self-revelation but in revealing the Son) do we pierce God's judgment and arrive at mercy.

Beginning the Trinity with the Holy Spirit—defined as Luther did ("I believe that I cannot believe")—means that any attempt to begin Trinitarian theology with God in God's own being and self or in creation or—amazing to say—in Christ will fail, because there is no way to account for the human element in the very theologian (to say nothing of everyone else) who decides to begin there. To the claim "I think I'll start with God" comes the harsh query of Romans (and Job): "Who are you to answer back to God?" To begin theology in anthropology (the nature of the human being), however, will also fail because it inevitably glorifies the human being. As Lutheran theologian Oswald Bayer has demonstrated, "Faith seeking understanding" (the famous phrase of Anselm: "fides quaerens intellectum") always means "*my* faith seeking *my* understanding" ("Fides mea quaerens intellectum meum") and makes us the center of the universe.[5] But the Holy Spirit, who contends with the world concerning sin (John 16:8-10), wrests a different confession out of us—"I believe that I cannot believe"—and thus destroys *both* an anthropocentric and a theocentric beginning point for theology and instead insists and drives us to join our voices with possibly the best theologian of the New Testament (Mark 9:24), the father who cried out, "I believe; help my unbelief!" and another, equally good theologian, who cried, "The good that I would do, that I do not; the evil that I would not,

that I do" (Rom. 7:14-25), and "No one can say Lord Jesus except by
the Holy Spirit" (1 Cor. 12:3).

Yet this is no evangelicalistic theology, which is grounded in the
same triumphalistic anthropology of the "I" ("*I* have decided to follow Jesus—no turning back, no turning back"). Instead—I believe
that I cannot believe—the reversed Trinity of Luther's catechism
holds in tension the human inability in theology, faith, and life with
the Holy Spirit's work through Word and Sacrament. Thus, the third
article is the actual turning point of the entire catechism, because
everything that follows (prayer, sacraments, living in community)
is precisely what happens to unbelievers when the Holy Spirit acts
on them, turning our "Woe is me!" into "Kyrie, eleison" (Lord, have
mercy!). The theology of the reversed Trinity is literally "theo-logy"
(God word), where God speaks to us and by speaking declares the
old new, the sinner a saint, the unbeliever a believer—God's service
to us, not ours to God.

At the same time, this reversed Trinity means that theology cannot begin with knowledge or principles but must begin with experience. Moreover, this experience is not just some epistemological
principle (that is, a theory about how human beings understand and
experience things) but is an actual experience of the gospel (that is,
with the Holy Spirit using the unconditional word of promise placed
in the mouth of a human being). Thus, the reversed Trinity also
undermines all forms of mystical, "self-chosen" spirituality, as the
author of Colossians (2:23) puts it. The experience of God is not a
mystical ladder climbing into the divine energy (no more than it is
an intellectual ladder climbing into the great mind or a moral ladder
climbing to the eternal good).

The experience of God, as the stories in the Bible so often demonstrate, comes as pure "surprise," a curious loan word into English
from French and Latin that means literally "to be overtaken." Thus,
when we read the Lukan account of Paul being overtaken on the
road to Damascus, two things jump out: that Paul was not forming
an experience but having one, being literally overtaken by the one he
was aiming to persecute, and that we cannot "have" or manufacture
the same experience, despite the many pious attempts to pour one's
expectations of how God ought to act into the framework of Paul's
experience. In fact, the community's response to Paul's experience was

to give him the same experience all Christians have had: baptism in the name of the Trinity. At Pentecost, in the course of Peter's speech, the listeners, overtaken by the rush of a mighty wind, experience God (they were cut to the heart, the text tells us), and again Peter offers them water and the Trinity: the forgiveness of sins through Christ. Jesus' encounters with people in the Gospels also always surprise the crowd, the disciples, or the person being healed or addressed. That is the nature of the Holy Spirit's work: to create the surprising experience of God with us and for us.

The First Article: The Creator for the Farmer in the Dell

Of course, one would expect, after such an introduction, that Luther would begin with the Holy Spirit in the catechisms, but in fact, having uncovered the heart of Luther's Trinitarian theology, we must also begin where Luther does, with the first article, so that his exposition of the Creed can pull the reversal off all on its own as the Trinity overtakes us or, rather, takes us over. That is to say, we must begin precisely the way we expect (from past to present: from creation to redemption to being made holy—Father, Son, and Holy Spirit) in order to encounter the unexpected God (Holy Spirit, Son, Father).

Although it is not the first word in the explanation to the first article, we must, further, begin with an "ought." In the Small Catechism, Luther made it clear that we owe God something, and he uses the word *schuldig*, which is translated as "owe," "debt," or "guilt." Later, he will use its opposite, *Unschuld*, which means "not guilty," "free from debt," or, since we often employ Latin words, "innocent" (where *in* means "not" and *nocens* means "guilty"). In the Large Catechism, we discover the exposition of this debt when Luther writes, in what must be surprising language to many today, "This article would humble and terrify us all, if we believed it."

Humble? Terrify? How is this possible? Is not creation all about beautiful sunsets, human beings made in God's image with infinite possibilities, babies nestling in their mothers' arms—and a whiff of apple pie in the kitchen? Not for Luther. The first article—that we live in a created world that comes to us as sheer gift from God and that we ourselves are creatures, not creators—comes instead with an enormous burden. If all that is around us and in us is good bestowed by a good God and received as sheer gift, then we are in trouble—given what we actually do with creation. In the Large Catechism, Luther began with our own limbs—the gifts of our arms, legs, mouths, brains, eyes, ears—and looked at how we use them against our neighbor, sometimes even against our very selves! Then, if one considers the other gifts of creation—air, water, earth, fire (to name the four elements Luther knew about)—where do we stand? If one could somehow survive Luther's exposition of the Ten Commandments and remain sinless, this article would finally put the lie to our rebellious, self-centered ways. This article *would* humble and terrify us!

But Luther made matters even worse by adding a stipulation: "If we believed it!" Already here we can hear echoes of the third article in the Small Catechism: "I believe that I cannot believe"—that is, the very first words of the first article (and the two subsequent ones), "I believe," already push us toward the crisis that has been brewing since the first commandment first demanded of us the one thing we could not deliver: "to fear, love, and trust in God above everything else," that is, faith. If we believed the simple words of this article (God creates everything), then we would be terrified, given our actual experience with and use of these gifts. But we cannot believe it and go on operating as if we were the center of the universe, as if we created life and meaning and all the rest.

With this word confessing terror and unbelief, however, Luther actually confessed, at the same time, his faith. This is perhaps the most difficult thing to come to terms with in Luther's exposition. Luther was not expounding facts to be learned or outlining doctrines to be believed; instead, he was confessing his faith. "I believe that God created me." Where did these words come from? They did not come from meditating on sunsets or thinking deeply about life; they did not arise from the classical proofs of God's existence or the practical logic of first causes. Instead, Luther's words came from experience—not the experience of creation (cf. Rom. 1:18-31) but the experience of God: Holy Spirit, Son, and Father. That is, the "I believe I cannot believe" of the third article, which continues "but the Holy Spirit has called me . . . ," made Luther a believer who could state the unbelievable, terrifying (to the sinner) truth: God made me.

If the impossibility of the first words of Luther's explanation of the Creed in the Small Catechism ("I believe God made me") and their connection to what we owe (and what, therefore, terrifies us) do not first strike us, we will always ask the wrong questions of this article and find Luther's paraphrase of it completely dissatisfying. It is precisely the experiential edge that is most scandalous here. "God made me!" It was this phrase, not the confession of God as creator of the world, that gave my own catechetical students the most trouble. One way or another, most all of them could believe God created the world—whether in six days or in billions of big bang years. But what none could fathom is how God could create them individually. Did the pastor (or Luther) not know anything about biology? There are sperm cells and eggs and intercourse and zygotes and all the rest that they had just learned in sex education class. Of course, at some basic level, arguing from first causes, they could always end up with the Enlightenment's benign God and say, "Well, where did the sperm or egg, the gene, the DNA, the carbon or hydrogen or whatever else finally come from?" But Luther, like the psalmist who has us being "knit together in my mother's womb" (Ps. 139:13) or like the author of Genesis, who insists that God scoops up mud and takes extra ribs (Gen 2:7, 21), seemed terribly uninterested in such safe speculation. "God makes me and then gives a whole host of very specific things and takes care of me." This is not a god of first causes but the God who created me—a terrifying thought, if we believed it.

Of course, this very closeness of God to creation begs another question that Luther never asked—namely, what about evil? Instead, he blithely moved from a long list of created blessing to insisting, in both catechisms, that God takes care of us, guards us, protects us, sustains us. The question of theodicy, as only modern thinkers could pose it, assumes a kind of leisure, of course, that Luther never had. In fact, for those interested in excusing God from this world's injustice, Luther made matters worse, not better, when he wrote in the Small Catechism, "He protects me from *every* evil." At least Luther could have had the presence of mind to say "most" or even just "evil" and left the rest up to the imagination of the reader. And, worse yet, how could Luther get away with saying that God gives me "body, soul, limbs, reason, senses," and all the rest, when he knew full well that some people are born with, or end up with, missing body parts,

mental problems, and so forth. Yet there is not one word about this
in either the Small or the Large Catechism.

Yet, far from being Pollyannaish, Luther had something else
in mind—"I believe that I cannot believe, but the Holy Spirit"—
namely, he was confessing as a believer. Thus, Luther was not interested—despite the demands from, among others, eighth graders
who, having just become abstract thinkers, love to toy with ideas
(and hapless confirmation instructors)—in providing a general theory about the universe and how God acts according to certain fixed
principles (usually called attributes in older catechisms). Instead, he
described the simple experience of the believer, the true believer, who
believes God created heaven and earth (and, therefore, me). After
all, the real problem with Luther's explanation lurks already in the
words of the Creed itself, as those early Christians rejected the enticing dream world of the gnostics and insisted that God created not
just the immaterial (heaven) but also the material (earth). As with
their insistence on Christ's bodily death, bodily resurrection, and,
finally, the resurrection of bodies, these Christians turned their backs
on speculation and theories and insisted on the experience of faith:
"God created me."

So, too, Luther described this simple experience of faith: I believe
that I am created and that this Creator gives, protects, guards, and
keeps. This, of course, means something rather disconcerting for
those of us who like to call God "Father." Calling God "Father" in
Luther's comments in the Small and Large Catechisms is a result
of faith, not a cause. In the first two sets of catechetical sermons
from 1528, Luther centered his remarks on the first article around
the word *Father*. But then, for some unstated reason, he shifted his
emphasis in the final set of sermons in 1528 to the word *Creator* and,
especially in the Small Catechism but also in the Large, proceeded
to turn that noun (*Creator*) into a verb (*created*). Only at the end of
the list of verbs—creates, gives, protects, guards, and keeps—did he
provide the appropriate adjective: "fatherly and divine goodness and
mercy." "Father" for Luther did get to the heart of God, to be sure,
but only through those verbs and, hence, only through faith. The
notion that "Father" is some sort of fixed, immovable principle in
Trinitarian thought was as far removed from Luther's encounter with
the Trinity as was the notion for him that (on the basis of another

set of principles) he should have called God "Mother." In such arguments (where the same unspoken anthropological principle plays a key role on both sides of the fence), finally it is not faith's experience but reason's ideology that sets the language. But, for Luther, the God experienced as creating "me and all that exists" was "fatherly and divine."

At this very point, however, a remarkable insight into Luther's language and theology suddenly shines through these words. The word *fatherly*, used here of God, demands human experience. An adjective like this one is and can only be a metaphor—worse yet, a simile—for, as everyone knows, *fatherly* means and is etymologically derived from "father like." (The German *väterlich* is even more helpful since the "lich" ending is clearly related to our word "like.")[6] But here many assume that the experience of their own father is the appropriate referent, which leaves many—not only women but also men—begging for a different metaphor altogether—"I hope God is not like *my* father." As Birgit Stolt, perhaps the most noted scholar of Luther's German of her generation, has noted, Luther's early use of the word *Father* for God was often connected to God as judge, which makes sense when we hear about Luther's father or even see his portrait. But, in 1526, Luther became a father, and according to Stolt, a marked change took place in Luther's use of the word *Father* for God. Why? Luther had discovered what it meant to be a father! "Father-like" was not a simile for Luther's father but the experience of Luther himself as father, especially with the death of his second child, Elizabeth, as an infant.

In one letter from the time of her death, Luther marked the depth of his grief in what may sound sexist to us but actually reveals the limits of his own masculine experience and language: "How womanish I have become," he wrote. That is, he cried, sobbed, wept, bawled, and thereby discovered a father's "womanish" heart. This adjectival movement culminated in 1531, when he added only one explanation to the first three parts of the Small Catechism: an explanation of "Our Father in heaven." There he portrayed "dear children coming to their dear father," surely a picture of what Luther saw in his own fatherly heart.

Luther was so loath to speculate about God that not only did he turn *Father* into a simile but he also paraphrased the word *Almighty* with the word *divine*. In German, this word, too, is metaphorical in nature: *Göttlich*, meaning "God-like." Luther refuses to speculate about the attributes of God or the doings of the Almighty One, the Pantocrator. Instead, all Luther seemed to know is that "all this the Creator does out of fatherly and divine goodness and mercy." Again, we are left with a confession of faith—very dissatisfying to those for whom knowing a thing signifies that we can control it but a great comfort to those who have come to know nothing about the inner nature of God.

Worse yet, there is a third word, an adverb this time, *purely*. God does this *purely* out of fatherly and divine goodness and mercy. Here, there is no room for works, no room for judgment or wrath. All is goodness and mercy. That German word *mercy* (*Barmherzigkeit*; literally, "mercy-heartedness") stands at the end of an interesting development in Luther's language.[7] In his early career, Luther, like all of his contemporaries, considered *gratia* (grace) to be a power or force (not unrelated to the Star Wars line "May the Force be with you"), which God infused into the soul. To be sure, there was also a more general grace, "given freely," which made *gratia* more closely related to "gift," but it was the *gratia infusa* that made a person acceptable to God by changing his or her very being. In 1519, however, the famous Greek scholar Erasmus of Rotterdam published the second edition of his Greek New Testament, in which he placed in parallel columns not the standard Latin translation (the Vulgate) but his own translation. Moreover, in a separate volume of annotations, he explained (and defended) why he had made certain changes to the highly regarded, nearly sacrosanct (in some quarters, at least) Vulgate. One of these changes came to the attention of Luther's young colleague and student Philip Melanchthon, who passed it on to Luther. The Greek word *charis*, translated as *gratia* in the Vulgate, Erasmus argued, should rather be translated *favor Dei*, that is, "God's favor." By 1521, both Luther and Melanchthon began using the new rendering of the Greek word and, over the years, came to replace "God's favor" with the more biblical phrase "God's mercy." Thus, when we teach our children that "Grace is undeserved love," we have Luther and Melanchthon (and Erasmus) to thank for rescuing that word from the philosophers and putting it back into God's heart where it belongs.

We have, however, skipped over one thing in this explanation of the first article, hinted at in the title of this section. In both the Small and the Large Catechisms, once he got beyond the immediate gift of "body and soul," Luther got rather personal, literally talking about shoes, drink, "house and farm, wife and children, fields, livestock and all property." How odd! Surely Luther knew that none of the children or women or servants or day laborers had such things. Why suddenly this turn toward, well, toward landed, male farmers?

The answer does not simply lie with the fact that, as was certainly the case, Luther was a product of his age and thought in terms of male property owners. There is also another, far more interesting reason that Luther made such a specific, exclusive list: he was talking about himself or, rather, he was confessing *his* faith. The "I believe God made me" points to a very specific "me," namely, Luther himself. We make a serious error when we think that Luther's faith rested on vague generalities here (God made everything). He was, to make the point even clearer, confessing that God made *his* body and soul, with all their accoutrements, so it would be best to read it thus: "I, Martin Luther, believe that God made me . . . my body and soul . . . and my brown eyes, my big ears, my limbs and senses, my sharp mind and clever wit." But then, "in addition," Luther wrote—as if, having once started listing God's blessings, he couldn't stop—"shoes and clothing"! An older "contemporary" translation dropped the shoes, but that is exactly to miss the point. God's care of us goes right down to our shoes! Who believes that?

And the rest of the list is nothing but vintage Luther: house and farm. Luther really had a house and, in German, *Hof*, or outbuildings, we might say (garage and tool shed and garden). He now, thanks to Katharina von Bora, had a wife of four years and a growing three-year-old Hans. By the end of his life, he also had fields, livestock, and all other kinds of property (thanks to a wife who managed the household with an iron hand). Although it was "illegal," he tried to pass everything on to his dear "rib" in a will that, against the law, bequeathed it all to her. Despite the best efforts of the executors (Philip Melanchthon and Justus Jonas), the courts disallowed such a radical step. One can almost hear Luther yelling at the lawyers from the grave.

Why not make this paraphrase/confession of the first article more general? Precisely because a confessing faith would not allow it! Luther's embarrassing specificity in this article reminds us that, in the Small Catechism especially, he was caught in the act of confessing his faith. The example that he set for the fathers of the houses, for whom the Small Catechism was originally written (and who, thus, could well have identified with much in Luther's list), and also for the other members of the household, was not "You must be thankful for things you do not have," but rather "God made me; gave me this and this and that." Such a confession is rather like hearing what a child received for his or her birthday or Christmas and celebrating along with the child, perhaps even getting caught up in the moment and saying to him or her, "And do you know what I got?"

This does not imply, however, that we should ignore Luther's list and just start making our own (or forcing unsuspecting eighth graders to write up theirs). Rather, one should learn as much as possible about Luther's list until, in its very specificity, it forces us to start making our own or comparing our list with Luther's. Some pastors wonder when or whether to teach anything about Martin Luther's life in their catechetical instruction. Perhaps this is the place. And then, when we know as much as possible about Luther's "birthday presents," our faith can spontaneously start making our own lists.

In the Large Catechism, Luther truly seemed incapable of bringing his list to an end. After covering much of what we find in the Small Catechism, he then listed the sun, moon, stars, day and night, the four elements (lucky for us he did not know about the table of elements or the list would have gone on even longer), and everything the earth produces. As if that were not enough, he included things like good government, peace, and security. "Thus we learn from this article that none of us has life—or anything else that has been mentioned here *or can be mentioned* [see how long a list it could be!]—from ourselves, nor can we by ourselves preserve any of them, however small and unimportant. All this is comprehended in the word 'Creator.'"[8]

Thus, again, even from Luther's laundry list of blessings, we are caught up in the third article ("I believe that I cannot believe") and the remarkable turnaround, or confession of faith, that the Holy Spirit creates. The whole universe—despite its threat ("This article should humble and terrify us all")—is finally *by faith alone* grace and mercy.

The Second Article: Ransom from Evil Kidnappers

On May 31, 1544, Jerome Baumgartner, while on his way home from representing the city of Nuremberg at an imperial diet in Speyer, was kidnapped by a rogue knight, Albrecht von Rosenberg, as part of the knight's feud against the Swabian League. Baumgartner was not only a scion of a wealthy Nuremberg patrician family but also a friend to Philip Melanchthon and Martin Luther, with whom he had studied in the early 1520s. Kidnapping for ransom was not an unknown occupation in early modern Germany. Not only brigands but, as in Baumgartner's case, rogue lords got into the act. If your castle was impregnable and your cause just (in your own eyes, of course), you could use kidnapping to carry out feuds or simply to enhance your revenue stream.

The reaction from Wittenberg to Baumgartner's misfortune was swift and predictable. Upon hearing of his confinement, both Melanchthon and Luther sprang into action.[9] They contacted overlords, especially Philip of Hesse, to pressure them into intervening. They wrote letters of consolation to Baumgartner's wife, whom at least Melanchthon had met on several visits to Nuremberg in the 1520s and 1530s. They even pleaded with friends in Nuremberg to expedite the paying of the ransom. In short, as in our day, when businesspersons may get whisked away in foreign lands where security is lax, family and friends of Jerome Baumgartner did what they could, until finally, on August 21, 1545, he was released.

In the Middle Ages and into the early modern era, the relation between lords (or cities) and their subjects was marked by mutuality. To be sure, the lord was over his subjects. But this did not translate into absolute power. That came later in the seventeenth and eighteenth centuries, when the Enlightenment's social theories combined with the French monarchy's ambitions to create Europe's first absolutist ruler in Louis XIV. In the sixteenth century, however, mutuality was still the standard by which to measure a lord's behavior. Moreover, in Luther's day, people would have expected that lords were responsible to protect their subjects and, should it happen, to rescue them from false imprisonment or kidnapping.

This single fact of sixteenth-century life illumines Luther's comments in his explanation of the second article of the Creed. In the first two sets of sermons from 1528, this connection was not made very clearly. In fact, Luther said very little about the Creed, especially the second article, since he thought it could best be covered in the Sunday sermons, based on the standard assigned texts (especially from Advent through Pentecost). However, in the third set of sermons and, hence, in the Small and Large Catechisms, we find that the image upon which Luther dwells is that of Christ's lordship. Here he stood in Wittenberg's pulpit, surrounded by the townsfolk and their children and household servants, and he chose a simple down-to-earth approach to explain the second article of the Creed: a good lord rescuing us from an evil tyrant.

> The second article follows, which we will also explain in a childlike way and only stress the word "our Lord." If you are asked, "What do you mean when you say, 'I believe in Jesus Christ . . ." respond: "This is what I mean by saying this, that Jesus Christ true Son of God has been made my Lord." How? "He has freed (*liberavit*) me from death, sin, hell and all evil, etc. For before this I did not have a king or lord. But the devil was our lord and king. Blindness, death, sin, flesh, and the world were our lords and we served them. Now they all have been expelled (*expulsi*) and in their place Christ is given—he who is Lord of righteousness, salvation, all good, etc."
>
> This article you always hear being explained, chiefly on Sundays: "Behold your king!" and the like.[10] Therefore you may believe in Jesus, that he has become your Lord, that is, that he redeemed you from death, sin and set you on his lap. Thus, I have rightly said that the first article teaches about Creation and the second concerning liberation, etc. For when we were created, the devil deceived us and was made our lord. Now, Christ frees us from death, devil, sins and gives us righteousness, life, faith, power, salvation, wisdom, etc. Because of this article we are called Christians. For those who acknowledge and call upon Christ are called Christians.
>
> What follows (namely, "conceived by the Holy Spirit . . .") are also sections that explain this faith in detail and show what Christ became and what our Lord did to free us, what it cost him, what he risked. So it happened that he was conceived by the Holy Spirit without any sin . . . , so that he might become my Lord and free me. . . . He did all these things so that he might become my Lord, because it was necessary for him to be so holy that the devil had no right over him. These

sections show what kind of Lord[11] he is and how he purchased [this lordship], so that I come under his lordship, namely through his own body, through which he established his kingdom.

The whole gospel is summarized in this article. For the Gospel is nothing other than the preaching of the conception, birth, etc. of Christ. Therefore, learn to understand this phrase: "Our Lord." I ought to believe and do believe that Christ is my Lord, that is, that he redeemed me, because the second article [of the Creed] talks about this. He defeats death and sin and frees me from them. First, when I was created, I had all kinds of blessings (the body, etc.), but I served sin, death, etc. Then Christ came, who suffered death so that I might be freed from death and become his son and be led into righteousness, life, etc. "Lord" means the same as "Redeemer" etc. The other sections [of this article] show how he set up the whole thing and what price he paid: not with gold, silver or equities [nor with arms, swords, and human powers] but with himself, that is with his own body [and blood], conceived by the Holy Spirit, born, [suffered and rose]. Now I will not say more about this article, for I do not want to overwhelm you. This is the truly Christian article, which neither the Jews, the Papists, nor the sectarians believe. For whoever believes that they are saved by works [and] not through Christ, [does not believe this article] and vice versa. But this belongs to another sermon.[12]

Luther painted this same image in his catechisms of 1529. The Large Catechism revealed his thought processes very clearly. The second article focused on the word *lord*. Jesus has become my lord: "What is it 'to become a lord'? It means that he has redeemed and released me from sin, from the devil, from death, and from all misfortune. Before this I had no lord or king, but was captive under the power of the devil."[13] While we faced God's wrath and displeasure for our sin, Luther went on, Christ had mercy on us: "Those tyrants and jailers have now been routed, and their place has been taken by Jesus Christ, the Lord of life."[14] For Luther, then, the word *lord* meant "redeemer." The rest of the article simply demonstrated how this redemption took place: through Christ's incarnation ("that he might become Lord over sin"), suffering, death, and resurrection: "And he did all this so that he might become my Lord."[15] The victory of this Lord occurred in his resurrection.

If the Large Catechism scatters references to Christ's lordship throughout its explanation, the Small Catechism represents a distillation of the same argument. The traditional christological arguments are reduced to an appositive clause ("true God . . . true human being") in order to concentrate on the metaphor of lordship ("I believe that Jesus Christ . . . is my Lord"). Even before these words, however, the reader is put on notice that this article concerns redemption. What Philip Melanchthon had famously stated in his theological handbook ("To know Christ is to know his benefits") Luther now put in the Small Catechism. This article is about the benefits of Christ's two natures in one person: redemption ("who has redeemed me").

The German word for redemption (already used in the ancient Gothic translation of the Bible), *erlösung*, has within it the word for being freed or "loosened" from captivity,[16] whereas the Latin *redemptio* means to be bought back. These two concepts came together for Luther in the single word *lord*, the one who both frees the kidnap victim and pays the ransom. Indeed, Luther employed three verbs (*erlösen, erwerben,* and *gewonnen*; redeemed, purchased, and freed) to describe this lord's activities. Both the fiercely metaphorical use of the term *lord* (*Herr*) and the heaping up of verbs here warn us against constructing some sort of "theory" of the atonement that Luther is using here. It is the opposite of a theory (that is, here is what God is doing for humanity); rather, it is the actual experience of God at work in Christ: loosening, buying back, freeing.

Moreover, the means of payment ("his holy, precious blood . . . and innocent suffering and death") destroys the enemies that hold us captive ("sin . . . death . . . the power of the devil"). But it also frees us from the curse of the law, for here weakness ("blood . . . and . . . death") is under no law ("innocent," which in German is *unschueldigen*—something not owed to God). The purpose would have been clear to any sixteenth-century person, child or adult: that I may receive a new lord! Thus, Luther's language at the end of the explanation is even clearer: "that I may belong to him, live under him in his kingdom, and serve him in eternal righteousness, innocence [German: *Unschuld*], and blessedness." The lord who rescues us now owns us, puts us in his kingdom, and frees us to serve. We, too, are no longer under the law and its eternal "ought" but under grace and now serve not because we must but because we are freed to do it. The proof of this triumph over our kidnapping enemies is, as always for Luther, the resurrection, through which Christ "lives and rules."[17]

The question that this explanation poses for twenty-first-century Lutherans is simple: In a world without "lords a-leaping," except in quaint Christmas carols, what picture can we find that carries the same weight? How do we unlock the remarkable heart of the Christian message, ensconced in the Nicene Creed—"who for us and for our salvation came down"? Our failure to do this will simply reduce Christ to mythology or moralism and rob us of the comfort (and freedom!) of the gospel. Moreover, this Lord Christ is not like other lords, but one who pays the ransom with blood and defeats evil with an evil death (crucifixion) and destroys death by dying. It is this One who is the "mirror of the Father's heart," showing once and for all by dying and rising that associating "Father" with power and force is to miss the point and destroy the very picture of God the catechisms' explanations of the Creed so beautifully paint.

The Third Article: God in Action Today

Finally, we arrive at the beginning of God's work with us: the Holy Spirit. This is the climax of Luther's explanation of the commandments and the Creed. The first and foremost commandment demands what we cannot deliver: faith. The Creed's first article revealed yet more human sin, "terrifying and humbling" us with the mere fact that we are created and yet abuse the Creator's gifts. The second article, even while proclaiming that "Jesus is Lord," failed to give us the faith to believe it. And without faith, we are left with the Oslo syndrome, where we have spent so much time with our captives that we fall for them. So we arrive with Luther at the third article. Now the requirement of faith, demanded in the first commandment, reaches its crisis point: faith makes both God and idol. However, the greatest idol Christians erect these days makes faith a human work and insists on our freedom to choose God. Take this one claim away from the hucksters in the American religious marketplace, and the airways would be nearly devoid of so-called Christian broadcasting.[18] Indeed, so pervasive is the insistence on choice for American religiosity today that eliminating it would destroy the Christian veneer in our culture and turn us into what we truly are: a pre-Christian society. By far the most subversive words of the Small Catechism, then, are simply these: "I believe that I cannot believe."

The impossibility of self-generated faith in the Small Catechism comes down to two words: "understanding or strength" (*Vernunft oder Kraft*). With them, Luther summarized the only other book (alongside the Small Catechism) that he once said was worth saving for posterity: *The Bondage of the Will*, his sophisticated argument against his age's most acclaimed defender of free choice, Erasmus of Rotterdam.[19] *Vernunft* (understanding or, better, reason) was the German equivalent of the technical philosophical term *ratio*, which (at least according to Philip Melanchthon's *Loci communes theologici*) was Plato's term for what medieval theologians (and Erasmus), under the influence of Aristotle, called the *liberum arbitrium* (free choice, a power [*Kraft*!] of the soul that allowed the will freely to determine the mind's course of action). If *ratio* placed freedom in the intellect, the *liberum arbitrium* centered it in the human will. But Luther, in surprisingly simple language, eliminated all such misconstruals of human potential. "I believe that I cannot believe!" Praise human mental power or will-power all you wish, he claimed, but you still cannot believe. It was not, please note, that Luther was eliminating the role of reasoning or willing in the human being. Instead, he was simply putting these faculties in their place: to work in this world for the good of the neighbor and the preservation of this garden we call earth. As soon as they become an object of trust vis-à-vis God, then we have replaced God with an idol: our reason and our choice. When it comes to God, we cannot get there from here; God must come to us.

God's coming to us is precisely the point of this article. Luther not only eliminated human willing and choosing ("I believe that I cannot believe") but also eliminated an old monastic heresy called *enthusiasmus*. There were monks who finally came to neglect or even reject the outward means of grace (Word and sacraments) for the sake of their own inner illumination, direct from God. They worshiped the God within (Greek: *en theou*; hence, en-thusiasm). These "ravers" (*Schwärmer*), as Luther often called them, were actually no different from those who defended free choice in matters of faith (or those who defended the authority of some specially designated [papal] magisterium). After all, they, too, placed their confidence in something within them. Contrary to such ravings, the Christian

God came in the flesh, destroying every form of Gnosticism (knowledge worship) or voluntarism (will worship) humanity can cook up. No wonder, in the lengthiest addition to the printed version of the Smalcald Articles, Luther wrote:

> In these matters, which concern the spoken, external Word, it must be firmly maintained that God gives no one his Spirit or grace apart from the external Word which goes before. We say this to protect ourselves from the Enthusiasts, that is the "spirits," who boast that they have the Spirit apart from and before contact with the Word. On this basis, they judge, interpret, and twist the Scripture or oral Word according to their pleasure. . . . The papacy is also purely religious raving in that the pope boasts that "all laws are in the shrine of his heart." . . . This is all the old devil and old snake, who also turned Adam and Eve into Enthusiasts and led them from the external Word of God to "spirituality" and their own presumption. . . . In short: Enthusiasm clings to Adam and his children from the beginning to the end of the world—fed a spread among them as poison by the old dragon.[20]

Thus, in the Small Catechism, Luther wrote not simply that the Holy Spirit calls in general but, more specifically, that the Holy Spirit "calls me *through the gospel.*" Saying both that we cannot believe and that the Holy Spirit calls through means puts the reader smack dab up against the paradox of the incarnation all over again. God in the flesh and an unbeliever who believes through an external word are equally scandalous—so much so that reason and the powers of choice cannot believe it. As one teacher put it, faith for Luther is falling in love when we hear the true love's voice proclaim, "You're mine."[21] Thus, we fall and confess that this marriage of faith was made in heaven ("I believe that I cannot believe, but the Holy Spirit . . .").

The concreteness of the encounter with Christ in the gospel, however, is reflected in Luther's verbs: the Holy Spirit has "called, enlightened, made holy, and kept in the true faith." Of course, defenders of free choice will latch onto "called" and argue that this implies choice ("We have to answer, don't we?"), but only, of course, if Luther suffered short-term memory loss and did not mean to say, "I . . . cannot believe *or come to him.*" The "called by the Gospel" is just what it sounds like, to those who have ears to hear. Faith, Paul wrote in Rom. 10:17, comes by hearing—not by deciding or willing or coming to God (see also Rom. 9:16). Thus, in the Large Catechism, Luther wrote, "Neither you nor I could ever know anything about Christ, or believe in him and receive him as Lord, unless these were offered to us *and bestowed on our hearts* through the preaching of the gospel by the Holy Spirit."[22]

Here is where Lutherans and some Reformed Christians part ways: the incarnation insists that our election takes place not simply "before the world was made" (Eph. 1:4) but in our very hearing: "God chooses you; you are forgiven; Jesus is your Lord." God in Christ comes to us through the power of the Holy Spirit. So the Holy Spirit calls through the gospel (Word *and* Sacrament) and thereby puts an end to our works. Faith is not a work or even a "response"; it is an event, what happens when we hear the lover's voice and fall in love.

"Enlightened with the Holy Spirit's gifts" gives the old creature yet another chance to use its "understanding and power" by turning the matter into a spiritual project. Thus, not surprisingly, much ink has been spilled over the meaning of this phrase in Luther.[23] Of course, it shows Luther's profound debt to his theological forebears, including the rich hymnody to the Holy Spirit, "who dost thy sevenfold gifts impart."[24] But even his rendering of this verse of *Veni Creator Spiritus* ties the gifts back to the gospel: "You give the Father's Word." In the Small Catechism, too, this enlightenment is not separate from the gospel's call, nor is it a separate stage on the way to full salvation (first called, then enlightened, and so forth). Rather, these verbs are all Luther's way of explicating the opposite of our bondage to reason and choice. In the midst of our deafness, God speaks; in our blindness, God shines.

The next verb, "made holy," gives translators and theologians fits. For Luther, this verb summarized everything the Holy Spirit does, so that it became the caption for the entire article: "On Being Made Holy." The trouble is that English, with its hankering after the prettiness of Latin speech (or, using Latin words: the addiction to beautification employing the Latin language), would have us use "sanctify" and "sanctification," thereby destroying the obvious connection, made explicit in the Large Catechism, between *Holy* Spirit and being made *holy*: "If someone asks, What do you mean by the

words 'I believe in the Holy Spirit'? you can answer, 'I believe that
the Holy Spirit makes me holy, as his name states.'" Moreover, the
word *sanctification* took on a very narrow meaning in the course of
the sixteenth century and beyond, until it became so divorced from
justification as to define a separate part of the Christian life.[25] Luther
and the young Melanchthon operated with no such fixed categories
(much to the chagrin of the authors of the Formula of Concord).
Thus, for Luther, to be made holy meant, first and foremost, to be
forgiven and, right on its heels, to be "kept in the true faith." That
is, the entire Christian life (predestined, elected, called, justified,
sanctified, and glorified, to use Paul's verbs from Romans 8) is lived
between the promise (called *by the gospel*) and faith (kept in the true
faith) by the work of the Holy Spirit. Everything else is just gravy.

But precisely here, at the conjunction of holiness and forgiveness, a second subversive element arose in Luther's explanation of the
third article. Not only did he wrest faith from the hands of the all-
controlling old creature; he also put believers in the church. Bucking
the centuries-old tradition of dividing the Creed into twelve parts
(one for each apostle), Luther gave it back to the Trinity, reducing his explanation to three. This has profound significance for his
pneumatology *and* ecclesiology, since it forced him to connect the
Holy Spirit to the church or, rather, the church to the work of the
Holy Spirit. In the Small Catechism, this linkage is shown in two
phrases: "just as" and "in this Christian church." Despite the worship of individualism in almost all forms of American Christianity
(witness our infatuation with the first-person singular pronouns in
current hymnody and "praise songs"), Luther knew no such piety.
He began with the individual because the Creed begins "Credo" (I
believe) and because baptism, which is the Creed's watery version, is
poured on each person individually. But he immediately placed this
person in the church. Indeed, the individual is as closely united with
the church as Christ's death is united with his resurrection! In both
places, Luther said, "gleich wie": "*just as* he is risen" and "*just as* the
Holy Spirit calls."

The centrality of the church as the Holy Spirit's workshop, to
borrow a phrase, is shown in the single addition to the list of verbs,
"Gathers."[26] The church, like faith itself, is not an institution or a
theory but an event or, to use a phrase from the 1960s, a happening.[27]

We are pulled in to hear the Word, to be washed in baptism, and to eat the Supper together. This gathering is not an institution but a gathering of believers ("In this Christian church the Holy Spirit forgives my sins and the sins of all *believers*"), precisely the chief work of the Holy Spirit ("I believe I cannot believe").

Luther elucidated this point much more fully in the Large Catechism. The church is truly the means the Holy Spirit uses to make us holy; it is the Holy Spirit's "unique community in the world, which is the mother that begets and bears every Christian through the Word of God." This maternal language, quite traditional for the time, stands out for the way it, once again, takes control of our Christian life out of our hands and entrusts it to the Spirit, the midwife for the church. Here it is mother not as threat (do not betray "mother church") but as comfort. Moreover, the church is not an independent operator, a fourth person in the Trinity, but completely dependent on the Holy Spirit. Here, Luther called to mind the absence of good preaching under the papacy: "What was lacking there? There was no Holy Spirit present to reveal this truth and have it preached."

What caught Luther's attention in the Large Catechism, however, was the phrase *communio sanctorum*, which he knew was not in the earliest versions of the Creed. Here, he demonstrated, for one thing, his gift for sense translation and not simply literal translation.[28] The Latin and Greek word for church, *ecclesia*, meant an assembly, and the German word for church (*Kirche*) derived from (and here Luther actually has been proven correct) the Greek word *kyria* (actually *kyriakos*: belonging to the Lord). Thus, he concluded, it should be translated "a holy Christian people." Likewise, the word *communio* simply meant "community" to Luther. Therefore, the phrase *communio sanctorum* simply meant "a holy community" and was added to explain what church meant. Yet it was not in his etymologies but in his almost lyrical confession of faith that the true impact of this very un-Roman definition of church became clear.

> This is the meaning and substance of this phrase: I believe that there is on earth a holy little flock and community of pure saints under one head, Christ. It is called together by the Holy Spirit in one faith, mind, and understanding. It possesses a variety of gifts, and yet is united in love without sect or schism. Of this community I also am a part and

member, a participant and co-partner in all the blessings it possesses. I was brought into it by the Holy Spirit and incorporated into it through the fact that I have heard and still hear God's Word, which is the beginning point for entering it. . . . The Holy Spirit will remain with the holy community or Christian people until the Last Day. Through it he gathers us, using it to teach and preach the Word. By it he creates and increases holiness, causing it daily to grow and become strong in the faith and in its fruits, which the Spirit produces. Further we believe that in this Christian community we have the forgiveness of sins, which takes place through the holy sacraments and absolution as well as through all the comforting words of the entire gospel. . . . Forgiveness is constantly needed, for although God's grace has been acquired by Christ, and holiness has been wrought by the Holy Spirit through God's Word in the unity of the Christian church, yet we are never without sin because we carry our flesh around our neck. Therefore everything in this Christian community is so ordered that everyone may daily obtain full forgiveness of sins through the Word and signs appointed to comfort and encourage our consciences as long as we live on earth. Although we have sin, the Holy Spirit sees to it that it does not harm us because we are a part of this Christian community. Here there is full forgiveness of sins, both in that God forgives us and that we forgive, bear with, and aid one another.[29]

When Luther wrote that there is no sect or schism, he was referring not to some sort of Platonic ideal but to the event of hearing the Word by faith, an event that unites all believers of every time and place. Moreover, he spoke the language of the believer, ignoring the divisions of the church much the way he ignored evil in the first article. To say, "I believe in the Holy Christian Church," is not to believe in what human beings do but to confess what God the Holy Spirit does. More clearly than in the Small Catechism, Luther here also moved seamlessly from the church to forgiveness of sins through Word and Sacrament. Thus, the unity of the third article occurs both through the Holy Spirit, who does all that is listed, and through the church, which is the place the Holy Spirit works on us. For Luther, there were no churchlets in the institutional church (*ecclesiolae in ecclesia*), as the Pietists invented and then used to tear people away from the Word and sacraments into their own "self-chosen spirituality" (Col. 2:23). There was, rather, this remarkable assembly of holy sinners, on whom the Holy Spirit is busy working to make holy—that is, ever-forgiven forgivers.

We return to the Small Catechism. As if to summarize what the Holy Spirit does to make us believers in church, Luther proceeded to the next phrase in the third article: forgiveness of sins. Luther's was not a project for human emancipation and self-actualization or other schemes that destroy all human environments in nature and society. Instead, he confessed, "I believe in the forgiveness of sins." As if it were not already clear that the Christian life takes place in community around Word and Sacrament, Luther added that "in this Christian Church" God forgives me and all believers.[30] Christianity's calling is simply forgiving sins and comforting the weak and terrified. And, Luther inserted, doing it *daily*, so that no one imagines that the church somehow ends when the people leave on Sunday and return home. Instead, Luther depicted the church as continuing in the home and workplace, where the stricken conscience can (alone) pray the Lord's Prayer together with all other Christians on earth or ask the pastor or the neighbor (beginning with parents, spouse, and children) for this gospel, and even constitute a house church as part of the same event of Word, table, bath, and prayer. God is not so miserly as to deprive Christians of this comfort but rather surrounds them with church throughout their lives. All this is church, and all of this tends toward the unity in the faith kept by the Holy Spirit. Thus, the individualized, isolated prayer and meditation of the hermit is more a danger to the Spirit's work than a help, and everything that happens in Word and Sacrament must draw Christians together, rather than sending them off into their private encounters with the divine.[31]

Finally, Luther described the Holy Spirit's work in terms of the end. Here, the eschatological nature of his thought snapped into focus. The Holy Spirit raises the dead and gives "me and all believers in Christ" eternal life. Luther would have found little to interest him in our grand theories of religious convergence, born in the Enlightenment and come to age in postmodernism. Where is the comfort in knowing, theoretically at least, that there are hundreds of ways up the mountain—especially if it would seem (and is, in fact, the case) that we are all headed for the pit? The Creed does not speculate about evil or about the fate of unbelievers (although Luther does not hesitate to talk about such things elsewhere). The reason is simple: "I believe that I cannot believe, but the Holy Spirit calls." That is, the Holy Spirit's goal is to make me holy, to forgive sins, and to give life—full, abundant, and free life—in Christ. Nothing can stand in the Holy Spirit's way in making the dead alive: here, daily, by faith and forgiveness and, one day, eternally, in the resurrection of the dead.

Thus, because we experience the Trinity backward, when we begin with the Holy Spirit, we actually begin at the end: the end of the old creature, the self-believer, and the resurrection in baptism through the Word of the new creature of faith. And the gnawing threat of the first commandment ("believe or else") finally reaches its true end: faith in Christ, the mirror of the Father's heart, as created by the Holy Spirit through the gospel. "Now the Spirit's visitation, now the Son's epiphany, now the Father's blessing, now, now, now."

"Our Father in Heaven": John 16[:23-24] (Jesus Explaining Prayer to the Father). Earlier versions depicted a sixteenth-century preacher in the pulpit (also used for the first petition) with no biblical reference.

CHAPTER 4

The Lord's Prayer and Believers' Needs[1]

For whenever a good Christian prays, 'Dear Father, your will be done,' God replies from above, 'Yes, dear child, it shall be done indeed in spite of the devil and the entire world.'"[2] In this way, Martin Luther brought to a close his most trenchant exposition of prayer: a brief introduction to the subject in the Large Catechism. It gets to the heart of Luther's theology of prayer, doing it in simple terms for his intended audience.[3] In this chapter, we will briefly describe Luther's own life of prayer, examine how he defined prayer in the Large Catechism, and give a detailed commentary on his explanations in the Small Catechism.

The Praying Luther

Luther's understanding of prayer arose out of his own experience, first as a monk, then as a pastor, and always as a Christian believer.[4] Fascination with Luther and prayer began long before his death. Not only did his barber, Master Peter Beskendorf, request Luther's instruction on how to pray,[5] but already Veit Dietrich, Luther's companion at the Fortress Coburg during the 1530 Diet of Augsburg, described to Philip Melanchthon the effect of Luther's praying.

> One time I had the opportunity to hear him praying. Good God, what spirit, what faith was in his words! He prayed for things with such reverence—as befits God—and with such hope and faith that he seemed to be holding a conversation with a father or a friend. "I know," he said, "that you are our Father and God. Therefore I am sure that you will destroy the persecutors of your children. If you do

not do this, the result will be disaster for us. The whole affair is yours. We are constrained to implore you for this. Therefore, defend us, and so on." I was standing nearby and heard him praying in a clear voice using words to that effect. My soul was set on fire with such a singular passion to hear him speak with God in such a friendly, serious, and reverent manner. And throughout the prayer he interjected psalms, so that he was quite certain that everything for which he prayed would come about.[6]

Luther's life was littered with examples of answered and unanswered prayer. By far the most famous example of Luther praying occurred in 1540.[7] In June 1540, Philip Melanchthon had taken sick on his way to the religious colloquy in Haguenau. He stopped in Weimar on June 12, unable to travel farther and too weak to return to Wittenberg. By the time his concerned colleagues, including Martin Luther and Justus Jonas, arrived in Weimar on June 23 with Melanchthon's son Philip, the poor man was in a semiconscious state.[8] After assessing the situation, Luther walked over to a window and started praying. As Luther later described it (according to Matthäus Ratzeberger): "There [in Weimar], the Lord God had to stretch out his hand to me. For I threw the entire sack in front of his door and rubbed his ears with all the *promissiones to hear prayers* that I was able to recall from the Holy Scripture, so that he had to hear me, were I to believe all those other promises."[9]

Luther's chutzpah toward God in that moment was a sign not so much of hubris (although it may at first glance appear as such) as of faith. "Throwing sacks" and "rubbing ears" were almost playful ways for Luther to express the urgency of the situation, the dire need for God's help, and the joy of being answered. Thus, upon entering the room, Luther had exclaimed, "May God protect us! Look how the devil has mistreated this *instrument* of mine."[10] The inordinate joy Luther derived from this answered prayer and Melanchthon's recovery may be seen in Luther's letter to his wife, Katie, ten days later. There, however, we also hear less of Luther's faith and more of God's surprising mercy.

Grace and Peace! Dear Maiden Käthie, gracious Lady von Zolsdorf[11] (and whatever other titles that pertain to Your Grace)! I wish to inform

You and Your Grace most submissively that I am doing well here. I eat like a Bohemian and drink like a German. Thanks be to God! Amen! This is because Master Philip was truly dead and has arisen from the dead just like Lazarus! God, the dear Father, hears our prayer—that we see and experience—even though we still do not believe it. Let no one say "Amen" to our terrible unbelief![12]

Of course, the notion that God hears prayer did not mean for Luther that absolutely everything was answered according to human expectations. Already in the fall of 1532, he could exclaim, "We have this advantage: that our prayer is always heard. Even if it is not heard according to our will, nevertheless it is heard according to the will of God, which is better than our will. If I did not know that my prayer would be heard, it would be the devil praying in my place."[13]

For Luther, alongside God's promise to hear and answer prayer was faith. Thus, in a not-well-documented comment at table, he may have said, "As a cobbler makes shoes and a tailor sews clothes, so should a Christian pray. The handiwork of a Christian is prayer."[14] Nevertheless, this faith in prayer is hard to come by. As we shall see below, the link among faith, need, and earnestness, as something coming through external necessity and experience, was crucial to Luther's approach to prayer in the Large Catechism.[15]

Another concrete incident in Luther's life, this time involving unanswered prayer, shows how consistent Luther's understanding of the interaction of God's promise and faith was. In the summer of 1537, the electoress of Brandenburg, Elizabeth von Dänemark, fell sick and ended up in Luther's home.[16] Several insights into prayer come from this stressful time in the Luther household. On August 18, Luther prayed:

Dear Lord God, now hear our prayer according to your promise! Do not let us throw the keys at your feet,[17] so that in the end we get angry at you and do not give you proper honor and what is your due.[18] Where will you be then? Ach, dear Lord, we are yours. Do what you will, only give us patience.[19]

Two days later, Anton Lauterbach recorded another prayer: "Dear God, you possess this name, that you are the Answerer of prayers, as David said [Ps. 145:19], 'He fulfills the desire of those who fear him and hears their groans.' Ach, Lord, we are not praying for anything evil! Do not make us throw the keys at the door."[20] Thus, Luther's comment about prayer for Melanchthon, preserved by Ratzeberger, was typical of the way his faith understood God's promise to hear prayer. What he refused to do was to pray timidly.

Around the same time, in the summer of 1537, he again reflected on prayer and faith, but this time with a sense of awe that God even bothers to hear a believer.

> Ach, what a great thing the prayer of the godly is! How powerful it is before God, that a poor soul should talk with God and not be frightened in his presence, but instead know that God smiles at him in a friendly manner because of Jesus Christ. The conscience must not run away on account of its unworthiness or be overwhelmed with doubts or let itself be frightened.[21]

This, too, was one of Luther's foci in the Large Catechism, where he used both law and gospel to solve the problem of the conscience fleeing prayer.

At the same time, Luther contrasted late-medieval piety and uncertain prayers to the saints to faith based on Christ's promise. Moreover, he admitted the human tendency, which he himself had shared as a monk, to turn prayer into a work, an ascent of the soul that human beings can accomplish. As will become clear, such contrasts also played a role in the Large Catechism. As the following shows, with respect to prayers for the electoress, Luther simply refused to pray, as late-medieval piety taught, "conditionally and hypothetically."

> Thus, the ancient [Christians] well defined prayer: '*Oratio est ascensus mentis ad Deum*' (prayer is the ascent of the mind to God).[22] It is well said, but I and everyone else did not understand that definition. We boasted about the ascent of the mind, but we missed out on the syntax, that we have to bring the *ad Deum* to it. On the contrary, we fled from God. We could not freely and with certainty pray to God through Christ, in whom the certainty of prayer exists, but we always prayed conditionally and hypothetically, not categorically. Therefore,

my brothers, who can pray, pray without ceasing, that is, from the heart and also at certain times orally. For, in the presence of our dear God, prayer upholds the world; otherwise things would be quite different.[23]

A third specific incident revealed yet another aspect of Luther's understanding of prayer. In the spring of 1539, the imperial princes gathered in Frankfurt am Main in an attempt to avoid what seemed by then to be inevitable: armed conflict over religion, exacerbated by the growing dispute between Philip of Hesse and Henry of Braunschweig-Wolfenbüttel. The result was the Frankfurt Truce (*Stillstand*) of 1539, which set in motion the religious colloquies of the 1540s and prevented all-out war until 1547. Philip Melanchthon, part of the Saxon entourage, was in Frankfurt from February 13 until April 20, returning home on May 9, when he dined with Luther.[24]

Luther, as always, remained at home and stewed about the prospects for peace in the face of political rumors and papal machinations. Throughout this time, his companions recorded his prayers, especially in worship[25] but also upon the receipt of a letter from Melanchthon.[26] As he had already expressed in his exposition to the fourth petition of the Lord's Prayer, "Civic peace is the highest gift of God on earth,"[27] the only defense against such warlike enemies was prayer.[28] Here, as in the other cases, there was nothing that could not be brought before God's throne. Faith and God's promises again combined to encourage Luther even in the midst of his own pessimism. Luther also voiced this attitude in the introduction to prayer in the Large Catechism. Although the negotiations did not resolve the underlying tensions in the empire, the crisis did reveal the role that prayer played for Luther in political matters. As personal as prayer could be for Luther, it was never caught in the kind of solipsism that so often marks teachings about prayer in the twenty-first century.

The Large Catechism

The Large Catechism arose out of Luther's catechetical sermons of 1528, especially the set produced in late November and early December.[29] The introduction to the section on prayer, which is the chief concern here, had direct connection to these sermons and to the Visitation Articles of 1527 and 1528.[30] In the Large Catechism, Luther used substantial space to give a more detailed overview of the topic, something that he also did in a less expansive way to begin the Creed. Here, however, Luther sensed how important prayer was for the Christian's daily life, much as he did later in the Large Catechism when he added a lengthy admonition on the reception of the Lord's Supper and, in a section added to the second edition, on private confession.[31]

In his exhaustive analysis of Luther's catechisms, Albrecht Peters lists five parts to this admonition. A more careful examination of Luther's grammar and his intention, however, reveals only three, plus a short opening transition from the preceding sections of the catechism. This will serve here as an appropriate outline for the following analysis.

Luther's Catechetical Order: Diagnosis, Treatment, Medication

As discussed in chapter 1, already Luther's *Betbüchlein* (*Personal Prayer Book*) of 1522 dealt with the question of the catechism's order. He used an Augustinian metaphor of sickness and healing to explain his reordering the parts of the catechism (moving from law to gospel to prayer).[32] Although his language was still much more in keeping with late-medieval piety, it demonstrated clearly how important the catechism's order was for Luther: diagnosis of the illness; declaration of the cure; procurement of the medicine. This movement from diagnosis of the human condition (sin) through the law, to treatment through the announcement of God's mercy and grace, to the reception of medication through prayer, marked all of Luther's catechesis and even his private prayer.[33]

Luther's comments on prayer in the Large Catechism thus began with a brief recitation of the relation between the Lord's Prayer and the earlier sections of the catechism.[34] The Decalogue described "what we are to do." However, as tempting as it may be to turn the commandments into a project for the old creature to achieve, it is important to note the force of the verb *sollen*, translated here as "are to." We should do this, but as Luther said to Erasmus, an "ought" never implies a "can." Earlier in the Large Catechism, Luther took this hubris head-on, as expressed by those who, thinking the Ten

Commandments easy to fulfill, wanted to graduate to "Christian counsels." Wrote Luther: "They fail to see, these miserable blind fools, that no one is able to keep even one of the Ten Commandments as it ought to be kept. Both the Creed and the Lord's Prayer must come to our aid."[35] Not only did Luther reiterate this very point in introducing the Lord's Prayer ("No one can keep the Ten Commandments perfectly"), but he added an even more devastating blow to the old creature ("even though he or she has begun to believe").[36] The faith created through the gospel as confessed in the Creed does not cure the illness. Instead, the believer, as believer, is immediately driven to pray. Luther added to this the big three: devil, world, and flesh. This medieval and patristic trio combined in Luther's view to fight the gospel tooth and nail.[37]

In light of humanity's deep illness and the creedal gospel (cure), Luther was driven to prayer: that desperate call to the pharmacy in the middle of the night. The chutzpah of his prayer for Melanchthon had already found expression in the Large Catechism: "Consequently, nothing is so necessary as to call upon God incessantly and to drum into his ears our prayer."[38] What was the content of this ear rubbing? "That [God] may give, preserve, and increase in us faith and the fulfillment of the Ten Commandments and remove all that stands in our way and hinders us in this regard." This need for faith and fulfillment of the commandments drove Luther finally to the Lord's Prayer itself, which provided him with "what and how to pray."[39] In this way, the Christian finally demands from God, the Great Physician, the very medicine without which one cannot live in faith.

The Command to Pray

As in the catechism overall, Luther structured his comments on prayer in the Large Catechism under the rubrics of diagnosis (law), treatment (gospel), and medicine (Lord's Prayer). Thus, paragraphs 4–18 examine Christ's command to pray. Here, Luther's comments were much richer than many later discussions of "law and gospel," because for him they were encounters with God's word, which was working on Luther as he wrote.

Luther first discussed prayer under the second commandment because he never encountered a text of Scripture where he did not immediately think of its opposite. As he once said: "When I preach, I make antitheses."[40] If a text forbids something, it means God is promoting the opposite. If a text promises something, it also means it is excluding something harmful. Regarding the explanations to the commandments in both the Small and Large Catechisms, this meant for Luther that negative commandments had a positive side and vice versa.[41] Specifically, the second commandment for Luther not only forbade the misuse of God's name but included the proper use of it.

Here, the explanation of the second commandment in the Small Catechism is particularly instructive: "We are to fear and love God, so that we . . . instead use that very name in every time of need to call on, pray to, praise, and give thanks to God."[42] Luther linked need with prayer. He also separated prayer from praise and thanksgiving, something that an English-speaking audience may not readily appreciate, where prayer is often defined as a general term for "words thrown in God's direction," thus including praise and thanksgiving. This is unfortunate if for no other reason than that the original, nonreligious meaning of the word *pray* in English, etymologically related to the German *fragen* ("to ask") and the Latin *precare* ("to beg"), was "to ask."[43]

The explanation in the Large Catechism also considered this positive side.[44] Luther even provided some examples of good prayers for children: "One must urge and encourage children again and again to honor God's name and to keep it constantly upon their lips in all circumstances and experiences."[45] Here is where the Christian receives consolation (par. 70) and where the devil gets chased away (par. 71–72). In the same way, each day should be commended to God (par. 73).[46] But Luther also had in mind making the sign of the cross in danger and uttering short prayers in dire need or blessing: "'Lord God, save me!' or 'Help, dear Lord Christ!' . . . 'God be praised and thanked!' 'God has bestowed this upon me' etc."[47] In a world where religious gurus and experts overspiritualize everything and where only the hyper-pious seem prepared to write on prayer, Luther's "simple and playful methods," as he called them (par. 75), come as a breath of fresh air. This advice was coming from someone who, according to Veit Dietrich, could spend three hours a day in prayer!

In the Large Catechism's introduction to prayer, Luther initiated the discussion of the command to pray with a look back at this discussion on the second commandment.[48] Again, the command *not* to take God's name in vain led Luther immediately to the opposite (par. 5): "We are required to praise the holy name and to pray or call upon it in every need. For calling upon it is nothing else than praying."[49] However, Luther's emphasis on the command to pray also arose out of his pastoral experience and his desire to contrast true prayer with what passed for prayer in late-medieval piety. One senses this already in his insistence that prayer meant "calling upon God's name." This meant clearly that it was not simply a matter of reciting proper religious formulas, creating the proper religious attitude, or observing the proper religious exercises. Later in the section, he addressed this problem directly.

The commandment, however, also eliminated all the old creature's excuses for not praying. In the Large Catechism, Luther focused first on "vulgar people" and their delusions that others would pray for them. This, too, arose from certain aspects of late-medieval piety, where thousands of masses, to say nothing of other prayers, could be purchased from "the religious" (professionals), whose spiritual exercises put them closer to God. Luther's comments at table included at least one concrete example of this attitude. Even the Large Catechism (par. 6) echoed this problem: "Vulgar people who say in their delusion, 'If I do not pray, someone else will.'" The gross antinomianism against which Luther reacted in other sections of the Large Catechism also shows up here: "Thus they fall into the habit of never praying, claiming that because we reject false and hypocritical prayers, we teach that there is no duty or need to pray." Against such contempt, Luther could only preach the law as judgment.[50]

As with all of his comments on late-medieval piety, Luther faced a problem. He had to preach the law in such a way that did not, to use his words elsewhere in the Large Catechism, "institute a new slaughter of souls."[51] Here, he had first to reject (using rather gruff terms) "the kind of babbling and bellowing that used to pass for prayers."[52] Recitation of words—even beautiful or meaningful words—could not be prayer for Luther because it did not come from the heart and its deepest needs. Of course, Luther knew this practice firsthand from the monastery. In later life, he even admitted that he continued to try to recite the daily office after the Reformation had begun, until Nicholas von Amsdorff and others convinced him to desist.[53] Despite his bad experience, however, Luther did not fully reject such recitation in the Large Catechism. It was good practice for children and the illiterate, but for Luther this was not yet prayer. True prayer, as he repeated throughout this introduction, was born of deep-felt need.

The command to pray also defined the Christian life. To be Christian and not to pray (now understood in the sense of crying out in our need to God) was a logical impossibility. After all, a true Christian was someone who had been worked over by the law and driven to the gospel. Refusing to pray was as unthinkable for Luther (to borrow an earlier analogy) as refusing to fill a prescription for the life-giving medicine after hearing the diagnosis and learning the treatment. Luther used a variety of images to get his point across. First, he likened the command to pray and the command to obey authorities (the fourth commandment). Second, he made clear that prayer has to do with God, not with us. It is a matter of glorying God's name. The law, then, functioned for Luther to "silence and repel" (par. 8) the old creature's excuses and allow faith the victory. Thus, he returned to the fourth commandment in paragraph 9, now to describe the relation between father and son. Luther, who at this time was both father and son, could speak with some authority out of this analogy. Thus, the obedience accorded the command arose not out of some slavish notion of compliance but from the relation of faith. No wonder that, in 1531, Luther added to the Small Catechism an explanation to the introduction of the Lord's Prayer and emphasized the trusting relationship of parent and child out of which true prayer arises.[54]

At this point in the explanation of prayer in the Large Catechism, Luther inserted two paragraphs (par. 10–11) into the second edition, also printed in 1529. He still focused on the same issue (par. 10: "as though it made no difference if we do not pray, or as though prayer were commanded for those who are holier and in better favor with God"). However, in the additional comments (the only important addition to the Large Catechism outside of a completely new section on confession and a new preface), he delved even deeper into the commandment, finding at its center God's gracious heart. Here,

Luther expressed his pastoral concern for the damaging effect of the law on the weak by turning the law inside out.

Luther managed to find gospel in the center of the second commandment. The human heart always flees from God (par. 10), "thinking that he neither wants nor cares for our prayers because we are sinners." Instead of pitting God's promise to be father against such fears, Luther turned first to God's command to pray (par. 11). For one thing, Luther thought that the command would make us pray out of fear ("so that we may not increase his anger by such disobedience"). More surprisingly, however, Luther insisted that "by this commandment [God] makes it clear that he will not cast us out or drive us away, even though we are sinners; he wishes rather to draw us to himself so that we may humble ourselves before him, lament our misery and plight, and pray for grace and help." Underneath the command "Call on me" sounds the voice of the ever-inviting Love of the sinner's life. Even the anger described here is that of a spurned lover, not simply an angry judge: "Therefore we read in the Scriptures that [God] is angry because those who were struck down for their sin did not return to him and through prayer set aside his wrath [for their sin] and seek grace."[55]

In the paragraphs following this later insertion, Luther made the same point in a less radical way by focusing not on God's heart but on the prayer itself (pars. 12–13). The command to pray, like the fourth commandment, actually gives meaning and worth to something that has no worth in itself. Obedience to parents gains worth only from God's commandment (not from the worth of either parent or child), because the commandment, as word of God, is the only thing on which the person "can rely and depend." In the same way, the one praying can trust the word of God, now in the form of a commandment, to turn what is unworthy into something worthy. Thus, those praying "should think, 'On my account this prayer would not amount to anything; but it is important because God has commanded it.'"[56]

Under this aspect of the commandment, Luther again criticized earlier practices. In the first place (par. 14), he attacked the notion that prayer was effective *ex opere operato*, by using a German equivalent of this Latin technical phrase, "if the act were performed" (*daß das Werk getan wäre*). Prayer became thereby a matter of luck and a completely uncertain occurrence, reduced to aimless mumbling. No wonder Luther could tell Master Peter in *A Simple Way to Pray* that the Lord's Prayer was the greatest martyr on earth![57] God, on the contrary, had commanded human beings to pour out their needs to him, in the expectation that God is actually listening to what they say and mean.

In the second place (pars. 15–16), the focus of prayer in late-medieval piety was always on one's own worthiness. The command to pray also overturned spiritual pride and its mirror image, despair; no one is worthier than another. Luther stated that everyone "should say, 'The prayer I offer is just as precious, holy, and pleasing to God as those of St. Paul and the holiest of saints. The reason is this: I freely admit that he is holier in respect to his person, but not on account of the commandment.'" The command, understood in this faith-filled light, leaves room for neither boasting nor despair and again functioned for Luther as good news.

Thus, Luther walked a tightrope between arrogance and despair, using the command of God to keep the balance. On the one side, he insisted (par. 17) that "our person" had no effect on God. Whether a prayer is spoken by a sinner or a saint, God hears any prayer uttered in obedience to the command to pray. Moreover (par. 18), the commandment guaranteed for Luther that God will not "allow our prayers to be futile or lost." Unlike attempts in elementary school to keep young children busy, the command to pray is not "busywork": "If [God] did not intend to answer you, he would not have ordered you to pray and backed it up with such a strict commandment." On the other side, Luther also insisted that God's command revealed the seriousness of the situation—especially in the face of the vulgar tomfoolery of the old creature. "God is not joking" (par. 18) and is angry and threatens punishment "if we do not pray."

The Promise to Hear and Answer Prayer

Luther spent only two paragraphs (19–20) on God's promise to hear and answer prayer and then a paragraph (21) summarizing his arguments in the first two sections of his introduction. However, as the examples above demonstrate, God's promise to answer prayer formed one of the central motivations for his praying. For Luther, God's promise was best summarized in Ps. 50:15 ("Call on me in the

day of trouble; I will deliver you") and Matt. 7:7-8 ("Ask, and it will
be given you. . . . For everyone who asks receives"). Perhaps one of
the most playful attempts to apply the latter verse to prayer came in
1542. Here, Luther revealed both the ground of his confidence in
asking God and the way in which the promise itself drove a person
to pray.

> Up until now, prayer has preserved the church. Thus we must continue
> to pray. That is why Christ says, "Ask, seek, knock!" First we are to
> ask. Now, as soon as we start asking, God sneaks away somewhere and
> doesn't want to hear or to be found. So, a person has to start search-
> ing, that is, keep on praying. When a person seeks for him, God shuts
> himself up in a closet. If someone wants to get in, that person has
> to start knocking. Of course, if someone knocks only once or twice,
> God ignores it. Finally, when the knocking gets to be too much, God
> opens the door and says, "Whatever do you want?" "Lord, I want this
> or that." Then God says, "All right! Go ahead and have it." Thus, you
> have to wake God up. I'm of the opinion that there are still a lot of
> godly people here [who pray this way], as sure as there are also a lot of
> evil jerks [who do not]. Thus, the verse 'Ask . . .' implies nothing less
> than: "Ask, shout, cry, search, knock, bang!" Moreover, a person has to
> keep it up without stopping.[58]

Despite Albrecht Peters's implication that Luther's comments
on prayer in the Large Catechism were somewhat domesticated and
lacked any hint of the problem of theodicy with which other comments wrestle,[59] this section on God's promise in its very brevity
placed the problem of unanswered prayer squarely where Luther
always placed it: in the promise of God. On the one hand, God's
promises work faith in us and "ought to awaken and kindle in our
hearts a longing and love for prayer." Here, too, Peters misconstrues
the term *sollen* and imagines that this is simply more law. Luther
said here not that the one praying "should" but that the promise
"should" have this effect. Its failure to do this may be a result of
human sin (and thus God's promise to hear works as law, showing
human unbelief), but it may also be a problem in God. Luther mag-
nified the problem by adding, "For by his Word, God testifies that
our prayer is heartily pleasing to him and will assuredly be heard

and granted, so that we may not despise, cast it to the winds, or pray uncertainly." Rather than using theology to solve the problem of unanswered prayer, Luther rested his case in the certain promise of God. It was his very silence about theodicy in the face of God's promise that allowed him room to pray with such chutzpah. What Peters does not realize is that the problem of unanswered prayer must always remain unanswered in theology, lest one abandon God's promises and, thus, faith itself for explanation.

The conclusion of the first two sections bears this out. Here, Luther expressed clearly his confidence and allowed his simple German pastors and people, the intended readers of this catechism, permission to do the same.

> You can hold such promises up to [God] and say: "Here I come, dear Father, and pray not of my own accord nor because of my own worthiness, but at your commandment and promise, which cannot fail or deceive me." Those who do not believe such a promise should again realize that they are angering God, grossly dishonoring him, and accusing him of lying.[60]

To "hold up such promises" (German: *ihm aufrücken*; literally, "throw back at God") expressed far more profoundly the heart of faith's struggle against unanswered prayer. Luther refused to allow an unresponsive God to send humanity back into itself, wondering whether it had done something wrong. Instead, everything rests on God's command and promise, the ground and "material" of faith. Believers could even tell God that if it were up to them, they would not be there praying. It is God's fault for commanding them to pray and for promising to "hear and grant" (German: *gewähren*, "fulfill," used in Luther's translation of the Bible only in Ps. 20:5) their requests.

The Words to Say

Luther introduced the final section of his remarks with a simple "furthermore."[61] In addition to the command and promise, Luther wrote (par. 22), "God takes the initiative and puts into our mouths the very words and approach we are to use." He immediately described the

two motives for God's actions: our needs and our certainty.[62] With
every prayer human beings cook up on their own, the question will
always arise whether it was done correctly. The issue of such "self-
chosen spirituality," as Luther translated Col. 2:23, has been dealt
with by others.[63] Here, it is enough to realize that, for Luther, the
Lord's Prayer was a treasure direct from Christ's lips to Christian
hearts. "God loves to hear it." The motif of "treasure" (German:
Schatz) figures significantly in the Large Catechism, particularly
in his description of the benefits of baptism and the Lord's Supper.[64] This highly affective language also marks paragraph 23, where
Luther used words like *edler* (here translated "noble" but which also
has deep association to jewels) and the phrase "trade for all the riches
in the world" (German: *der Welt Gut*).

What clearly caught Luther's imagination in this third section
(especially pars. 24–32), however, was human need and its reflection
in the petitions of the Lord's Prayer. This concern, already expressed
in opening comments on the command to pray, now takes center
stage. To be sure, in Luther's view, such needs varied according to
the individual's plight. However, they were intimately connected
with faith itself. Need was simply another, poignant way for Luther
to express the (eschatological) *Anfechtungen* (assaults) under which
all believers live.

Now it becomes clear that, for believers, the *sollen* of Luther's
discussion is out of their hands. God's word (command and promise) and human need conspire, in Luther's words "to drive and compel us to pray without ceasing." Now, as Peters also points out, it
was no longer a matter of some mechanical mantra that allowed
monks to pray without ceasing (and also without thinking); rather,
prayer had become for Luther the very breath of a Christian living
under the cross, in the midst of attacks, at the end of the world.[65] He
wrote, "Therefore we have rightly rejected the prayers of monks and
priests, who howl and growl frightfully day and night, but not one
of them thinks of asking for the least little thing [literally, "a hair's
breadth"]."[66] The final break with late-medieval piety and its insistence that prayer or the sacraments were effective *ex opere operato*
(by the mere performance of the rite) occurred here. Not only God's
word but also human experience put the lie to this form of piety. If

prayer is not asking and begging God out of true human needs, it is simply howling and growling, unwilling or unable to ask (par. 25) "even for a droplet of wine." Worse yet, it is one more form of works righteousness, so twisted that it never even occurs to the worker to ask God for anything.

Having broken with this late-medieval (and modern!) piety concerning prayer, what remains to the one praying is his or her need. Here, finally, Luther resolved the pastoral problem of turning prayer into one more "must" with which to slaughter souls. In one of the most paradoxical statements in the Large Catechism, Luther described human need this way.

> But where there is to be true prayer, there must be utter earnestness. We must feel our need, the distress that drives and impels us to cry out. Then prayer will come spontaneously, as it should, and no one will need to be taught how to prepare for it or how to create the proper devotion.[67]

In language strikingly similar to his later comments at table described above, Luther mixed human need and earnestness in such a way as to eliminate the "ought" of prayer and turn it into spontaneity. Whereas religious people tend to deny needs (and look down at anyone who suddenly begins to pray or comes to worship as a result of deep-felt needs), Luther reveled in them. Needs—one might say "God's law in the flesh"—drive and impel with the opposite result than one might expect. Literally in German, "Prayer just comes forth from itself, as it should." Now, finally, the *sollen* is quieted in the face of desperate, real earnestness. This groaning was, for Luther, the heart of all prayer.[68]

To reveal our needs, the Lord's Prayer comes to the believer's rescue and provides a complete listing of all human need (using the Small Catechism as a guide): for God's word, for the Holy Spirit and faith, for victory over evil, for all the necessities of daily life (especially peace), for forgiveness (especially in the face of conscience, which always thinks it has no business praying), for strength in *Anfechtung*, and for final deliverance from all evil in the "vale of tears."[69] Luther realized, of course, that the human heart was more devious than simply to fall to its knees in the midst of needs. The listing of needs in the Lord's Prayer aided human weakness: "For we are all lacking plenty of things: all that is missing is that we do not feel or see them. God therefore wants you to lament and express your needs and concerns, not because he is unaware of them, but in order that you may kindle your hearts to stronger and greater desires and open and spread your apron wide to receive many things."[70] This self-induced ignorance or denial finally comes to an end in the word of God, this time in the words of the Lord's Prayer itself, which sets the heart on fire—the very affective language Dietrich himself used to describe Luther's praying. Then God shakes loose more than humanity's outstretched ponchos can hold.[71] God knows human needs but allows our prayers, grounded in faith, to be the ground of that very faith.

It would seem that paragraphs 28–29 mark a fitting peroration for Luther's admonition. However, as is often the case, a single remark caused him to expand this section to include several other points. For one thing, here is the only place where Luther mentioned what otherwise was central to his understanding of prayer: that it never takes place in isolation from others.[72] So when he went to list needs (par. 28), he mentioned "anything that affects us or other people around us." Pastors, magistrates, neighbors, and servants come in for special mention. In the same breath, Luther reiterated his point in paragraph 21: that those praying needed to remind God of his commands and promises. The point of the admonition, Luther concluded (par. 29), was to prevent crude and cold prayers. People were daily becoming more inept in praying.

Luther clearly had summarized his chief arguments. Nevertheless, the off-hand mention of the devil caused him to break off the end of the admonition and give the reader a glimpse of the end of the world. The ineptness in prayer was not simply a human foible; it matched exactly the devil's own desires, since he knew what damage proper prayer could do to him. Here, in language that modern readers of Luther all too often ignore, Luther stated the serious, eschatological struggle in which prayer arose.[73]

Paragraphs 30–32 showed the other side of the coin, so to speak. The appearance of the devil, a very important part of the language in both the Small and Large Catechisms, illustrated to the reader just how much more is at stake in prayer than in academic or mystical conversations with God. The God who commanded Luther to pray, promised to answer, and gave him the words to pray was the very God who had redeemed him with his holy and precious blood "from sin, death, and the power of the devil."[74] Here, Luther brought the entire Reformation and all the struggles over church into focus with the comment about the devil. Here, a politicized Luther was praying in ways not unrelated to his later prayers in 1539. The only weapon the Christian had to wield against Satan was "prayer alone," a "*sola*" worth adding to Reformation stained-glass windows—but understood now not as mere howling or magic or a work but as arising out of God's word and human need. The only thing that had prevented a collapse of the Reformation movement itself was prayer (par. 31): "A few godly people intervened like an iron wall on our side." Otherwise, "the devil would have destroyed all Germany in its own blood." Enemies of the gospel might laugh and sneer, "but by prayer alone we shall be a match both for them and for the devil." There followed (par. 32) Luther's brief synopsis of the third petition, with which this chapter began. With respect to prayer, everything, finally, rested in God's hands: "Yes, dear child, it shall be done indeed." It is on this eschatological note that Luther concluded his remarks, rejecting all babbling, howling, and growling and concentrating instead on actual, concrete asking—"a great and precious thing."[75] It was on this remarkable canvas that Luther could then paint his exposition of the Lord's Prayer in the Large Catechism.[76]

The Small Catechism's List of Needs

The brilliance of the Small Catechism's explanations of prayer has often been missed by its users. In the nine explanations that Luther provided, he summarized everything that he had proposed in the introduction to prayer in the Large Catechism. One finds here a concentration and clarity of language that other catechisms by other Christians have rarely if ever attained. Luther reduced twenty-four years of monastic and evangelical prayer life to a few short sentences.

The Commands and Promises ("Our Father . . . Amen")

The explanation to "Amen" demonstrated just how profoundly the distinction between law and gospel influenced Luther's theology of prayer: "For [our Father in heaven] himself commanded us to pray like this and has promised to hear us." As with baptism (see chapter 5), Luther grounded the certainty of prayer ("that I should be certain that such petitions are acceptable to and heard") in God's word as command and promise.[77] Prayer is faith breathing, and its respiration is measured by the "amen," which for Luther could only mean, "Yes, yes, it is going to come about just like this." Rather than provide a lengthy explanation of why some prayers were not answered (prayer's equivalent of the discussion of theodicy), Luther was far more interested in rubbing God's ears in the promises. For the believer, all depends on God's *promise* to answer, not on the answers themselves. Thus, unanswered prayers might cause the believer *Anfechtung*, that sense of having one's faith assaulted, but they never resulted in speculation about one's own faith (as if by the work of faith one earned answers) or God's will (revealed for Luther in the promise to hear and answer prayer).

The other gospel note in the Small Catechism's exposition of the Lord's Prayer comes in the single section added to the five chief parts: an explanation of "Our Father in heaven." Luther's use of "Father language" for God, as Birgit Stolt has shown, changed over the course of the 1520s and mirrored Luther's own experience first as a son and then later, beginning in 1526, as a father.[78] Discovering the "father's heart" for children, especially with the death of his infant daughter, meant, for Luther, that calling God "Father" revealed God's very heart for us, infinitely more gracious and merciful than Luther's for his own children. Thus, in 1531, with Hans now in his fifth year, Luther wrote, "With these words God wants to entice us, so that we come to believe he is truly our Father and we are truly his children, in order that we may ask him boldly and with complete confidence, just as loving children ask their loving father."[79] Again, Luther's comments reflected the certainty that comes with the promise ("God is your loving father not your merciless judge"). Yet it is important to remember that this discussion of father comes after the third article of the Creed ("I believe that I cannot believe"), so that it is not Luther's experience of being a father or of having a father that made God merciful but, rather, the experience of the Trinity itself that made this happen (see chapter 3).

The First Three Petitions: The Believer's Basic Spiritual Needs
The interweaving of the first three petitions in the Small Catechism in terms of form, language, and content is quite striking. Each petition evokes from Luther two questions: "What is this?" and "How does this come about?" The explanations to the second and third petitions then reiterate language from the previous one or two. This, in turn, gives the three an underlying unity of meaning that states in simple terms the basic insights of Lutheran theology.

The three petitions undermine the very request being made to God. Luther saw in these strange, Hebraic sentences the end of any notion that our prayers are good works that merit God's response. "Hallowed be your name; your kingdom come; your will be done." Too late! The believer lives by God's grace alone and thus must pray these prayers as if having just tumbled out of the third article of the Creed ("I believe that I cannot believe"): "God's name is holy in itself. . . . God's kingdom comes on its own. . . . God's good and gracious will comes about without our prayer."[80] "I cannot believe."

Yet right on the heels of this claim that God's name, kingdom, and will are not ours to earn comes the "*I believe* that I cannot believe, but instead the Holy Spirit . . .*" This truly is a call to the pharmacy for medicine, in which case it is not that medicine is not there or needs to be earned—it just needs (thanks to the Holy Spirit) to be sent to the correct address. Thus, Luther added, "We ask in this prayer that [God's name] may also become holy in and among us . . . that [God's kingdom] may also come to us . . . that [God's will] may also come about in and among us."[81]

Exegetically speaking, the text of the Lord's Prayer itself gave Luther permission to make this kind of distinction. Luther simply took the final words of the third petition ("on earth as in heaven") and applied it to all three, something that is not impossible grammatically or theologically speaking. "May your name be hallowed on earth," that is, "in and among [German: *bei*] us"; "May your kingdom come on earth," that is, "to us"; "May your will come about on earth," that is, "in and among us." It was not that Luther abandoned the eschatological thrust of these petitions—his explanations in the Large Catechism made that clear—but rather that he saw the end crashing in through the Word, which ushered in the Last Judgment ahead of time. The Lord's Prayer was truly the prayer of the believer and the believer's most critical needs.

The second question—"How does this come about?"—reflects in clumsy English a remarkable linguistic feat in the German: the second question posed to each of the first three petitions employed the same word as the third petition itself—*geschehen*. Thus, one experiences in these petitions a unifying "How does this happen?" three times, connected with "May your will happen!" The answers to this second question once again take all control for the Christian life out of our hands and place it into God's hands ("but the Holy Spirit has called me . . ."). How does all this happen? God must act.

Indeed, the deepest needs of the believer caused Luther to pray the Creed backward in the Lord's Prayer. The believer's fundamental need is for the word of God. Without this Word, all is lost and the world sinks back into its own dreams of its own powers and its own schemes of wresting heaven from God. The third article's "called me through the gospel" and "daily . . . abundantly forgives all sins—mine and those of all believers" demanded that the Word be taught purely. Thus, the first petition begged God for the Word. Although Luther also tied this petition to God's name and the second commandment (without which there is no prayer), here he insisted that the fundamental need for God's name is simply the need for God's word. The woodcut for this commandment said much the same, depicting a sixteenth-century preacher with his congregation—already indicating a sea change of remarkable proportions for an age when the Eucharist and penance far overshadowed preaching. Moreover, and this is unique to the explanation of the first petition, Luther broke the boundary of explanation and returned much more clearly to paraphrase by breaking into prayer. Finally, he also brought echoes of the introduction ("Our Father") into the mix.

> How does this come about? Answer: Whenever the Word of God is taught clearly and purely and we, as God's children, also live holy lives

according to it. To this end help us, dear Father in heaven! However, whoever teaches and lives otherwise than the Word of God teaches profanes the name of God among us. Preserve us from this, heavenly Father![82]

Here the children are running to their heavenly Father for the Word and for life in the Word. Even "sanctification" (living a holy life) depended upon God answering a prayer and not upon our work.[83] The "clearly and purely" here, which later became an excuse to put children (to say nothing of candidates for ordination) on trial, misses the point when not directly derived from the third article. The Word creates faith, church, and all the rest; the church, faith, or, above all, the preacher does not create the Word. Indeed, the point of the petition is to pray to God for help![84]

The second petition's explanation, which Luther knew also was praying for the final kingdom, as his comments in the Large Catechism made clear, drove to the heart of the third article of the Creed while still echoing the gospel introduction ("Our heavenly Father") and the first petition (God's "Holy Word"): "whenever our heavenly Father gives us his Holy Spirit so that throug his grace we believe his Holy Word and live godly lives here in time and hereafter in eternity."[85] Thus, if the first petition begs for the Word—God's true medicine of forgiveness and life—the second begs for the Word to work—that is, for faith, which (as the third article insists) happens only through the Holy Spirit. At the end ("here in time and hereafter in eternity"), Luther even managed to hint at the eschatological edge to this prayer.

Having mentioned the Holy Spirit in the second petition, Luther—at least linguistically—moved to the second article of the Creed in the third petition. Although Christ is not mentioned by name here or anywhere else in Luther's explanation of the Lord's Prayer (Luther took seriously that this prayer was addressed to the Father), the language of defeat for the devil, world, and flesh (the traditional three enemies of the believer) echoed that of the second article, where Christ defeats "sin, death, and the power of the devil" with his suffering and death and rescues believers from their worst kidnappers.[86] Twice, in both the negative and the positive parts of this petition, Luther tied the struggle over God's will to the first two petitions themselves: "God breaks and hinders every evil scheme and will . . . that would not allow us to hallow God's name and would prevent the coming of his kingdom. . . . God strengthens us and keeps us steadfast in his Word and in faith." Although, on occasion, Luther could use the more traditional, almost Stoical notion that praying for God's will to be done meant preventing our will from being done, here he understood this petition not as a mystical "Let it be" but as a battle cry, so that the language here is not that far removed from "A Mighty Fortress," written at nearly this same time.

Praying for God's Left Hand: The Fourth Petition

The divide between the third and fourth petitions might seem at first glance to be rather artificial, especially since some in the tradition—including Luther in *The Personal Prayer Book*—insisted that the fourth petition was praying for God's word or, even, the Lord's Supper. However, developments in Luther's own theology led first, in 1521, to the definition of a first use of the law (to keep order in the world and to restrain evil) and then, in 1523, to the defining of two spheres of God's work with human beings (the left and right hands of God, bringing blessings, order, and restraint in this world and forgiveness, life, and salvation for the world to come). Already in 1526, in comments from the preface to the German Mass (*Deutsche Messe*), Luther began to connect the fourth petition with sustenance in this life. Indeed, Luther defined the third petition as the work of God's right hand in defeating evil for the final coming of the kingdom and contrasted this, especially in the Large Catechism, with prayers for temporal peace in the fourth petition.[87]

The fourth petition reflects in every way the language of the first article, as Luther (whether consciously or not) reversed the order of the Trinity in the explanations to the Lord's Prayer from the work of the Holy Spirit through the Word, through the defeat of evil (won for us in Christ's death and resurrection) to the work of the Creator. In one way, Luther's explanation to the fourth petition mirrored the first three. His answer to "What is this?" might confuse those looking for meaning, since Luther did not yet deign to

tell the reader what the words *daily bread* meant. Instead, he again
faced the fact that receiving daily bread, like receiving salvation,
did not depend on us: "God gives daily bread without our prayer."
Here, Luther confessed again what was already in the first article:
God's fatherly and divine goodness and mercy. Thus, as with the
first three petitions, the point is that the prayer reaches the believer's
heart: "We ask in this prayer that God cause us to recognize what
our daily bread is and to receive it with thanksgiving."[88] Faith opens
the believer's eyes to God's ever-abundant mercy and allows it to
pour forth praise. The very thing *demanded* in the first article ("we
owe it to God to thank, praise, serve, and obey") now comes in this
prayer as a desperate request for medicine, that is, recognizing God's
created mercies and thanking God for them. This is not an "ought,"
but because of the gospel ("I believe that I cannot believe . . ."), it
becomes a fervent prayer.

With the second question, Luther asked, for the first time in
the Small Catechism, what something actually meant, namely, the
words *daily bread*. He summarized the list in the first few words
("everything included in the necessities and nourishment for our
bodies") and then gave some examples. Both here and in the Large
Catechism, where the list is even more all encompassing,[89] one hears
echoes of the first article with its confession of Luther's faith or, at
least, the faith of the head of the household. He prayed for upright
spouse, children, household members, and rulers, where the word
upright (German: *fromm*) had both religious and worldly conno-
tations in the sixteenth century. In the household and in society,
one prayed for justice and godliness. The other adjective Luther
employed several times ("good") reminds one again of creation and
even of his (incorrect) derivation of the name God (*Gott*) from *good*
(*gut*). Luther's list was once again a brief confession of faith and
therefore cannot simply be the same for everyone who prays this
prayer. Thus, in the Large Catechism, he summarized this petition
with these words: "Thus, you see, God wishes to show us how he
cares for us in all our needs and faithfully provides for our daily sustenance. Although he gives and provides these blessings bountifully,
even to the godless and rogues, yet he wishes us to ask for them so
that we may realize that we have received them from his hand and

may recognize in them his fatherly good toward us."[90] Before this summary, Luther concentrated in the Large Catechism on the gift of good government and peace, without which no one could eat the bread, and the fury of the devil, who not only attacks faith but also wants the whole world to collapse in war and starvation.

Baptized, We Live: The Final Three Petitions
So far, Luther's explanations reduced human need to these things: the Word, faith and the Holy Spirit; the triumph of the Word and faith over all evil working against them; and sustenance for our bodies. With the final petitions, Luther sketched the life of the baptized: living from God's forgiving grace alone, in the midst of struggle, yearning for deliverance in the end.[91] As he stated in the preface to the baptismal service, it is no joke "to take action against the devil and not only to drive him away from the little child but also to hang around the child's neck such a mighty, lifelong enemy."[92] The Lord's Prayer confronted the threats to the baptized: wills contrary to the saving will of God (third petition), the lack of peace and daily sustenance (fourth petition), sin (fifth petition), assault to one's faith (sixth petition), and, in a final summation, all evil (seventh petition).

With the fifth petition, Luther did not simply focus on forgiveness in general—after all, the first three petitions also do battle with the devil, the world, and our flesh—but precisely on the guilt that would block believers from praying at all and would undermine all faith in God's promise (as a gracious father) to answer this very prayer. Suddenly, believers who call on God for help also acknowledge that, at the same time (*simul*!), they are sinners: "We ask in this prayer that our heavenly Father would not regard our sin nor deny these petitions on their account." For Luther, the devil was a master of syllogisms, always arguing: "God punishes sinners; you are a sinner; therefore, etc." Here, in Luther's explanation, that very syllogism was destroyed. Christ put into the believer's mouth the very thing the sinner cannot believe: that God forgives sin.

The undeserved nature of creation's blessings, underscored in the first article and the fourth petition, was now translated into the language of God's forgiving mercy, which made the unworthy worthy:

"For we are worthy of nothing for which we ask, nor have we earned it. Instead we ask that God would give us all things by grace, for we daily sin much and indeed deserve only punishment."[93] This petition of the sinner-declared-righteous expressed the grace lurking behind every petition of this prayer: here is medicine for human illness of sin, a true "balm in Gilead." The *simul iustus et peccator* (at the same time righteous and sinner) was the only thing that made sense of the Lord's Prayer. If the believer is not truly a sinner, what sense would it make to pray this petition? When Paul stated in Romans 7, "The good that I would do, that I cannot, and the evil that I would not, that I do," it could not, despite all the warm wishes of pious and enlightened exegetes, past and present, simply have referred to Paul's problem before conversion. No! "Forgive us!" comes the cry of the Holy Spirit, crying, "Abba, Father!" as Paul says then in Romans 8. "All things by grace" finally puts the lie to every pious-sounding scheme. We do not progress in the Christian life; we remain sinners until that "Great Gettin' Up Morning."

Of course, many consciences have been crushed by what follows in the Lord's Prayer: "as we forgive." Luther's comments in the Small Catechism remain cryptic and, perhaps, even disconcerting to those who would read his explanation out of context, that is, without the explanations to the preceding parts of the Lord's Prayer and to the Ten Commandments and the Creed. From comments in the Large Catechism, we know that Luther realized the pastoral problem here. But Luther's language here is peculiarly comforting. To rob folks of the comfort of this petition, the devil comes with this syllogism: "You must forgive or you will not be forgiven; you have not forgiven; therefore despair!" Luther brushed this aside by writing: "So, on the other hand, we, too, truly want to forgive heartily and to do good gladly to those who sin against us." Here faith speaks its will ("We, too, truly want to"), but without the Holy Spirit, the death of the old creature (through the Ten Commandments), and the birth of the new (through the Creed's gospel), we remain trapped (*simul iustus et peccator*). Thus, the demonic threat of the addition to this petition loses its force in the face of faith, where the one sinned against wants to do exactly what God has already done: forgive.[94]

In the Large Catechism, Luther investigated the matter in more detail. The *simul* is as starkly put as anywhere in Luther's writings. That is, he first stated the law of this phrase: "If you do not forgive, do not think that God forgives you." But then, in the event that someone did forgive the neighbor, Luther found himself driven to confess the gospel: "But if you forgive, you have the comfort and assurance that you are forgiven in heaven—not on account of your forgiving (for [God] does it altogether freely, out of pure grace, because he has promised it, as the gospel teaches) but instead because he has set this up for our strengthening and assurance as a sign along with the promise."[95] Not only did Luther struggle to make grace the heart of the petition ("God forgives altogether freely"), but he also turned the phrase into a sign to the believer—surely the last thing one would expect. Comparing it to baptism and the Lord's Supper, Luther indicates that forgiving one's neighbor is something people can do anytime they feel at all uncertain about whether God forgives them, receiving a sign or "seal" of God's willingness to forgive them. It is the continual presence of this sign that indicates that Luther finally left the legalism of "Forgive everyone or else" for the grace of "Every time I forgive someone, this is a sign of God's grace as much as baptism or the Supper is." As he wrote: "Moreover, above and beyond the other signs [baptism and the Lord's Supper], it [forgiving others] has been instituted precisely so that we can use and practice it every hour, keeping it with us at all times."[96] Forgiveness of others is not a work of the sinner but the fruit of the Spirit and a sign of God's grace.

The sixth petition continued Luther's theme of describing the baptized believer's life of faith. Here, too, the *simul* of Christian existence comes to expression, especially when Luther wrote, "Yet such is life that one stands today and falls tomorrow." This remarkably realistic view of human existence contrasted with the medieval anxiety over whether one was in a state of sin or grace (or perfection) and contrasts with the modern American addiction to conversion experiences, decisions for Jesus, and the striving for holiness and perfection. Those who are always both sinners and believers now pray to be preserved and kept from those things that would do them in. Of course, the reference to "the devil, the world and our flesh" recalls the third petition and a cry that God would be victorious.

Now, on an even more personal level, the believer cries for protection. Here, remarkable words in the Small Catechism's explanation come in what it lists as the chief sins: false belief and despair.[97] Once again, Luther sent the reader back to the third article and, indeed, to the first commandment. The commandment demands trust, and the third article ("I believe that I cannot believe") fulfills that demand. Then the first three petitions pray to God for the Word, faith and the Holy Spirit, and victory. Finally, in the daily grind of the Christian life, where the old creature dies daily and the new creature of faith comes to life, the believer cries for protection from the one thing that could ruin it all: false belief and despair. Even so, Luther's realism shone forth, in that he admitted that the believer is under attack (using the verbal form of *Anfechtung*: "although we may be attacked by them"). This kind of realism may not fill old basketball arenas with false hopes of prosperity, and it certainly will not create best sellers dedicated to the mythical "purpose-driven" life, but it will bring comfort to those broken by life and living by faith in God's promise alone.

Finally, Luther viewed the seventh petition as a summary of the whole prayer and, thus, of the entire Christian life. In the Large Catechism, he noted that the Greek could also be translated "Deliver us from the Evil One," which certainly matched his baptismal theology.[98] But in the Small Catechism, he construed the term more broadly to include evil "affecting body or soul, property or reputation." For one under the empire's ban, living from the largesse of the elector, vilified in many corners of the church, and having in 1527 experienced the first major physical collapse of his life, Luther certainly hit upon those forces of evil that he was experiencing. Moreover, rather than rewrite the medieval obsession with a "blessed end," Luther swept it up into this petition, thereby ensuring that, as a summary of the entire prayer, the eschatological edge to the prayer would not be completely lost. What Luther would not allow, however, was a lessening of the role of God's grace in the life of the believer, and thus he wrote, "And at last, when our final hour comes, [God] may grant us a blessed end and take us *by grace* from this valley of tears to himself in heaven." Of course, medieval writers also thought that everything happened by God's grace, especially

God setting up the condition of merit. But by this point in Luther's explanation, the reader knows to look for God's grace in the Holy Spirit's work to reveal Christ, who is the mirror of the Father's heart. In the end, Luther managed in these brief explanations of the Small Catechism to discover and describe everything a baptized believer needs for the Christian life, surely worth rubbing God's ears in.

The Sacrament of Baptism: Matthew 4 (the Baptism of Jesus). Earlier versions of the Small Catechism used similar depictions of contemporary baptisms but linked to Matthew 28 and not to Jesus' Baptism which is not depicted here.

CHAPTER 5

Luther, Children, and Baptism[1]

Wittenberg's theological revolution, begun by Martin Luther in 1517, was fueled not only by the printing press but by the paintbrush—in particular that of Lucas Cranach Sr. He was an indefatigable worker, as noted by Melanchthon in his table talk,[2] which meant that he kept long hours, employed dozens of apprentices, and saw to it that the faces of Luther, Melanchthon, and other figures of the Reformation were spread all over Europe. That labor also produced several new types of images in Christian religious art.[3] Depictions of the Samaritan woman at the well, of the Last Supper and of the Lord's Supper with laypersons in sixteenth-century dress receiving the chalice, and of the raising of Lazarus with the Reformers in attendance were among his innovations.

Most striking were his paintings for baptismal fonts. In Augsburg's St. Anne's Church and in Weimar, among many other places, Cranach provided pictures of Jesus blessing the children from Mark 10, complete with women and babies in sixteenth-century garb, nursing mothers, shy children, and scowling apostles. This scene, without parallel in medieval art, doubtless arose from the same concern that drove Luther to urge painting the Last Supper over Wittenberg's altar: so that people might know what was taking place at the font. However, Cranach's art preserved more than Renaissance fashions in women's clothing. It also pointed to a fundamental shift in the assessment of baptism and of children that stands near the heart of Luther's Reformation theology.

Baptism: The Sacrament of the Christian Life

Throughout his career, Luther's theology was marked by discovery and reform, as he unearthed more and more profound insights based on God's surprising work of justifying sinners in the Crucified through faith in the living Word alone.[4] In 1519 and 1520, Luther first turned his attention toward the sacraments. Alongside profound criticism of Roman abuses of the Lord's Supper in the *Babylonian Captivity of the Church*, Luther had these remarkably positive words for Holy Baptism.

> Blessed be God and the Father of our Lord Jesus Christ, who according to the riches of his mercy [Eph. 1:3, 7] has preserved in his church this sacrament at least, untouched and untainted by the ordinances of men, and has made it free to all nations and classes of mankind, and has not permitted it to be oppressed by the filthy and godless monsters of greed and superstition. For he desired that by it little children, who were incapable of greed and superstition, might be initiated and sanctified in the simple faith of his Word; even today Baptism has its chief blessing for them.[5]

Baptism, a relatively neglected sacrament in late-medieval theology,[6] provided Luther the perfect reflection of justification by faith alone. In baptism, God links our destiny to that of Jesus Christ.[7] In baptism, Christ himself baptizes[8] and joins us to his death and resurrection, not just allegorically but, to use modern parlance, "for real."[9] In baptism, God ordains all to the royal priesthood we share in Christ.[10] Far from bestowing a magical power *ex opere operato*, which was easily sinned away when a person "came of age" and began sinning in earnest, baptism now remained a valid, irrevocable promise of God, creating and received in faith. Thus, Luther took on Jerome's hackneyed view of baptism and penance (the first and second planks after the shipwreck of sin) and turned it on its head. Baptism never sinks, because baptism constitutes the ship itself.

> You will likewise see how perilous, indeed, how false it is to suppose that penance is "the second plank after shipwreck," and how pernicious an error it is to believe that the power of Baptism is broken, and the

Top: The Second Commandment: Leviticus 24[:10-16] (The Blasphemy of Shelomith's Son)
Bottom: The Third Commandment: Numbers 15[:32-36] (Breaking the Sabbath)

Top: The Fourth Commandment: Genesis 9[:20-27] (The Drunk-
enness of Noah)
Bottom: The Fifth Commandment: Genesis 4[:1-16] (Cain Slaying
Abel)

Top: The Sixth Commandment: 2 Samuel 11 (David and Bath-
sheba)
Bottom: The Seventh Commandment: Joshua 7 (The Theft of
Achan)

Top: The Eighth Commandment: Daniel 13 (The Story of Suzanna, from the Apocrypha)
Bottom: The Ninth Commandment: Genesis 30[:25-43] (Jacob and Laban's Sheep)

The Tenth Commandment: Genesis 39 (Joseph and Potiphar's Wife)

Top: The First Petition: Mark 5 [=4] (Jesus Preaching to the Crowds). Earlier versions depicted sixteenth-century preaching with a reference to Exodus 20[:8-11, 19]

Bottom: The Second Petition: Luke 11[:13] (The Holy Spirit, Promised by Jesus, Comes upon the Apostles [Acts 2]) Earlier versions referred to Acts 2.

Top: The Third Petition: Matthew 26 [36-44 (Gethsemane)] (Jesus Carries the Cross) Earlier versions refer to Matthew 27:31-32.
Bottom: The Sixth Petition: Matthew 4[:1-11] (The Temptation of Jesus)

The Seventh Petition: Matthew 9[:20-22] (The Healing of the Woman with a Flow of Blood). Earlier versions depict the story of the Canaanite woman (Matthew 15:21-28)

ship dashed to pieces, because of sin. The ship remains one, solid, and invincible; it will never be broken up into separate "planks." In it are carried all those who are brought to the harbor of salvation, for it is the truth of God giving us its promise in the sacraments. Of course, it often happens that many rashly leap overboard into the sea and perish; these are those who abandon faith in the promise and plunge into sin. But the ship itself remains intact and holds its course unimpaired.[11]

Justification by faith alone implies that God is no respecter of persons. Baptism, as the sacrament of justification par excellence, becomes the great equalizer of Christians. Even age no longer divides them. This view of baptism fostered a completely different approach to children, already inherent in comments from the *Babylonian Captivity* itself. First, two years before the Zwickau prophets attacked infant baptism and five years before the first rebaptism by the Swiss Brethren in 1525, Luther defended the practice of infant baptism as central to justification by faith alone. Second, and perhaps even more important for the development of Reformation theology, Luther derived from baptism his first criticisms of monasticism, from which source arose his unique doctrine of vocation in daily life, including the vocation of children.

Infant Baptism

When the Zwickau prophets landed on Wittenberg's doorstep in late 1521 (while Luther was at the Wartburg throwing reams of ink-stained paper at the devil) and proclaimed an end to infant baptism, Philip Melanchthon (in need more of Luther's authority than his theological advice) wrote to his older mentor for support. "I have always expected Satan to touch this sore, but he did not want to do it through the papists," Luther responded.[12] The devil would do anything to undermine the promise of God in Christ! The certainty of God's unconditional, justifying word in baptism could not be broken by those who had "swallowed the Holy Spirit feathers and all," as Luther would later say.

When Luther returned to the question in his 1527 tract *On Rebaptism*, he wrote with even more assurance about baptism's central place in the Christian life.[13] Not deterred by texts like Mark 16:16

("The one who believes and is baptized . . ."), which seemed to imply that faith must precede baptism, Luther argued for infant faith on the basis of John the Baptist's handsprings in Elizabeth's womb. No wonder the children in Cranach's paintings seem so content! One is even pulling Jesus' beard. The more rational, grown-up perspectives of both Roman theologians (who argued that the mortal sins willed by adults destroyed baptismal grace) and Anabaptists (who reserved baptism for those old enough to decide) fell before Luther's childish point of view. Even if they had no faith, Luther argued, a baptized child was like a woman who had married without love. If five years later she fell in love, there was no reason to retie the knot. Nothing could thwart God's good promise: "Let the children come." It is no accident that prominent in both versions of Luther's baptismal service from the 1520s, the second version of which was appended to virtually every Wittenberg printing of the Small Catechism during his lifetime, was the Markan story depicted later by Cranach for evangelical baptistries.[14] As we shall see below, this defense of infant baptism had profound implications for Luther's pedagogy.

Luther also summarized his arguments from *On Rebaptism* in an excursus in the Large Catechism.[15] First, he argued from results. It seemed easy for him to prove that Christians baptized as infants showed all the signs of the Holy Spirit's work (he cited the examples of Bernard of Clairvaux, Jean Gerson, and John Huss) and that, since God had promised that the church would endure throughout all time, it must have existed when only infants were being baptized. Of course, this argument could be taken to mean that baptism's validity depended on faith. As a result, Luther hastened to add a second, in his view stronger, argument: "Everything depends upon the Word and commandment of God."[16] He admitted that this argument was a bit subtle (indeed, he began this excursus by instructing the "simple" to leave the entire question to the "learned"), but he also indicated that many of his earlier statements about baptism (see below) were aimed at making this very point. He distinguished baptism's validity from its effectiveness and clearly separated the roles of faith and the word of God: "For my faith does not make baptism; rather, it receives baptism. Baptism does not become invalid if it is not properly received or used, as I have said, for it is not bound to our faith but to the Word."[17] Even if infants did not believe, this would not invalidate baptism. One builds baptism not on faith—even the faith of the gathered community—but on God's word and command. He would use a similar argument regarding the Lord's Supper.

Luther suspected that those opposed to infant baptism were entertaining what he called in *On Rebaptism* a *Werkteufel* (works devil)—that is, they had turned faith into the object of faith and thus argued against the centrality of God's grace in Christ (and, by extension, in the sacraments). To have faith in faith (a phrase also found in *On Rebaptism*) was to destroy Christianity completely. This argument still rings true against all forms of "decision theology" today. Luther wrote, "Therefore only presumptuous and stupid spirits draw the conclusion that where there is no true faith, there also can be no true baptism. Likewise I might argue, 'If I have no faith, then Christ is nothing.' Or again, 'If I am not obedient, then father, mother, and magistrates are nothing.'"[18] He urged his readers to reverse the argument, arguing that charges of the abuse of baptism actually in themselves proved that baptism had existence and value apart from use, since otherwise it could not be misused. Quoting a Latin adage, he concluded that "misuse does not destroy the substance, but confirms its existence."[19] The problem with believers' baptism was, for Luther, quite simple and horribly destructive: it put believers in charge of their faith and denigrated God's word, turning baptism into an empty sign.[20] In this way, the medieval conviction that baptism could be sinned away and the Anabaptist conviction that baptism arose from faith were simply two sides of the same coin, undermining both God's grace and human vocation.

From Baptism to Vocation

In the *Babylonian Captivity*, Luther began an attack on monastic vows by contrasting such human traditions to the truly godly character of the baptismal vow.[21] In 1521, while at the Wartburg, Luther turned his full attention to the problem in his work *Martin Luther's Judgment on Monastic Vows*, where he intensified his onslaught. Monasticism of Luther's day, like claims of pietism or spirituality in later generations, implied a division of Christians into the truly spiritual (or *perfecti*) Christians and the carnal Christians. Children, parents, outcasts, and the real poor came off as second-class

Christians, able only in a state of grace to fulfill the Ten Commandments, compared to the "converted" (as the monastic life was called)
and their oblates, whose very vows, Thomas Aquinas had argued,
fulfilled not only the commands but also the counsels of the New
Testament. Over against such holiness, Luther placed the universal,
law-free gospel, which claimed no special advantage to any person's
works. God is no respecter of persons.[22] Especially in the preface,
addressed to his father, he also accorded new authority to the fourth
commandment.

By eliminating the bifurcation of medieval spiritual life, Luther
created a serious spiritual crisis for his listeners. Suddenly, the counsels of the New Testament, once safely left only for those under a
vow, now became the responsibility of all. By Luther's own testimony
in his 1523 tract *On Secular Authority*, this crisis led to the development of his notion of God's two hands, or governments, and to the
idea of vocation in daily life.[23] Baptism makes us priests before God
and frees us to serve our neighbor in our particular arenas of life.
Vocatio, another technical term used almost exclusively in the late
Middle Ages for the call to the monastic life, had become in Luther's
hands a word for the day-to-day world in which all Christians found
themselves: a world divided between household and work, society
and government, church and school. The single introductory sentence to what is mistakenly called the "Table of Duties" in the Small
Catechism summarized this insight: "A Chart of Some Bible Passages
for the Household: Through these verses all kinds of holy orders and
walks of life may be admonished, as through lessons particularly pertinent to their office and duty."[24] In one stroke, marriage, parenthood, childhood, and even widowhood had become holy orders!

Luther's defense of infant baptism and his innovative perspective on daily life as the locus of the Christian life shaped his view of
children. To be sure, there were other factors, which he held in common with contemporaries who held widely different theologies, that
also influenced his point of view. However, only in the light of the
theological underpinnings described here does Luther's approach to
children make sense.

Luther's Baptismal Pedagogy:
The Fourth Commandment

Claims by social historians regarding the pedagogical failure of Luther's reformation themselves fail adequately to account for Luther's view of baptism and its implications for the child.[25] As Klaus Pezold has pointed out, even medieval writers as sensitive as Jean Gerson viewed baptism as a preliminary to the true Christian life, asserting that baptized children must subsequently be led to Christ. Luther, by contrast, realized that children came to Christ in baptism, making baptism the sacrament of justification by faith alone par excellence.[26] This changed both the content and the tone of Christian education for Luther. His comments on the fourth commandment throughout the 1520s provide an example of this shift.

In 1520, Luther published his *Short Form of the Ten Commandments, the Creed, and the Lord's Prayer*, material that became the backbone of his *Personal Prayer Book* of 1522.[27] There, the medieval character of his comments on the fourth commandment still shone through.[28] There was no mention of vocation; the material centered on moral admonitions to care for and honor one's parents; and the limits of obedience were not spelled out. In contrast, the *Treatise on Good Works*, also produced in 1520, focused on the parents' responsibility. It outlined a form of dishonoring one's parents that arose from the parents' own permissiveness and failure to follow the first table of the Decalogue. In this laxity, children were not to obey their parents. Luther also sketched the good works parents can do by fulfilling this commandment. Parents fulfilled Matthew 25 when they cared for their children: "How many good works you have at hand in your own home with your own child who needs all such things as these like a hungry, thirsty, naked, poor, imprisoned, sick soul! O what a blessed marriage and home that would be with such parents! That home would indeed be a true church, a chosen cloister, yes, a paradise!"[29]

At the same time, Luther contrasted the God-given beauty of these works to the self-chosen vows and pilgrimages of the day: "Husbands run to St. James [of Compostella], wives make vows to Our Lady."[30] Moreover, he strongly emphasized the centrality of faith.

It has been said in reference to the other commandments that they are to be fulfilled in relation to faith, the chief work. It is the same in this instance. Nobody must think that the training and teaching of his children is sufficient in itself. It must be done in confidence of God's favor. A man must have no doubt that he is well pleasing to God in what he is doing, and he should let work of this kind be nothing else but an expression and exercise of his faith.[31]

From this beginning, Luther focused increasingly on the baptized believer's vocation implied in the fourth commandment. In his catechetical sermons of 1528, he linked the life of faith squarely to the everyday world of the household. He realized the radical implications of this approach, so he reminded his listeners that not only had the pope and scholastic theologians not grasped this commandment, but "nor did I understand or was ever taught what you are being taught now."[32] When parents perform their office, the old creature curses and refuses to honor them. God therefore "commands [children] not only that they should obey them but also honor them; that is, that the children think highly of them, not because they are beautiful or well clothed, but because of the first commandment, which commands that we fear God and trust him."[33] The following day, Luther returned to the fourth commandment, only this time to admonish parents: "For the fourth commandment calls you fathers and mothers, not tyrants, rascals, and scoundrels. . . . God does not give you your children to play with, nor does he give you servants for you to use them like donkeys for work."[34]

In reworking these themes for the Large Catechism, published in 1529, Luther applies this notion of Christian vocation directly to children.

If this could be impressed upon the poor people, a servant girl would dance for joy and praise and thank God; and with her careful work, for which she receives sustenance and wages, she would obtain a treasure such as all who pass for the greatest saints do not have. Is it not a tremendous honor to know this and to say, "If you do your daily household chores, that is better than the holiness and austere life of all the monks"? . . . In God's sight it is actually faith that makes a person holy; it alone serves God, while our works serve people.[35]

Baptism was no longer a far-removed stepping-stone in the child's life, easily lost in the struggle against sin. Instead, it had become the place where a child entered the realm of God's favor and, as the exorcisms in Luther's baptismal services made all too clear, gave the newly baptized a lifelong enemy, the devil.[36] This meant that, for Luther, the parents' responsibility for their baptized children became one of the central concerns of the fourth commandment. With dulling regularity, despite the fact that the fourth commandment itself addressed only children, Luther emphasized the responsibilities of parents and governmental officials in providing schooling for their charges to fight the devil.[37] In announcements for sermons on the catechism in December 1528, he pleaded, "Give them an hour off that they may come to know themselves and Christ more fully."[38] Otherwise, the parents would have to answer for their neglect. In the preface to the Small Catechism, Luther highlighted the fourth commandment as a text in need of emphasis in parish education. After a cursory mention of the obedience of children and subjects, he spent a paragraph describing the responsibility parents and governing authorities bore for education.[39] In the Large Catechism, too, Luther fulminated, "Therefore let all people know that it is their chief duty—at the risk of losing divine grace—first to bring up their children in the fear and knowledge of God, and, then, if they are so gifted, also to have them engage in formal study so that they may be of service wherever they are needed."[40]

Nowhere did Luther emphasize the office of child, especially the child as learner, and the concomitant office of parent as educator more strongly than in *A Sermon on Keeping Children in School.* There, in highly eschatological language, he explained to pastors and preachers in the preface what the neglect of schools really portended. It provides a good summary of Luther's view of children.

> Among [Satan's] wiles, one of the very greatest, if not the greatest of all, is this—he deludes and deceives the common people so that they are not willing to keep their children in school or expose them to instruction. He puts into their minds the dastardly notion that because monkery, nunning, and priestcraft no longer hold out the hope they once did, there is no more need for study and for learned men, that instead we need to give thought only to how to make a living and get rich.[41]

Such advice may also ring true in the present, where children and parents alike are consumed by our consumer society, a process that stifles both faith toward God and care for the neighbor. Luther's solution, grounded in God's calling in and through baptism, may also provide surprisingly good news for children and parents in our day, too.

Baptism in the Catechisms

The foregoing discussion may help reground Luther's comments in the catechisms within their proper theological and social context. He asked in both the Small and Large Catechisms four basic questions of baptism, adding to the Large Catechism an excursus on infant baptism similar to his comments in *On Rebaptism* from the previous year. The first question is "Was ist das?" ("What is baptism?"). The Small Catechism's answer is remarkable for its encapsulation of Wittenberg's understanding of sacraments. Indeed, there were two definitions of sacraments rattling around Wittenberg, both dependent on the Augustinian and medieval tradition. One emphasized God's word connected to a physical element; the other stressed God's command connected with a divine promise.[42] Luther here combined both in a single sentence: "Baptism is not simply plain water. Instead it is water enclosed in God's command and connected with God's Word."[43] The command comes in Matthew 28, quoted here, and the promise comes in Mark 16, which Luther first quoted in connection with the second question. In 1529, smarting under the outrageous things that he had heard rumored were part of Anabaptists' rejection of infant baptism, Luther insisted that baptism was not a "bathkeeper's baptism." It was not about the water in itself.[44]

Modern "historical" critics have called into question whether Matthew 28 and its command to baptize all nations really reflect the *ipsissima verba* of Christ. But this is to miss the point. Matthew, Mark, and Luke all place baptism in the sending commands of the risen Christ. No Christian church fails to baptize. One is reminded of the debate over whether Shakespeare wrote his plays. If he did not, someone once said, we would have to invent another Shakespeare who did. Moreover, the commands to spread the good news, to celebrate the Supper, to forgive sins, and to baptize are all of a kind, so that one can speak of audible sacraments and visible words to describe Luther's understanding of preaching and the sacraments.[45]

Luther underscored the point he wanted to make by beginning with Matthew 28 in comments in the Large Catechism: "Observe, first, that these words contain God's commandment and institution, so that no one may doubt that baptism is of divine origin."[46] It was not, he went on, a human plaything or an indifferent matter. Its externality cannot offend in the face of God's word and command. Again, the sweep of Luther's comments here is astounding, in that within a single paragraph he touched on the certainty of God's promise, the notion of adiaphora, and a sacramentology of the cross (that is, God revealed in the last place we would reasonably look). He even saw fit to heighten this scandal by concluding: "To be baptized in God's name is to be baptized not by human being but by God himself. Although it is performed by human hands, it is nevertheless truly God's own act."[47] The notion of God using human means, already introduced in comments on the first commandment, echoed forth here.

There was, for Luther, a close connection between the incarnation and the sacraments and thus to the theology of the cross: God comes in the flesh, in water (in bread and wine), to save. Although the term *theology of the cross* disappears from Luther's later writings, the concept (defined as God's revelation under the appearance of the opposite) made a remarkable reappearance here, as Luther contrasted human works and the ploys of Satan to God's work in baptism: "The devil sets to work to blind us with false appearances and to lead us away from God's work to our own." The example Luther provided was of the Carthusian monk, again using baptism to criticize, as already in 1520, monastic vows and piety: "Here one must evaluate not the person according to the works, but the works according to the person, from whom they must derive their worth. But mad reason rushes forth and, because baptism is not dazzling like the works that we do, regards it as worthless."[48]

On the basis of this introductory reflection in the Large Catechism, Luther then posed his first question: "What is baptism?" Here, we glimpse the true impact of Luther's theology of the Word

in his thought. It was not a worship of the Bible but an encounter
with God's own speech, giving meaning and value to every weak
thing it touched. For those who might be looking for a complicated
explanation of baptism, Luther's words will always disappoint. He
simply stated the obvious. If a person stumbles in on a baptism, he
or she will notice two things: water and words. That is what baptism
is. The question, then, for Luther was, "What kind of Word?" What
makes this water so special, "different from all other water"? The
answer lay for him in the Word, "something nobler" than water,
which turns natural water into "a divine, heavenly, holy, and blessed
water . . . all by virtue of the Word."[49] In this connection, Luther
quoted Augustine's definition from his sermons on John, often used
in medieval discussions of sacraments, that "'when the Word is
added to the element or the natural substance, it becomes a sacrament,' that is, a holy divine thing and sign."[50] Look not at the husk,
Luther urged his readers, but at the kernel, just as is the case with
parenthood or governmental authority. Parents (to say nothing of
politicians) do not look like much until God's command ("Honor
your parents") comes and clothes them in God's majesty. Wrote
Luther: "In the same manner, and to an even greater extent, you
should give honor and glory to baptism on account of the Word."[51]
Furthermore, these two things (water and the Word) must not be
separated.

Second, Luther asked about baptism's purpose, "that is, what
benefits, gifts, and effects it brings."[52] This move from definition to
effect could be thought of as defining the very heart of Lutheran
hermeneutics. The true, full meaning of a thing (whether a sacrament
or a text from Scripture) could not be measured simply by its definition but must always include its effect. Here, to be sure, both Luther
and his colleague Melanchthon were beholden to Aristotle, who in
his *Analytics* had outlined a host of questions that one must ask about
a thing: whether it exists, what it is, what are its genus and species,
what are its parts, what is similar or different from it, what are its
causes, and what are its effects. In his effort to sum up Lutheran theology, Melanchthon concentrated on just two of these questions: what
a thing is and what its effects are. Thus, in his *Loci communes theologici* of 1521, the first organized summary of Wittenberg theology,

Melanchthon asked not only what were the law and gospel but also what was their power or effect. Luther, who once said that he had learned "dialectics," as this branch of Aristotelian thinking was known, from Melanchthon, also often used these two questions. In the first edition of his theological textbook, the *Loci communes theologici* of 1521, Melanchthon famously wrote, "To know Christ is to know his benefits." In the catechisms, Luther's first two questions on the sacraments made the same point: to know baptism is to know its benefits. He wrote, "It brings about forgiveness of sins, redeems from death and the devil, and gives eternal salvation to all who believe it, as the words and promise of God declare."[53]

To prove his point, Luther pointed to Mark 16:16: "The one who believes and is baptized will be saved." This verse, already cited in the *Booklet for the Laity and Children* of 1525, went far beyond Matthew 28 in demonstrating the connection between baptism and salvation itself, something further reflected in 1 Peter 3:21 ("Baptism . . . now saves you") and in a variety of passages in the Pauline corpus. The fact that Mark 16:16 is now known to be a later addition to Mark's gospel is of little consequence, since the point of this text goes beyond itself to the sacrament of baptism and its effect. As with his explanation of the benefits of the Lord's Supper, Luther changed his vocabulary to emphasize the giftedness of baptism: it is "precious," an "inexpressible treasure," and "a divine, blessed, fruitful, and gracious water."

In the Large Catechism, we get a hint of why tying the benefits of salvation was so important to Luther. There, he went after the "know-it-alls" and "new spirits," who were more than happy to crow about faith alone saving but who divorced it from any material things. This addiction to "spirituality" (falsely so called) infects modern Christianity as well, where the scandal of particularity (*this* baby; *this* water; *these* words) has lost out to a host of far more impressive forms of religiosity, all based in our commitments and abilities to figure theology (and God) out. In response, Luther hauled out the carnal (as in incarnation) side of his theology: "Now, these people are so foolish as to separate faith from the object to which faith is attached and secured, all on the grounds that the object is something external. Yes, it must be external so that it can be perceived and grasped by the senses and thus brought into the heart, just as the entire gospel is an external, oral proclamation."[54] In place of all this talk about spirituality, one might be wise to consider boasting instead in "Lutheran carnality," that is, God coming in the flesh, in the water, in the bread and wine, in my needy neighbor, and even to children and infants. In a world where religion is what we make of it, this external, watery word, with all of its benefits, comes from outside of us and gives what no self-imposed piety (Col. 2:23) can offer: God at work in the last place we would reasonably look.

The third question in the Large Catechism arose out of the second. Who then receives such benefits? The Small Catechism seems, at first glance, to pose a different question altogether, namely, how can water do such great things? Yet a careful examination of Luther's answer in the Small Catechism reveals that the benefits promised in baptism come only by faith: "Clearly the water does not do it, but the Word of God, which is with and alongside the water, and faith, which trust this Word of God in the water."[55] Thus, Luther's complete sacramentology becomes clear: external means (which scandalize reason), the command and promise of God (which make something out of nothing), "and faith, which trusts this Word of God in the water." This last phrase—that the Word is in the water— is itself remarkable in how closely it mirrors the incarnation (the Word in the flesh).

At this place in the Small Catechism, however, Luther had not forgotten the explanation to the third article of the Creed ("I believe that I cannot believe"). Thus, he concentrated not on faith (as if it were some sort of "work" that depended on human exertion) but on that faith-creating and faith-strengthening Word. Without the Word, we have only water; with the Word, "it is a baptism, that is a grace-filled water of life and a 'bath of the new birth in the Holy Spirit.'"[56] Not content to paraphrase Titus 3, Luther then quoted the text, using two phrases that link baptism to the Creed and, thus, to faith: "that through that very grace we may be justified [later versions change it to 'be righteous']. . . . This is most certainly true."[57] The paraphrase for "amen" at the end of each of the articles of the Creed ("This is most certainly true"), which is also reflected in the explanation to "Amen" in the Lord's Prayer ("Yes, yes, it is going to come about just like this"), now finds its rightful place in the connection between baptism and faith: "This is most certainly true." Baptism is not a mere sign that points to something else, an allegory, but is the real thing: justification itself.

In the Large Catechism, Luther concentrated even more fiercely on the role of faith. First, Mark 16, with its "whoever believes," "is so powerful that it excludes and drives out all works."[58] For Luther, faith is not a work but, rather, the opposite of works, an insight into Christianity that is by and large lost on Americans intent on "deciding to follow Jesus." As if to anticipate just such a confusion of faith and works, Luther went on to say:

> But some are accustomed to ask, "If baptism is itself a work and you say that works are of no use for salvation, what place is there for faith?" Answer: Yes, it is true that our works are of no use for salvation. Baptism, however, is not our work, but God's work (for, as was said, you must distinguish Christ's baptism quite clearly from a bath-keeper's baptism). God's works are salutary and necessary for salvation, and they do not exclude but rather demand [or: further] faith, for without faith one cannot grasp them. . . . Neither the hand nor the body can [receive in the water the promised salvation], but rather the heart must believe it. Thus you see plainly that baptism is not a work that we do but that it is a treasure that God gives us and faith grasps, just as the LORD Christ upon the cross is not a work but a treasure placed in the setting of the Word and offered to us in the Word and received by faith.[59]

Here, Luther made explicit the connection to Christ's saving death and portrayed faith as a matter not of the free will but of the transformed heart. Baptism (especially the baptism of infants) is, of all the sacraments, the one most clearly *not* a human work. Only when faith becomes a work and baptism becomes a sign of human commitment do we lose the treasure in this amazing sacrament. No wonder Luther never used the term *baptismal vow* (or even *baptismal covenant*) in his catechisms, an unfortunate (and unbiblical) term that can only imply works in modern parlance. For Luther, in these writings, baptism is sheer grace and treasure, a splendid antidote for a work-happy (or, rather, work-infested) church.

The fourth and final question in both the Small and Large Catechisms dealt with the signification of water baptism, namely, the daily drowning of the old creature and the rising of the new. Because this was acted out specifically in the Sacrament of Absolution, the next chapter will deal with this theme. As argued in chapter 1, this question actually determined the catechisms' structure, as a movement from law to gospel.

Before coming to this question in the Large Catechism, however, Luther provided two additional sections. The second was the excursus on infant baptism discussed above. In the first excursus, Luther summarized his arguments up to that point, treating his readers to a baptism-centered view of the entire Christian life.[60] In a few paragraphs, he summarized the work of the entire Trinity, the central baptismal promises, and the profligacy of God's unmerited grace given to all people without regard to their persons. Baptism, far from being an easily discarded piece of God's grace, lost in the shipwreck of sin, had become for Luther the very center ("no greater jewel") of the Christian life—a proposal that few who call themselves Lutherans, let alone other Christians, have ever fully appreciated.

> In baptism, therefore, every Christian has enough to study and practice all his or her life. Christians always have enough to do to believe firmly what baptism promises and brings—victory over death and the devil, forgiveness of sin, God's grace, the entire Christ, and the Holy Spirit with his gifts. In short, the blessings of baptism are so boundless that if our timid nature considers them, it may well doubt whether they could all be true. Suppose there were a physician who had so much skill that people would not die, or even though they died would afterward live eternally. Just think how the world would snow and rain money upon such a person! Because of the throng of rich people crowding around, no one else would be able to get near. Now here in baptism there is brought, free of charge, to every person's door just such a treasure and medicine that swallows up death and keeps all people alive.
>
> Thus, we must regard baptism and put it to use in such a way that we may draw strength and comfort from it when our sins or conscience oppress us, and say, "But I am baptized! And if I have been baptized, I have the promise that I shall be saved and have eternal life, both in soul

and body." . . . No greater jewel, therefore, can adorn our body and soul than baptism, for through it we become completely holy and blessed, which no other kind of life and no work on earth can acquire.[61]

May Christians today learn anew to cover themselves daily in this jewel!

Fifth Petition of the Lord's Prayer: Matthew 18[:23-35] (the Parable of the Unforgiving Steward)

CHAPTER 6

The Daily Sacrament
of Baptismal Absolution

We are *simul iustus et peccator* (at the same time a righteous person and a sinner). This remarkably Lutheran insight found expression throughout the catechisms but nowhere more clearly than in Luther's comment on the signification of baptism with water. Daily, the old dies; daily, the new creature of faith comes forth to live. One of the first times Luther stated this in print was in comments on Galatians 2 in his 1519 *Annotations on Galatians*. In explaining that we are justified by faith and not by works (Gal. 2:16), Luther paraphrased Paul's comments this way: "We [Jews] seek to be justified by faith in Christ: now at the same time sinners with the Gentiles and at the same time justified with the Gentiles."[1] Later, in comments on verse 18, Luther described the suffering Job as "at the same time righteous; at the same time sinner."[2]

This kind of talk was seen to contradict the heart of the sacraments—that the grace contained in them moved a person from a state of sin into a state of grace. While the "matter" of sin, defined as concupiscence, remained in the baptized, it was not sin without the proper form. This was a serious enough charge against Luther to be included in the papal indictment of 1520, which Luther then refuted in his *Assertion of All the Articles of Martin Luther Condemned in the Recent Bull of Leo X*. Using Romans 7, Luther insisted, "Every person was at the same time sinner while being righteous."[3] In 1521, he would argue the same points in his refutation of Latomus.[4] Fast-forward to 1530, and Luther, now in near isolation at the Castle Coburg, wrote short expositions of the first twenty-five psalms, explaining Ps. 25:11 ("For your name's sake, pardon my sin") with a shot at his opponents: "The sophists cannot understand that the

Christian is at the same time righteous and has sins."[5] Not surprisingly, in the second, much larger commentary on Galatians, published in 1535, Luther stated (this time commenting on Gal. 3:6), "Thus, the Christian person is at the same time righteous and sinner, holy and profane, an enemy and a son of God."[6]

One of the most important places Luther used the concept (though not the exact phrasing) was in the preface to Romans in the 1522 translation of the New Testament. In commenting on Romans 7 again, Luther noted:

> After this [Paul] shows how the spirit and the flesh struggle against each other in a person, and he presents himself as an example, so that we learn how to recognize properly the work of putting sin to death in us. . . . Yet the entire person is both spirit and flesh completely, which struggles against its flesh until the person becomes completely spiritual [in the Resurrection].[7]

The Small Catechism and Private Absolution

In 1531, this insight also found its place in the Small Catechism, not only in the fourth question of baptism but also in an appendix to baptism that provided a simple way to confess sins before the pastor and receive forgiveness. But the place of confession and forgiveness or, as sixteenth-century Lutherans preferred to call it, the Sacrament of Absolution was by no means certain in the catechisms. The first edition of the Large Catechism omitted any explanation of the topic, adding it to the second edition produced later in 1529.[8] Since no copies of the original booklet form of the Small Catechism printed in Wittenberg in 1529 have come down to us, historians rely on reprints from other cities to indicate its content. The 1529 translation of Luther's catechetical broadsides into the dialect of the German lowlands (called Niederdeutsch) and published in Hamburg in booklet form had no mention of confession either. As late as 1535, the Latin/German version of the Small Catechism also omitted any reference to confession.

According to a handwritten copy from 1530 of the original sheets, there was a sheet entitled, "Who wants to take or receive the Sacrament of the Altar should be able to give answers to these five questions. Why do you take the sacrament? [Answer: communion with Christ.] What do you confess is in this sacrament? [A: body and blood under bread and wine given by Christ as a testament.] What are the words of this testament? [A: Take and eat and drink, and so forth.] Why do you take this sacrament, isn't faith enough? [A: To strengthen faith according to God's gift, which I don't want to despise.] How will you take it? [A: Eat, drink, and believe the promise Christ gave to his disciples.]" However, the scholarly literature is divided on whether this stemmed from Luther's pen, although everyone agrees that it certainly reflected catechetical and penitential practice in Wittenberg at the time.

A printing of the Small Catechism in Erfurt, patterned after a Latin translation from Wittenberg, has at the very end a prayer of private confession (labeled, oddly, the second prayer of confession [for which there is no first; see below]) but with no explanation of what confession is. In the earliest German Wittenberg catechism of 1529, a quite different form of confession from the 1531 form was placed at the very end of the booklet, after the baptismal service (the marriage service was lacking altogether), almost as an afterthought (see below). This form was translated in the second Latin version printed in Wittenberg in 1529. Only in 1531, where the original printer of the Small Catechism, Nicholas Schirlentz, undertook a complete revision of it presumably under Luther's direction, do we find a brief explanation of confession and forgiveness along with a quite different order for private confession—one that was placed, for the first time, immediately after baptism, so that the fourth question of baptism now introduced the Sacrament of Absolution.

It would seem that, being *simul iustus et peccator*, sixteenth-century Lutherans could not count. Some documents, such as Luther's *Babylonian Captivity of the Church* from 1520, counted only baptism and the Lord's Supper as sacraments. Thus, Lutherans ought to have two. Yet in the Augsburg Confession, in its Apology, and in other documents, Lutherans seemed intent on adding "penance" or, as they preferred, "the Sacrament of Absolution" as a third sacrament. Luther's comments on baptism in the Large Catechism clarified the problem and, actually, made it a nonissue for his colleagues, if not for later Lutherans. Commenting on the signification of baptizing with water, he wrote, "Here you see that baptism, both by its power and by its signification, comprehends also the third sacrament, formerly called penance, which is really nothing else than baptism. What is 'penance' [translated in the *Book of Concord* as 'repentance'] but an earnest attack on the old creature and an entering into a new life?"[9] In this light, baptism becomes for Christians a "daily garment that they are to wear all the time."[10] This daily baptism is nothing other than to be found in faith, in suppressing the old creature and growing up in the new. Luther's last line in this section reflected a lifetime of living *simul iustus et peccator*: "As we have once obtained forgiveness of sins in baptism, so forgiveness remains day by day as long as we live, that is, as long as we carry the old creature around our necks."[11]

Luther clearly derived penance from baptism, as we have seen, but, in medieval fashion, he also still linked it to the Lord's Supper, assuming that those who underwent penance would then come to the Supper. This linkage may be seen in one of the booklet editions of the catechism from 1529 (referred to above). It provided an entire dialogue meant for the confessional and for preparation for the Lord's Supper.

A Short Way for the Simple to Make Confession to the Priest from Luther's Small Catechism of 1529

Penitent: Dear reverend Lord, I beseech you for God's sake to give me good counsel for the comfort of my soul.

Confessor: What do you desire?

P: I, a poor human being, confess and lament to you before God my Lord, that I am a sinful and frail human. I have not kept the commands of God. I have also not believed the gospel. I do nothing good. I cannot suffer evil being done to me. In particular I have done X, and that which burdens me in my conscience. Therefore I ask you, that you would in God's place speak forgiveness to me and comfort me with God's word.[12]

Another form of confessing for penance:

P: I confess before God and you that I am a poor sinner and full of every sin of unbelief and blaspheming God. I also feel that God's word is not bringing forth fruit in me. I hear it, but do not take it seriously. I do not show to my neighbors the works of love. I am

angry, full of hate and envious of them. I am impatient, miserly
and inclined toward all kinds of malice. For this reason my heart
and conscience are weighed down and long to be free of sin. I
beseech you to strengthen my little faith and comfort my weak
conscience with the divine word and promise.

C: Why do you want to receive the Sacrament [of the Altar]?

P: Because I want to strengthen my soul with God's word and sign and
obtain grace.

C: Don't you have forgiveness of sins in Confession?

P: What does it hurt? I also want to get the sign of God added to the
Word. And the more times God's word is gotten, so much the
better.[13]

Although there is some debate about the origin of this material,
still it sounds like vintage Luther (perhaps with the help of other
Wittenberg theologians). It showed a clear concern for the first
commandment and for law and gospel. It also, in the word *miserly*,
showed a concern for impoverished neighbors. It also connected the
Sacrament of Penance to the Sacrament of the Altar. The more word
of God, the better.

In 1529, when this version was being printed, Wittenberg theologians were just recovering from their first serious internal dispute,
which involved John Agricola, a former student of Luther who was
now the rector of the Latin school in Eisleben, and Philip Melanchthon.[14] What was the nature of true penance? (In both German
and Latin, the same word, *poenitentia* or *Buße*, could be translated
"penance," "penitence," or "repentance.") Did it arise out of fear of
punishment (that is, the preaching of the law) or love of God (that
is, the promise of the gospel)? When the Latin version of the Visitation Articles, published in 1527, included the former view, Agricola
raised objections with its author, Philip Melanchthon. Luther proposed a compromise, arguing that the believer scarcely could distinguish his or her motivation for sorrow for sin and claiming that
although faith (and thus God's promise) in some attenuated way
preceded repentance (after all, one had to believe that there was a
God), it was better to place the law, which condemns sin, before
the gospel. Melanchthon was delighted with this proposal, since it
in fact supported his position (that the sinner moved from law to

gospel) far more than Agricola's, which was not far from his later antinomian perspective. The compromise language found its way, word for word, into the German version of the Visitation Articles, published early in 1528.[15] The uncertainty over penance and, hence, private confession spilled over into the curious lack of clear statements about this third sacrament in either the first edition of the Large Catechism or that of the Small.

In the 1531 version of the Small Catechism, all of that changed as the Wittenbergers took a different tack.[16] First, it was expressly catechetical, telling people not simply how to make confession but also how to clarify what confession was. In comparison to medieval understanding, the 1531 version redefined confession. Scholastic theologians had divided penance into three parts: contrition (defined as sorrow for sin out of love of God, as opposed to attrition, which was sorrow for sin out of fear of punishment), rigorous confession to a priest of all known sins, and satisfaction of the temporal punishment that remained after the penitent's guilt and eternal punishment had been removed. Late-medieval theology had placed special emphasis on contrition, arguing that persons in a state of sin, who could love God above all else and their neighbors as themselves, could certainly, by doing what was in them, show true sorrow for sin out of love of God and thus merit God's grace. Whereas earlier theologians had argued that first in hearing the absolution in the confessional was one infused with the grace that makes the sinner acceptable to God (this grace being understood as a disposition or habit of charity [love]), late-medieval theologians, such as Gabriel Biel, argued that already in contrition one was infused with such a disposition and went to the priest not to receive grace but to make sure that the contrition was true. Once in a state of grace, a person then said prayers, gave alms, fasted, or did other good works to merit the reduction of the temporal punishment that remained for sin.[17]

In this basic Reformation approach to the sacrament, Luther dismissed the notion that one had to confess all one's sins or show "proper" contrition, and he had elsewhere (for example, in the Visitation Articles) completely eliminated satisfaction, claiming that Christ had made complete satisfaction for all of our sins. Instead, for him, this sacrament consisted primarily of confession of sin and, especially, absolution—that is, receiving the comfort of God's forgiveness. As in the rest of the Small Catechism, the categories of law and gospel are at work. The 1531 version also incorporated the important Lutheran notion that enumeration of sins is not necessary: "However, before the confessor we are to confess only those sins of which we have knowledge and which trouble us."[18] Luther was not out to torture consciences. Those who could not think of any serious sins "are not to worry, nor are they to search for or invent further sins and thereby turn confession into torture."[19] Luther also tied the Ten Commandments explicitly to the so-called second use of the law and such confession. "Here reflect on your walk of life in light of the Ten Commandments," he advised.[20]

The actual form of confession omitted references to unbelief found in the earlier form. Perhaps this had the effect of eliminating the torture of people who were weak in faith. It did, however, reflect more fully on the different estates of people (servant/master, which we would better translate employee/employer) and their particular sins, an indication of just how practical and balanced these theologians were trying to be. (The Latin version listed possible sins of students.) In contrast to the previous form from 1529, the absolution itself was clearly spelled out. Notice that Luther did not imagine that praying for God to be merciful actually meant a true absolution. It was, rather, a part of the confessor's acknowledgment of the confession ("God be gracious to you and strengthen your faith. Amen").[21]

The absolution proper began with what might be termed a small installation service. The confessor first asked the penitent whether he or she thought that the pastor could do this forgiving in God's place. Only then did Luther add the direct word of forgiveness, based on this simple, sacramental faith (namely, that a human being could forgive sins in God's name) and parallel to those used in the medieval penance, except that he did not connect this word with some sort of infusion of grace and power to perform the law and become righteous. Instead, its fruit was comfort for the stricken conscience. In this vein, Luther instructed the confessor to add specific passages of Scripture, through which he "will in fact be able to comfort and encourage to faith those whose consciences are heavily burdened or who are stressed and under attack."[22] This, for Luther, was the Christian life in a nutshell: the believer under attack (using the verbal form of *Anfechtung*) and in need of consolation. It is a theme first sounded in the explanation of the sixth petition of the Lord's Prayer and now repeated here in this daily return to baptism.

The Large Catechism

To the second 1529 edition of the Large Catechism, Luther added a new preface, several sentences to his introduction to the Lord's Prayer, and the entire section on confession. The positioning of this section at the very end of the document may well have had as much to do with the printer's decision as anything else, and it followed similar formatting in Small Catechisms of that year, as noted above. This section also contained numerous parallels to Luther's sermon on confession, preached on Palm Sunday 1529.[23] This sermon was the first of a series preached during Holy Week and was designed to encourage people to receive the Lord's Supper, since such confession was generally understood as a prerequisite to reception of the Eucharist. Thus, the particular positioning of this section had as much to do with these practical factors as with any theological decision by Luther.

In the Large Catechism, one hears more clearly echoes of the historical background for Luther's statements on penance. Luther began with a declaration of independence from the "pope's tyranny," his "coercion," and the "intolerable weight and burden" of compulsory confession and of the requirement for enumerating all of one's sins, so that "no one was able to confess purely enough." But Luther's biggest complaint centered in the lack of proper instruction: "No one taught or understood what confession is and how useful and comforting it is."[24] In Luther's view, comfort was robbed from consciences both coming and going by the pope and restored to people through Wittenberg's reforms. Now one was under no compulsion, could confess only what was bothering one, and knew what was really going on there.

Of course, while these papal problems had been "solved," another pastoral dilemma had been created: people were not coming to private confession at all. The contemptuous language highlighted Luther's quandary. The people "do whatever they please and take advantage of their freedom." Since they immediately understood that whatever in the gospel is mild and gentle, "such pigs . . . should not have the gospel or any part of it" and should instead remain under the pope.[25] Those who refused to believe the gospel or live according to it should not be allowed to enjoy its benefits: "For such people we shall provide no preaching, nor will they have our permission to share and enjoy any part of our liberty, but we shall let the pope or his kind bring them back into subjection and coerce them like a true tyrant."[26] This "rabble" deserved such a jailer "who is God's devil and hangman." At the same time, Luther admitted that there were also "others" who hear the gospel gladly. To these people, Luther was obliged to preach, "exhorting, encouraging, and persuading them not to ignore such a precious and comforting treasure."[27] For these simple people, then, Luther prepared this exhortation.

Having laid out the pastoral issues, Luther turned to instruction, describing the results of several years of debate over the nature of penance.[28] Without eliminating private confession to a priest, Luther commenced his discussion by identifying two other forms of confession, either directly to God alone or to the neighbor alone, both of which Luther derived from the fifth petition. The first, confession to God, happens each time a person recites the Lord's Prayer. Indeed, the *entire* Lord's Prayer was such a confession: "that we neither have nor do what we ought and a plea for grace and a joyful conscience. This kind of confession should and must take place continuously as long as we live." In fact, here Luther appealed to the notion of *simul iustus et peccator* as the very basis of the Christian life: "For this is the essence of a genuinely Christian life, to acknowledge that we are sinners and to pray for grace."[29]

As to the second kind, confession to the neighbor, Luther uncovered two instances of this, derived from the second half of the fifth petition. On the one hand, in the general confession of sin, especially as a congregation prayed the fifth petition together, everyone admitted to God and to their neighbors their sinfulness. With respect to individual sins, one must take steps to confess to and reconcile with a particular neighbor.

On the other hand, however, there was the secret confession to an individual brother or sister for a particular issue, "eating away at us until we can have no peace."[30] Unlike confession to God and the neighbor, this type did not fall under God's command but was free to be used "as often as we wish [to] lay our troubles before a brother or sister, seeking advice, comfort, and strength." Already in introducing this final type, Luther stressed the absolution and its comfort: "Thus, by divine ordinance Christ himself has placed absolution in the mouths of his Christian community and commanded us to absolve one another from sins."[31]

Luther defined this third form of confession in terms of confession and absolution, contrasting it to what was done under the pope and making clear that the point of it was not to burden consciences but to unburden them, something that happened only in hearing the promise/absolution. As in the beginning of this section of the Catechism, so here he hammered away at the contrast between this new understanding of confession and what had previously been taught: "In the past we placed all the emphasis on our work alone. . . . It was just as if our confession were simply a good work with which we could pay off God. . . . People were driven to the point that everyone despaired of confessing that purely. . . . [It became] not only useless to us but also burdensome and bitter, to the manifest harm and destruction of souls."[32]

Luther solved this monumental pastoral dilemma by dividing confession and absolution: "We should set little value on our work but exalt and magnify God's Word." One went to confession to receive a gift from God. Here, Luther wrestled with the same dilemma expressed in comments on prayer and the Lord's Supper: how to preserve the gracious center of the absolution without turning confession into a "magnificent work to present to God." Luther concluded, "We urge you, however, to confess and express your needs, not for the purpose of performing a work but to hear what God wishes to say to you."[33]

Luther was convinced that the very treasure present in the absolution would be enough to draw people to this sacrament: "If all this were clearly laid out, and along with that if the needs that ought to move and induce us to confession were clearly indicated, there would be no need of coercion or force."[34] He then painted the picture of beggars rushing to receive a rich gift of money or clothes somewhere. There would be no need to drive and beat them; they would run as fast as they could for such a gift. If, however, the command to appear somewhere was all that was given, with no promise, how could the beggars go except with resentment? In applying this to the contrast between past practices and the present, Luther shifted metaphors. Rather than hearing about this rich treasure, people had simply been taught to concentrate on their own filthiness. Then, returning to the metaphor of healing, which, after all, had defined the order and thrust of Luther's catechesis since 1522 as a movement from law to gospel (diagnosis to cure), Luther stated, "If you are poor and miserable, then go and make use of the healing medicine. Those who feel their misery and need will no doubt develop such a desire for confession that they will run to it with joy."[35] This emphasis, not so much on human beggarliness as on God's prodigal grace, marked even the very last words from Luther's pen, found on his writing desk in Eisleben in 1546 by Justus Jonas: "We are beggars; this is true."[36] If one considered one's great need (the work of the law), one would need no external compulsion but would force oneself to go to confession in order to hear the absolution.

Using yet another metaphor, Luther argued that, while those who do not come to confession should have no part in the gospel, "if you are a Christian you should be glad to run more than a hundred miles for confession, not under compulsion but rather coming and compelling us to offer it." This matched comments about the Lord's Supper in the preface to the Small Catechism, where Luther was also convinced that recognizing one's need and knowing the great treasure in the Supper would make Christians compel their pastor to offer it to them.[37] Indeed, life between the law of our need for forgiveness and the gospel of God's free absolution in Christ marked the entire Christian life in Luther's view: "Therefore, when I exhort you to go to confession, I am doing nothing but exhorting you to be a Christian. If I bring you to this point, I have also brought you to confession."[38] Luther then employed a final metaphor, that of hunger and thirst, as described of a deer in Psalm 42, which Luther glossed in this way: "That is, as a deer trembles with eagerness for a fresh spring, so I yearn and tremble for God's Word or absolution and for the sacrament, etc. In this way, you see, confession would be taught properly, and such a desire and love for it would be aroused that people would come running after us to get it, more than we would like."[39]

What Ever Became of Absolution?

What happened to confession and absolution in the Lutheran Church?[40] Among American Lutherans, this sacrament has survived in the public form of confession and absolution practiced in many Lutheran congregations.[41] In a delightful irony, the Lutheran who helped to found Alcoholics Anonymous made the fifth step in the Twelve-Step program (confession to God, self, and another human being the exact nature of one's wrongs) one of the few places where a person might seek out a pastor for private confession. Of course, not being a Christian assembly, the program does not demand absolution. What often happened among Lutherans, however, is that private confession became a thing of the past—so much so that some Lutherans think of it as exclusively Roman Catholic. Attempts to revive the practice, for example as part of the movement of Pietism, focused much more squarely on confession of sins and attempted to "fence the Table" by not allowing unrepentant sinners to Holy Communion and thus reverting to the very thing Luther had tried to avoid.

Perhaps the only place this sacrament survives is in pastoral care, where, if pastors are sharp enough to realize that they have just heard a confession of sin, they may actually think to give not just a seldom-heard encouraging word but a declaration of forgiveness, perhaps even with the laying on of hands, in order to give this sacrament even more physicality. In crises, at the end of life, or surrounded by anxiety, people still thirst for a word of comfort. In those moments, when pastors fulfill their calling by delivering an unconditional promise, this sacrament comes back to life much as Luther had envisioned it.

In their commentary on the catechism for young people, *Free to Be*, Gerhard Forde and James Nestingen concluded that the devil stole it.[42] To be sure, unlike baptism and the Lord's Supper, there is no absolute necessity for this sacrament. Granted, it survives in a public form in some Lutheran churches and some still avail themselves of this sacrament, especially in connection with Twelve-Step programs, or simply seek pastoral advice without realizing that they get an entire sacrament thrown in for free. But for the most part, Christians are left to fend for themselves, thirsty, sick beggars that they are, driven by guilt or shame or simply fear and uncertain where to go.

The challenge for Lutherans today is not to reintroduce a medieval private confession, which would invariably start slaughtering souls again, but to bring the absolution front and center for all kinds of pastoral conversations: at the beginning of each worship service as a true return to one's baptism and its unconditional promises, in crisis counseling (where not just good psychology but good theology ought to reign), and in the "mutual conversation and consolation of the brothers and sisters," which would include not only pastors but the entire people of God in sharing the best news beggars can hear: "Food and money; cooling drink and medicine—all free—and you do not have to run a hundred miles to get it."

The Lord's Supper: Matthew 26[:26-28], Mark 14[:22-24], Luke 22[:19-20] (the Last Supper)

CHAPTER 7

Treasuring the Lord's Supper[1]

E arly in 1529, as Luther was well on the way to finishing the texts of the Large and Small Catechisms, he fell ill, leaving material on the sacraments uncompleted until around Easter. As a result, at the very time he was writing the final sections of the catechisms, he was also preaching during Holy Week.[2] The sermons from Sunday through Thursday focused on confession and the Lord's Supper and formed the backbone of the comments in the Large Catechism. The proximity of these sermonic and catechetical works to one another heightened the pastoral tone in this portion of the Large Catechism, especially, as we shall see, in Luther's concluding exhortation on receiving the Lord's Supper regularly. For this reason, Luther's remarks on the Supper still provide helpful insights and needed critique for our teaching and practice today.

Historical Background

Until 1520, the Lord's Supper, in its late-medieval manifestation as the Mass, was a feast for the eyes and a ceremony for the dead. The words of institution were whispered sotto voce by a richly attired, distant priest. The worshipers were often fenced off from the officiant by means of ornately carved rood screens. The buildings not only contained imposing tabernacles for the consecrated host but were themselves often designed as ostentatious markers for the miracle of God's coming to earth in the "unbloody sacrifice" of the mass. Chronicles even recorded Sunday-morning stampedes from one church to another, as the faithful rushed to catch a glimpse of the central act of the Mass, the elevation, when the priest's offering to

God was consummated. And every day, at the countless altars dotting the interior of many churches, thousands upon thousands of masses were recited privately for dead souls languishing in purgatory. Thus, as Helmar Junghans recounts, in 1519, in Wittenberg's Castle Church, with its twenty altars, nearly nine thousand masses were said for the souls of the departed princely family of Saxony and other wealthy donors.[3]

In 1520, however, an Augustinian friar, Martin Luther, changed all of that for many in the church. In his tract *On the Babylonian Captivity of the Church*, Luther insisted that the Mass—far from being a visual feast and sacrifice—was a real feast, meant to be eaten and drunk while hearing the Word of Christ's forgiving presence. This Word revealed that, far from being empty symbols or spiritual magic, the Supper was the promise of its dying Lord: a last testament in which all that Christ's death accomplished was offered to the communicants and received by faith in that Word alone.[4]

In 1524, a preacher in Zurich, Ulrich Zwingli, judged these same late-medieval practices in the light of a "newly discovered" second commandment that prohibited the making and worshiping of graven images.[5] From the perspective of a theology that insisted on a radical polarization of the material and the spiritual, Zwingli argued that the Mass pulled people away from the spirit into the world of flesh and matter. The Supper was supposed to be a sign (another visual image!) of the communicant's faith and a mnemonic device for remembering Christ's death, not a means of grace or the locus of Christ's presence on earth. Christ's bodily ascension made his presence in the Supper impossible. Moreover, in John 6:63, Jesus had warned against such a materialistic view of the Eucharist when he said, "The flesh [in the Supper] profits nothing; the Spirit makes alive." As a result, the words "This is my Body" must be understood metaphorically or symbolically[6] to mean "This signifies my Body" or "This is like my Body." These points made up the heart of objections to Luther's understanding of the Lord's Supper by Zwingli and his supporters.

Against this equally visual construal of the Lord's Supper, Luther also entered the lists, again insisting on the priority of Christ's words, this time not against the work of the Mass but against the workings of reason, which could not imagine how the whole Christ could be present in the bread and wine. Here, as in his criticism of the Anabaptist understanding of baptism, Luther suspected the presence of a *Werkteufel* (works devil) and the concomitant absence of faith in the word and promise of Christ. In fact, his battle with Zwingli was taking place directly alongside his writing of the catechisms. In October 1529, the two theologians met face-to-face in Marburg for an unsuccessful colloquy to solve their differences.

Luther's Catechetical Response

In his catechetical sermons of 1528 and 1529 and in the catechisms, Luther situated his understanding of the Lord's Supper directly between these two opposing points of view. On the one hand, with the papal party, Luther agreed wholeheartedly that Christ is present "in" or "under" the bread and wine.[7] On the other hand, with Zwingli and other Reformers from south Germany, he insisted that faith was the goal and effect of the sacrament. Where both sides went wrong, he believed, was in their denigration of the actual words and promises of Christ. To those who denied that Christ was present in or under the bread and wine, Luther pointed to Christ's words "This is my Body." To those who had made the sacrament into a sacrifice, effective by its mere performance (and, thus, not needing faith), he hammered away at the promise "Given for you . . . shed for you for the forgiveness of sins," and the faith that that promise engenders.[8]

Lutherans have often succumbed to the temptation of reducing Luther's statements on the Lord's Supper to doctrine: timeless truths to be memorized by unsuspecting, impressionable eighth graders. However, the Large Catechism reveals that Luther aimed to use God's word and promise in the sacrament to make believers out of his readers and comfort them with the presence and forgiveness of Christ. Far from giving an esoteric exercise in right doctrine and practice, Luther speaks as a pastor, even in the midst of hefty polemic.

In all, Luther posed three questions in the Large Catechism. A fourth question in the Small Catechism about fasting was actually subsumed under the third in the Large. As he had in the section on baptism, Luther prefaced his remarks here with an insistence that the sacrament had to be understood as God's ordinance, arising from God's word and command. "Do you think God cares so much about our faith and conduct that he would permit them to affect his ordinance?" he asked.[9] Indeed, all of Luther's comments arose out of this central claim: the Supper grew not in our garden but in God's. It is something God wants to do for us, not something we do for God.

With the first catechetical question ("Was ist das?" or "What is this?"), Luther defined the essence of the sacrament. "It is," he wrote in the Small Catechism, "the true body and blood of our Lord Jesus Christ under the bread and wine, instituted by Christ himself for us Christians to eat and to drink."[10] As we will see in a moment, Luther aimed this pointedly traditional definition of Christ's presence in the Supper (*under* the bread and wine) at those who would deny that Christ comes to us in the meal.[11] However, the last phrase, "for us Christians to eat and to drink," was aimed at the late-medieval piety of watching the sacrament rather than receiving it. Luther had reason to return to this problem in his exhortation from the Large Catechism.

He immediately drew another parallel to his explanation of baptism, noting that just as baptism was not "mere" water, so the Supper was not "mere" bread and wine: "Rather, it is bread and wine set within God's Word and bound to it."[12] Likewise, Luther again cited Augustine's definition of the relation between the elements and the Word, already mentioned in the exposition of baptism. This "word and ordinance . . . of the divine Majesty" immediately brought Luther to a critique of reason, once again revealing his "sacramentology of the cross."

> With this Word ["This is my Body"] you can strengthen your conscience and declare: "Let a hundred thousand devils, with all the fanatics, come forward and say, "How can bread and wine be Christ's body and blood?" etc. Still I know that all the spirits and scholars put together have less wisdom than the divine Majesty has in his littlest finger. Here we have Christ's word. . . . Here we shall take our stand and see who dares instruct Christ and alter what he has spoken. . . . For as Christ's lips speak and say, so it is; he cannot lie or deceive.[13]

Luther's thought forged an iron chain linking Christ's promised presence to the certainty of faith and the untrustworthiness of human reason and works. Luther insisted here on the dependability of God's word in order to strengthen the conscience and to destroy all attempts to turn the sacrament's unconditional promise into something that depends on the recipient. The sacrament, he wrote,

> is not founded on human holiness but on the Word of God. . . . For the Word by which it was constituted a sacrament is not rendered false because of an individual's unworthiness or unbelief. Christ does not say, "If you believe or if you are worthy, you have my body and blood," but rather, "Take, eat and drink, this is my body and blood." Likewise, when he says, "Do this" . . . this is as much as to say, "no matter whether you are worthy or unworthy, you have here his body and blood by the power of these words that are connected to the bread and wine."[14]

As the controversy with the Zwinglians unfolded, discussion also centered on whether those who were "eating and drinking the Supper unworthily" received mere bread and wine while sanctified believers received Christ's body and blood or whether all received Christ—believers to their benefit and unbelievers to their harm.[15] For Luther, that unworthy or even ungodly people received Christ's body was first and foremost a pastoral issue of assuring the weak that Christ comes to them. Everyone, even those who feel unworthy when they approach the Supper, can be certain that Christ does not abandon them at the altar. (Luther addressed this issue more squarely in the exhortation.)

The second catechetical question focused on what Luther viewed as the other weakness in the Zwinglian understanding of the sacraments: that they depended on human remembering and faith and did not actually offer any benefits in themselves.[16] For Luther, any word of God also carried with it a "power and benefit, for which purpose the sacrament was really instituted."[17] Here, his very name for the Lord's Supper changed, so to speak, from "sacrament" to "treasure."[18] He wrote, "That is to say, in brief, that we go to the sacrament because there we receive a great treasure, through and in which we obtain the forgiveness of sins."[19] Indeed, Luther immediately added that the Supper provided the believer "food for the soul" to be used against sin, death, and all evils as a daily living out of one's baptism.

For it nourishes and strengthens the new creature. For in the first instance, we are born anew through baptism. However, our human flesh and blood, as I have said, have not lost their old skin. There are so many hindrances and attacks of the devil and the world that we often grow weary and faint and at times even stumble. Therefore the Lord's Supper is given as a daily food and sustenance so that our faith may be refreshed and strengthened and that it may not succumb in the struggle but become ever stronger and stronger. For the new life should be one that continually develops and progresses. But it has to suffer a great deal of opposition. The devil is a furious enemy; when he sees that we resist him and attack the old creature, and when he cannot rout us by force, he sneaks and skulks about at every turn, trying all kinds of tricks, and does not stop until he has finally worn us out so that we either renounce our faith or lose heart and become indifferent or impatient. For times like these, when our heart feels too sorely pressed, this comfort of the Lord's Supper is given to bring us new strength and refreshment.[20]

"For times like these." These words demonstrate a completely different approach to the Supper than Luther's heirs generally practiced. By the eighteenth century, if not before, the Lord's Supper became a four-times-a-year rite, effective for the Christian by mere participation. After more than half a century of liturgical renewal, twenty-first-century American Lutherans have increased the frequency of celebration and participation dramatically, but with little more attention paid to the "times" than that of their pious predecessors. Just because people receive the Supper more often and congregations celebrate it even weekly, as was the case in Luther's Wittenberg, it does not mean that the urgent, eschatological edge (the devil's "sneaking and skulking") is present. Here sermon, liturgy, and catechesis must combine to reveal our need until, as Luther wrote in the preface to the Small Catechism, people "would come on their own, rushing and running to it; they would compel themselves to come and would insist that you give them the sacrament."[21]

In the Small Catechism, then, Luther reduced the benefits of the Supper to three: forgiveness of sins, life, and salvation, arguing that where the one was literally promised ("given for you . . . shed for you *for the forgiveness of sins*"), the others quite naturally came along. In the Large Catechism, besides making the direct connection to baptism, as we have seen, Luther also went after his Zwinglian opponents, who denied that forgiveness came with the Supper itself but insisted that it was a far more spiritual thing, given directly to the human spirit through the Holy Spirit. Luther, as he had done with baptism, tied these effects to the Word. After all, how could one know what God was up to there or seek it if the Supper was not a treasure "set within the Word"?[22] The work of Christ's death took place on the cross, to be sure, but, Luther argued, "it cannot come to us in any other way than through the Word."[23] Otherwise, he wondered, how would we know that this salvation and forgiveness is for us? Luther tied the gospel of the Creed (believing in the church and the forgiveness of sins) to preaching the Word and celebrating the sacraments: "Now, the whole gospel and the article of the Creed . . . are embodied in this sacrament and offered to us through the Word."[24]

Always the equal-opportunity reformer, Luther then turned his attention in the third question ("Who receives such benefits?") and proceeded to attack the sacrifice of the Mass. Some, including Zwingli, had interpreted Luther's emphasis on Christ's presence and the Supper's benefits as a return to a late-medieval insistence that the sacrament was effective by its mere performance (*ex opere operato*) or, in this case, by the mere recitation of the words. Here, too, Luther centered his answer on the Word and, more precisely, on who receives the Word's promises. If the one side rejected the presence of Christ and questioned the sacrament's benefits, the other completely eliminated faith. Masses for the dead especially had eliminated the importance of faith (let alone actually eating and drinking).

Luther attacked this third question by turning attention to the recipient of the meal. This Supper and its promises "are not spoken or preached to stone and wood but to those who hear them, those to whom [Christ] says, 'Take, eat, etc.'"[25] What Luther was going after here was any theoretical approach to the meal that imagined it was not a real meal with real elements and real promises addressed to real people with real ears and mouths. As with baptism, the answer to the question "Who receives these benefits?" went back to the Word and "the one who believes what the words say and what they give." This is why some current debates over the first age of communion miss the point. The question Luther asked was not "How old is the person?" but "Who believes?" and "How would receiving this sacrament benefit this specific believer?" Christ did not institute the sacrament as a spectacle, to be carried around in a monstrance and adored, or as postmortem medicine, but precisely for each sinner in the assembled community of believers. The pastoral question must precede all other concerns: "How may I deliver the unmerited forgiving presence of Christ to this person without turning the Supper into magic on the one side or memory work on the other?" Luther concluded, "The treasure is opened and placed at everyone's door, yes, upon the table, but it also belongs to the sacrament to take it and confidently believe that it is just as the words tell you."[26] Luther's comments relieve the celebrant of the responsibility of checking each person's worthiness (as if a human being could determine such a thing); rather, they allow the celebrant to place the gift in the hands and upon the lips of those who receive. It also means that preaching includes true invitation, similar to what Luther saw going on in the introduction to the Lord's Prayer—that God here "wants to entice us." To paraphrase a new Eucharistic hymn: "Pass the word around, forgiveness, life and salvation abound!"

The fourth question in the Small Catechism, not found in this form in the Large, revealed another aspect of Luther's pastoral approach to the Supper. His people were used to certain practices, especially fasting, before receiving the Lord's Supper, but they had learned to do these things in order to be worthy of the Sacrament. Luther did not simply dismiss century-old practices in the name of novelty or reform—an example people may wish to follow today. Instead, he called them what they were and are: "fine external discipline." But worthiness for Luther did not consist of our works but of faith in the promises, "given for you . . . shed for you for the forgiveness of sins."

Of course, the history of Lutheran celebration of the sacrament among both Orthodox and Pietist Lutherans came to place the quest for worthiness at the table back at the center of the Supper. Then the old creature once again wondered: "Have I done enough? Am I worthy?" And those who did come forward were often thought to be "uppity," spiritually proud of their worthiness. Yet Luther seemed to have unchained this beast with his comments: "However, a person who does not believe these words or doubts them is unworthy and unprepared, because the words 'for you' require truly believing hearts."[27] To some degree, Luther's point can be mitigated by the ambiguity of the German, where sixteenth-century German did not distinguish between "require" and "promote" (now in German: *fordern* and *fördern*, respectively). Thus, it could be that the words do not require but rather encourage or promote believing hearts. Unfortunately, both Latin translators of 1529 read the terms as "require" (*requirat* or *postulat*). However, the dilemma only arises when one again imagines that Luther did not remember what he had already written: "I believe that I cannot believe." Faith is not some sort of difficult (if not impossible) work that God puts in the way to block all access to mercy and grace. It is exactly what happens when the Holy Spirit "calls through the gospel." The "for you" in the Supper is precisely that call. Moreover, this call is not a demand to comprehend all the intricacies of the Lutheran doctrine of the real presence but rather a gentle, enticing invitation from the savior of the world: "Here I am for you."

In today's American Lutheran churches, practice varies widely: from restricting the table to members or believers only to offering it to everyone and anyone; from quarterly communion to weekly communion; from using the bare words of institution to reinserting them in a wide variety of eucharistic prayers; from indoctrinating our children and adults about the Supper to assuming that they will "get it" if they just participate. In this welter of customs, Luther's approach may offer a breath of fresh air. In the catechisms, he cuts through our most reasonable and most ritualistic approaches to this sacrament and refocuses the discussion on what matters: the word of Christ, this treasure, and faith in that word. When we lose this focus, we always turn in upon ourselves to what we can offer: either what we bring to the altar or what we do at the altar. Either way, we bury the treasure and lose the very comfort it conveys.

Luther's Advice on Dealing with Spiritually Anorexic Christians

In Luther's approach to the Lord's Supper in the Large Catechism, he first emphasized Christ's presence in the sacrament. Then he stressed the "treasure" of forgiveness and faith in that promise. Finally, he concluded with a lengthy plea to make use of "so great a treasure." Similarly, in the preface to the Small Catechism, Luther also included an exhortation to receive the Supper. Overlooking these comments would miss the most pastoral part of all. Here, Luther took an actual exhortation to his own congregation during Holy Week 1529 and turned it into a general reflection on how to deal with Christians who neglect the Supper, what we today call "inactive members" of Christian congregations.[28]

In the church in which Luther grew up, yearly confession and communion were required to remain a member of the church. When Luther insisted that anything so important to faith could not be coerced, some people exercised their newfound freedom by not going to the Lord's Supper at all. Others, still burdened with the notion that unworthy sinners had no place at the table, also stayed away because of scruples of conscience. In this new world of Christian freedom, Luther and other Reformers traveled in uncharted waters, certain that they did not wish to return to the "slaughter of souls" (*Seelenmord*) under papal obligations, but equally convinced that our "old skin" had to be restrained.

To this highly complex theological and pastoral dilemma Luther turned his skills, first in a Holy Week sermon of 1529 and then in the Large Catechism itself.[29] The result was a succinct manual on how to deal with spiritually anorexic congregational members, who are starving themselves of one of the chief treasures that God provides believers. Because it is so easy to be judgmental and legalistic on this issue, Luther's approach, grounded in distinguishing law and gospel, may provide new light on this vexing problem.

When faced with the problem of inactive or, better, sleeping Christians, the old creature in active Christians (also known as the "Elder Brother" of Luke 15) is only too happy to moralize or equivocate. One wants either to "get tough" or to "take it easy." Either way, in Luther's view, God's word gets lost and believers are left to their own devices to fix the problem. Luther, on the contrary, used the law and gospel to sort matters out. He used the law not to moralize but to "tell it like it is." Thus, he wrote, "For we see that people are becoming lax and lazy about [the Supper's] observance. A great number of people . . . let a year, or two, three, or more years go by without receiving the sacrament, as if they were such strong Christians that they have no need of it."[30] All this was occurring under the pretext of Christian freedom. Others exempted themselves from the table because they felt no "hunger and thirst."

The temptation—expressed in the model constitutions of some modern American churches—is simply to lay down the law. But Luther knew firsthand the danger of that response: "Now it is true, as we have said, that no one under any circumstances should be forced or compelled, lest we institute a new slaughter of souls." Luther also realized that centuries of believing that watching the sacrament was a meritorious work meant that, at the same time, he had to remind his people that "Christ did not institute the sacrament for us to treat as a spectacle, but he commanded his Christians to eat and drink it and thereby remember him." Moreover, he refused to flinch from the fact that people who "abstain and absent themselves from the sacrament over a long period of time are not to be considered Christians."[31] So Luther had first to eliminate the old creature's favorite uses of law and gospel: moralistic murder of others, meritorious religiosity, and well-intentioned (but antinomian) permissiveness.

Having cleared the decks, so to speak, Luther was then ready to sail off in a very different direction. As in his opposition to the Zwinglian and the Roman parties, he struggled to let the Word speak for itself. At the same time, however, he understood, as a pastor, that the Word was being addressed to different people in different ways, depending on their situations in life. Thus, he immediately distinguished true Christians ("who cherish and honor the sacrament") from the weak ("who would also like to be Christians"). Even among the weak, however, he discerned three types: the "cold and indifferent," those who felt unworthy, and those who felt no need for the sacrament at all. Each of these three groups received special treatment from their pastor.[32]

To the first group, Luther preached the law—not *his* law but Christ's command to "do this in remembrance of me."[33] Similarly, in the preface to the Small Catechism, he wrote, "For Christ did not say, 'Omit this,' or 'Despise this,' but instead, 'Do this as often as you drink it.' He really wants it to be done and not completely omitted or despised."[34] These words, Luther went on to say in the Large Catechism, were addressed to Christ's followers, so that "whoever

wants to be a disciple of Christ . . . must faithfully hold to this sacrament, not from compulsion, forced by humans, but to obey and
please the Lord Christ."[35] The focus for Luther was not on rules for
cleaning the church rolls but on the invitation and command of
Christ. The Christian had no Christian liberty to despise the sacrament. Wrote Luther: "If you want such liberty, you may just as well
take the further liberty not to be a Christian; then you need not
believe or pray, for the one is just as much Christ's commandment
as the other."[36]

Luther then expressed another temptation, one perhaps even
more prevalent today than in Luther's day, where the pastor injects
his or her own personality into the mix: "Come to church to make
me happy." Luther concluded instead, "But we neither force nor
compel anyone, nor need anyone do so in order to serve or please us.
What should move and induce you is that he [Christ] desires it, and
it pleases him." No good work ever arose from *human* compulsion:
"You should not let yourself be forced by human beings either to
faith or to any good work." Our urging, he continued, was not for
our own sake "but for your own. He invites you and incites you, and
if you want to show contempt for his sacrament, you must answer
for it yourself."[37]

Luther concluded his discussion of the first group, which he now
named the "cold and indifferent," by revealing his own struggles.
Legalists reveal their deepest motivation for demanding obedience to
the law with a prayer: "I thank you, God, that I am not like that tax
collector (or even: not like that legalist)." Luther, far from lording it
over even this most hardened group with his superior Christian faith,
admitted instead that he himself had experienced how easily absent-
ing oneself from the Lord's Supper resulted in coldness and callous-
ness, so that he wrote, "As I have found in my own experience . . ."[38]
Part of the genius of Luther's pastoral care rested in his honest admis-
sion of solidarity with persons in trouble, under the law.

With the second group, those who feel they are unworthy,
Luther began by making the same confession: "This is my struggle
as well."[39] At first glance, the problem of unworthiness might seem
passé, "inherited from the old order," as Luther described it, where
people tortured themselves to become pure enough to receive the
sacrament. One then contrasted unworthiness to God's gift and

found it "as manure in contrast to jewels." One thinks, too, of a certain strain of Pietism, where people would commune at their confirmation (it was required) and then just before death. Otherwise, they were unworthy. Thus, this group might seem rather small in today's church—reduced to a few old, pious souls who still fret over whether they are worthy to receive the Supper. Yet it would seem that many folks, especially when something in their home life goes awry, become inactive because of guilt or shame. Divorce, abuse, and a host of other crises can easily drive one away from the Christian assembly and, hence, from the table. Shame, guilt, and despair are still powerful motivators of religious conviction or inactivity.[40]

To this second group, Luther preached both law *and* gospel, after distinguishing this group from the first.[41] After all, they already know that they must come (the law), but they cannot: "People with such misgivings must learn that it is the highest art to realize that this sacrament does not depend upon our worthiness." When people are overwhelmed with feelings of unworthiness, the command of Christ frees them to come. It frees them to say to Christ, "I would really like to be worthy, but I come not on account of any worthiness of mine, but on account of your Word, because you have commanded it, and I want to be your disciple, regardless of my worthiness."[42] Indeed, Luther transformed a command ("Do this!") into a gentle invitation that overcomes guilt and shame by revealing God's heart: "Christ wants me to come." (Similarly, the command to pray reveals God's desire to hear from us, as was made plain in chapter 4.)

Then follows the promise ("My Body *for you*"), "which should most powerfully draw and impel us." Here, as in the explanation of the introduction to the Lord's Prayer, God tenderly entices. When a person hears the words "for you" (words that Luther capitalized at this point in the text), Luther writes, "Ponder, then, and include yourself personally in the 'YOU' so that [Christ] may not speak to you in vain."[43] In calling on such broken people today, pastors would be well advised to bring the Lord's Supper along, as they do for those with bodily illnesses in hospitals or nursing homes, since it is medicine for sin-sick souls, perhaps even encouraging them with Luther's words.

In this sacrament [Christ] offers us all the treasures he brought from
heaven for us, to which he most graciously invites us. . . . We must
never regard the sacrament as a harmful thing from which we should
flee, but as a pure, wholesome, soothing medicine that aids you and
gives life in both soul and body. For where the soul is healed, the body
is helped as well. Why, then, do we act as if the sacrament were a poi-
son that would kill us if we ate of it?[44]

To the command and promise of Christ, Luther added a third
motivation for these weak souls to consider: "your own need, which
hangs around your neck, which is the very reason for this command,
invitation, and promise."[45] In the Small Catechism, he depicted this
need in much starker terms, contrasting those who thought they had
no need for the sacrament to the reality of the Christian life. Once
again, Luther brought his people to the final petitions of the Lord's
Prayer and the neediness that marks the entire Christian experience.

Those who do not hold the sacrament in high esteem indicate that
they have no sin, no flesh, no devil, no world, no death, no dangers,
no hell. That is, they *believe* they have none of these things, although
they are up to their neck in them and belong to the devil twice over.
On the other hand, they indicate that they need no grace, no life, no
paradise, no heaven, no Christ, no God, nor any other good thing. For
if they believed that they had so much evil and needed so much good,
they would not neglect the sacrament in which help against such evil is
provided and in which so much good is given.[46]

Finally, there is the third group: those who feel no need. These
people pose one of the most frustrating dilemmas for any pastor,
since neither law nor gospel seems to have any effect on them. They
are neither cold and indifferent nor guilt-ridden; they are numb,
spiritually comatose. Again, instead of seducing such people with
moralisms or entertainment, Luther ran to the Word and to human
experience. First, such people should "put their hands to their bosom
to determine whether they are made of flesh and blood."[47] Luther
correlated this odd bit of advice with a reference to Paul's description
of the flesh from Gal. 5:19-20 and the suggestion that "if you cannot
feel the need, at least believe the Scriptures."[48] In this way at least,

the Scripture, God's trustworthy word, outweighs one's feelings and experience. That Scripture for Luther did not simply contain "time-less truths" may be seen in the second Bible verse referred to here: Paul's own experience described in Rom. 7:18 ("For I know that nothing good dwells within me, that is, in my flesh"). If Paul experienced his life as *simul iustus et peccator* (simultaneously righteous and sinner), surely we are no better, Luther insisted. Our inability to experience the weakness of the flesh is also, he continued, great proof of just how weak it is.[49]

Luther's second bit of advice to such benumbed believers was to "look around you and see whether you are also in the world. If you do not know, ask your neighbors about it." Perhaps this is the equivalent of saying that if a man does not know whether he is a sin-ner, he should ask his wife, and vice versa. Again, if the Pollyannaish world in which we imagine we live fails to reveal itself to us, Luther led his readers again to Scripture and to its description of the world. Luther also suggested that simply trying to live a Christian life in the gospel would bring a host of troubles, "enemies who harm, wrong, and injure you and give you cause to sin and do wrong."[50]

Luther's final suggestion was to consider the work of the devil.[51] Throughout the catechisms, Luther's mention of the devil was hardly simply a throwback to a superstitious, medieval mind-set. Rather, as Heiko Oberman has shown, Luther discovered that as soon as he believed the gospel of the unmerited forgiveness of sins and pro-claimed it, all hell broke loose.[52] This appearance of evil was hardly simply the product of an unenlightened, fertile imagination; rather, it was the very center of the doctrine of justification by faith alone. Thus, discussion of the devil appeared all over Luther's catechisms, but especially in the second article of the Creed, in portions of the Lord's Prayer, and especially in discussions of baptism and the Lord's Supper. Only the justified live by God's grace alone and thus feel their need and experience true assaults from the "liar and murderer: A liar who entices the heart away from God's Word and blinds it, making you unable to feel your need or to come to Christ; a murderer who begrudges you every hour of your life."[53] If Christ could not avoid the devil, Luther wrote in the Large Catechism, how could his fol-lowers? Then came the pièce de résistance of Luther's argument: "If you could see how many daggers, spears, and arrows are aimed at you every moment, you would be glad to come to the sacrament as often as you can."[54]

Of course, defenders of the human will, who want to blame our will for what has gone wrong and thus expect human willing to fix things in the end, will find in Luther's comments too strong an antidote to their "just try harder" approach. Inactivity or, better, spiritual starvation, Luther insisted, was not simply a matter of bad upbringing or a failure of will. Its root causes cannot be fixed with PowerPoint presentations, more exciting worship, or fancy appeals. The absence of people around the Lord's table was a sure sign for Luther that we are in battle with the devil, where the only effective tools are Christ's word and work, not our own ("I believe that I cannot believe"). He wrote, "The only reason we go about so securely and heedlessly is that we neither imagine nor believe that we are in the flesh, in the wicked world, or under the kingdom of the devil."[55] Here, Luther put his readers back in the Garden of Eden, where the true temptation was denial: "You will not die; you will be like gods, deciding what is right and wrong."

But what if this dose of reality bears no fruit? Some might be tempted to cross the person off the mailing list, take them off the rolls, and send a smug letter wishing them a good life. But even at this point, even when all of this reality preaching (that is, the law) turned out to be no more than water off a duck's back, Luther took a much more evangelical and pastoral approach: "If even then you still feel nothing, you have all the more need to lament both to God and to your brother or sister. Take the advice of others and ask them to pray for you; never give up until the stone is removed from your heart."[56] The ones who feel nothing—and God knows that not just Luther's age but also our society is filled with such folk—were in Luther's eyes more miserable, more to be prayed for and pitied than anyone else. Perhaps they are the only ones a pastor dare not take off the membership roster! What a different way to view these people!

Luther's teaching on the Lord's Supper opened up an entirely new way to care pastorally (that is, with law and gospel) for all the people in Christian congregations. This wholly evangelical approach, so foreign to our "old skin," places Christ right where he belongs: in the center of his Supper, this treasure, where he gives himself for us.

In this meal, as first in baptism, the believer experiences the intimate connection between the "Holy Christian Church" and the "forgiveness of sins." In this meal, believers are ushered into the Holy Spirit's workshop, where they encounter Christ for them, not against them, who reflects God's glory and draws and entices into the Father's heart.

Fourth Petition of the Lord's Prayer: John 6[:1-15] (the Feeding of the Five Thousand)

CHAPTER 8

The Catechisms as
a Vocational School

In his book *The Reformation in the Cities* and elsewhere, Steven Ozment has consistently argued that the real appeal of the Reformation and Luther's theology was the renewed sense of the worth of ordinary work in the eyes of God.[1] Thus, to appreciate just how revolutionary Luther's proposal was, we have to remember what the general shape of Christian life was prior to the Reformation. Medieval theology had drawn a line through society dividing good and better Christians—that is, the laity on the one hand, bound to follow the Ten Commandments, generally incapable of higher acts of Christian good, caught in a world of soldiery, money, trade, marriage, and other such things; and those under a vow (monks, friars, and bishops) on the other. According to Thomas Aquinas, among other theologians, the monks and friars, on account of their vows (of poverty, chastity, and obedience), were bound to follow not only the Ten Commandments but also the counsels of the New Testament, especially those regarding turning the other cheek (no war), celibacy (no marriage), and selling all and giving the proceeds to the poor (no money or trade). That is, monks and friars embodied the so-called *vita apostolica*, the apostolic life.

In the fifteenth century, this division came under attack by followers of the *Devotio Moderna*, the Modern Devotion, a movement of lay and clerical piety that began in the Netherlands and included the quasi-monastic movement the Brethren of the Common Life. These brothers, both lay and ordained, did all the things monks did (they held property in common, were chaste, and obeyed their superior), but they refused to take a vow and, rather than be cloistered, worked in the community. Already in the fourteenth century, the dispute over whether Franciscans could own any property in common had brought some of the practices of monks into disrepute. But what remained was the ideal of a better, higher level of Christian life, marked by strict attention to the Sermon on the Mount and other sayings of Jesus.

Now, if the apostolic ideal moved toward monasticism in the Middle Ages, the early sixteenth century saw it take two rather different twists. On the one side, the Anabaptists, heavily influenced by the *Devotio Moderna*, especially as mediated by Erasmus, had as their goal bringing all Christians out of daily life and into the monastery.[2] That is, especially among such groups as the Swiss Brethren and the Hutterites, Anabaptists replaced the monastic vow with adult baptism, a sign that a person was ready to lead a life in which property was held in common, the government and society at large were held to be evil and thus oaths of fealty and soldiery were forbidden, and individuals were beholden to the will of the entire group as embodied in its leaders and enforced through the ban and shunning. Over time, because of their intense social conservatism, they even developed a habit (that is, peculiar dress) and, like Benedictines, imagined the city to be evil and the country to be the only place to live a Christian life.

Martin Luther, in contrast to this approach and as a direct result of his understanding of justification, brought the apostolic life, the monastery if you will, into daily life. In 1521, from the Wartburg, he wrote *The Judgment of Martin Luther concerning Monastic Vows*.[3] That tract, in combination with a commentary on 1 Corinthians 7 published in 1523 and sermonic helps on John 21 from 1522, gives the broad outline of his approach.[4] This final source, from Luther's Christmas *Kirchenpostil* (Church Postil: sermons on the appointed texts for the season of Christmas, composed in the Wartburg), had perhaps the most far-reaching effects, since it passed into the reading and preaching of nearly every Evangelical pastor after that time.[5] Luther stated his case as clearly as possible. Of the two teachings Luther discovered in this gospel, the first dealt with Christian vocation. Luther wrote, "The teaching is as follows: Notwithstanding the examples and lives of all the saints, every person should attend to the work entrusted to him and guard the honor of his calling. Oh, this is truly a needed and wholesome teaching." Like Peter, who was advised by Jesus not to worry about what would happen to John, we are to attend to our duties. In a single paragraph Luther attacked people who went on pilgrimages to saints while leaving wife and children behind, "not knowing that their calling and mission are quite different from that of the saint they are imitating. In the same way they do with their bequests, fastings, clothing, holidays, priestcraft, monasteries and cloisters."

Having completely gutted traditional piety, he then dealt with the following objection:

> "But how if I am not called, what shall I do then?" Answer: How is it possible that you are not called? You have always been in some state or station; you have always been a husband or wife, or boy or girl, or servant. Picture before you the humblest state. Are you a husband, and you think you have not enough to do in that sphere to govern your wife, children, domestics and property so that all may be obedient to God and you do no one any wrong? Yea, if you had five heads and ten hands, even then you would be too weak for your task, so that you would never dare to think of making a pilgrimage or doing any kind of saintly work.

Luther then ran the gamut of possible vocations—son or daughter, domestic or servant, prince or lord, bishop—and concluded, "Hence it is, that if a pious maid-servant goes forth with her orders, and sweeps the yard or cleans the stable; or a man-servant in the same spirit plows and drives a team: they travel direct to heaven in the right road; while another who goes to St. James [of Compostella] or to church, and lets his office and work lie, travels straight to Hell." Luther preached obedience all right, but obedience to Christ in a person's daily life and calling.

Vocation in the Large Catechism

This revolution, which has often been completely lost in the Lutheran Church of the twenty-first century, comes to expression nowhere more clearly in Luther's writings than in the catechisms.[6] Luther had discovered that justification by faith alone was nothing less than the promise of a coming new world. That world comes only through the gospel promise received by faith alone. Christians are declared righteous and forgiven of their sins, and they receive that promised righteousness by faith alone. The church exists precisely where the promise is proclaimed, coming into existence in a deeply hidden way: hidden in the Word and sacraments, which destroy human reason and proclaim the Crucified and Risen One as victorious Lord.

At the same time, Christians also live in this world. What does the Christian message have to say about that? Instead of separating believers from the earthly realm, the Christian message revealed for Luther that the God and Father of Jesus is also Creator and that Jesus is the one through whom all things were made. Thus, daily life is sanctified by faith alone.[7] Rather than trying to escape this world or imagining that this world is all that there is, the Christian finds in this world God's calling to love the neighbor. Thus, Christian faith, which frees a person from having to do works for God (*coram Deo*), sends one back to work in the world for the neighbor (*coram hominibus*). This work, arising out of God's will for creation and the neighbor's need, defined for Luther the Christian's calling (*Beruf*; Latin: *vocatio*). Indeed, Luther seems to have invented an entirely different way of understanding the term *vocatio*, which before the Reformation had been used almost exclusively for a calling in the church.

At the same time that he defined in his theology both an earthly and a heavenly realm, or this world and the world to come,[8] Luther also divided the world into the kingdom of Christ and the kingdom of Satan.[9] Because of sin and because God justifies sinners (that is, believers are *simul iustus et peccator*), God-given vocations are always under attack. The devil, the world, and the sinful self conspire to drive believers away from the neighbor—who is Christ in our midst—back into themselves. In this situation, then, the law, which was established to keep order in this world and to give plenty of opportunity to serve the neighbor in Christian freedom (the so-called first use of the law), must also drive persons to do it, killing the old creature and forcing it to help the neighbor. This second use of the law drives believers to Christ in two ways: both to the gospel's forgiveness and to the neighbor in need.

Luther's catechisms were written to explicate Christian life in just such a world: living between condemnation and forgiveness (law and gospel), expecting God's coming reign with feet firmly planted in this world (God's two hands), safe in Christ and under attack by Satan (two kingdoms), trusting Christ and serving the neighbor (Christian freedom). Suddenly, the need for a special, more committed brand of Christian or a higher Christian ethic disappears; all believers live equally under God's mercy in Christ. Special Christians under vows, Christian communities strictly separated from "the world," and (perhaps) even the need for mountaintop retreat centers are eliminated as the actual congregation, society, and household now stand at the heart of Christian living.

Luther resituated the monastery in the household. More specifically, borrowing medieval understandings of society, he defined three arenas, or walks of life, in which Christians experience their callings: the household (*oikonomia*, a term that embraced both family life and the workplace), the society and its governance (*politia*), and the church (*ecclesia*, understood as the visible gathering of believers around Word and Sacrament). Into this context he placed the catechisms. This threefold division of life was not so much a central theological principle as it was an assumption derived from medieval (Aristotelian) views of the world. It provided Luther with a down-to-earth way to view God's work among human beings. For example, Luther's exposition of the fourth commandment in the Large Catechism demonstrates how pragmatically these categories functioned to expand the literal meaning of "father." "So we have introduced three kinds of fathers in this commandment: fathers by blood, fathers of a household, and fathers of the nation. In addition there are also spiritual fathers . . . those who govern and guide us by the Word of God."[10]

Similarly, when it came to teaching the catechism, Luther distinguished his calling as pastor from that of the heads of households (fathers and mothers). Each heading in the original broadsheets of what became the Small Catechism, published in 1529, reminded people that these were instructions for the *oikonomia*: "In a simple way in which the head of a house is to present them to the household."[11] Luther did not ignore the facts of society, but rather coopted them for the gospel's sake. The housefather and housemother were, by virtue of baptism, the family's pastors and had to be enjoined and encouraged to train their children. This work was part of their Christian vocation. Thus, again in the explanation to the fourth commandment in the Large Catechism, which functions as a short essay on Christian vocations in the world, Luther admonished parents and governmental officials to see to their children's education, for the good of both the world and the church. "For if we want capable and qualified people for both the civil and the spiritual realms, we really must spare no effort, time, and expense in teaching and educating our children to serve God and the world."[12]

Luther's distinction and connection of faith and works meant that trivial, humble work was the heart of true Christian living. In comments on the fourth commandment, Luther laid to rest the myth of a "Christian ethic," especially as practiced by self-anointed speakers for the cause of some social or political agenda or another.

> If this could be impressed on the poor people, a servant girl would dance for joy and praise and thank God; and with her careful work, for which she receives sustenance and wages, she would obtain a treasure such as all who pass for the greatest saints do not have. Is it not a tremendous honor to know this and to say, "If you do your daily household chores, that is better than the holiness and austere life of all the monks"? Moreover, you have the promise that whatever you do will prosper and fare well. How could you be more blessed or lead a holier life, as far as works are concerned? In God's sight it is actually faith that makes a person holy; it alone serves God, while our works serve people. Here you have every blessing, protection, and shelter under the Lord and, what is more, a joyful conscience and a gracious God who will reward you a hundredfold. You are a true nobleman [*Junker*] if you are simply upright and obedient.[13]

Monasticism of one sort or another, including congregational monasticism, is still the order of the day in many forms of Christianity. Congregational service projects, not making beds, become the mark of truly committed Christians; going the extra mile in giving to the congregation (taking Jesus' comment about forced service by Roman soldiers in an opposite, self-serving direction) becomes holier than driving children to school; becoming a pastor or missionary is more blessed than being a good plumber. Instead of teaching children (and adults) to leap in praise around washed dishes or mown grass, we would rather sign them up for spiritual retreats or outreach, reinforcing the mistaken belief that such things are on a higher spiritual plane, when in fact they are simply different, not better, ways of serving one's neighbor.

So Lutherans are quietists? Only if one measures their activity on the basis of some liberal or conservative political agenda (read: ideal)! Lutherans raise children, marry, work, give, serve, and all the rest, but not up to the standards of governmental interference and busy-body activism that idealists on both sides of the political spectrum set for them. The irony that a relatively tiny group of Christians in the United States, the Lutherans, should have over the years created the single largest nonprofit, nongovernmental social service network in the nation, is one of the few signs that Luther's practical view of Christian service may still have some faint life. Helping real people in real-life situations defines true activism.

In Luther's comments on the Christian life, the word *obedience* gives some people pause, as if it demands the kind of blind sub-mission to authority that bedeviled Germany in the Third Reich. Such a distortion of Luther's position occurred when the distinc-tion between this world and the world to come had been destroyed through hundreds of years of governmental control of the church, to the point that Christian leaders imagined they were speaking for the nation. Instead, Lutheran history—from the resistance of Mel-anchthon in the Smalcald War to the Confession of Magdeburg in the 1550s, from the emigration of Missouri Synod Lutherans in the nineteenth century to the protests against the German Democratic Republic's regime—demonstrates that Lutheran obedience to gov-ernment depends upon obedience to God and care for the neighbor. As Luther wrote in the explanation to the fourth commandment of the Large Catechism, "*If* God's Word and will are placed first and are observed, nothing ought to be considered more important than the will and word of our parents, provided that these, too, are subordinated to God and are not set in opposition to the preced-ing commandments."[14] Similarly, at the end of his explanation, he noted that, although there was no mention of the duties of parents or others in authority, he needed to add such comments. "Everyone acts as if God gave us children for our own pleasure and amusement, gave us servants merely to put them to work like cows or donkeys, and gave us subjects to treat as we please, as if it were no concern of ours what they learn or how they live."[15] Luther lived and thought in a world where what he considered God-ordained inequality was tempered by reciprocity in relationships and the real threat of divine judgment. Thus, one of the most unique things about the catechisms was that, despite the fact that their main targets are the youth and subjects, Luther also gave advice to those in authority.

Luther used this distinction between the two realms (this world and the world to come) to criticize and instruct the princes and others in authority, which is nowhere more clearly indicated than in his comments on the eighth commandment in the Large Catechism. After eliminating any and all forms of slander, backbiting, and judging the neighbor, Luther looked at public sins of those in authority. Here others with the appropriate calling had no choice but to speak up. "For when something is exposed to the light of day, there can be no question of slander or injustice or false witness. For example, we now censure the pope and his teaching, which is publicly set forth in books and shouted throughout the world. Where the sin is public, appropriate public punishment should follow so that everyone may know how to guard against it."[16] The very public nature of the pope's crimes forced Luther to go public on the attack. On this basis, Lutherans would not be quietists at all but irritating "noisy-ists" in the face of public crimes.

What about all the counsels to turn the other cheek? Part of the reason for the medieval insistence on dividing the secular realm from the spiritual and placing monks and others under a vow in the latter was because it was deemed impossible for governmental officials to carry out Christ's commands not to judge, to turn the other cheek, and to be obedient. Luther, instead of dividing people into different groups, divided each person, shielding the officeholder from fulfilling this command in his (or her) office by the higher command of loving one's neighbor. Again, the Large Catechism demonstrates how Luther dealt with this, using the extreme example of the hangman.

> So you see that we are absolutely forbidden to speak evil of our neighbor. Exception is made, however, of civil magistrates, preachers, and fathers and mothers in order that we may interpret this commandment [the eighth] in such a way that evil does not go unpunished. We have seen that the Fifth Commandment forbids us to injure anyone physically,

and yet an exception is made of the hangman. By virtue of his office he does not do his neighbor good but only harm and evil, yet he does not sin against God's commandment because God of his own accord instituted that office, and, as he warns in the First Commandment [Luther here was referring to the summary], he has reserved to himself the right of punishment. Likewise, although no one personally has the right to judge and condemn anyone, yet if they are commanded to do so and fail to do it, they sin as much as those who take the law into their own hands apart from any office. In that case necessity requires one to report evil, to prefer charges, to give evidence, to examine witnesses, and to testify.[17]

For Luther, an office did not give a person power but rather placed upon them a different, but still God-given, set of responsibilities, leaving them answerable to God to love their neighbor. God as creator played for Luther a crucial role in the Christian's life in the world. The reason for order in this world is so God can answer the prayer, "Give us today our daily bread." Indeed, while the other six petitions deal with the coming rule of God and faith, this one alone dealt with the present life, showing God's love and concern for it, which the believer has already confessed in the first article of the Creed. Thus, he suggested that a prince's coat-of-arms or coins be emblazoned with a loaf of bread, to define more clearly what his office was.[18] At the same time that Luther was defining the role of the government (God's left hand) in providing bread, however, he also depicted the battle between God's will and the devil, who "also prevents and impedes the establishment of any kind of government or honorable and peaceful relations on earth. . . . In short, it pains him that anyone should receive even a mouthful of bread from God and eat it in peace."[19]

The Household Chart

The Small Catechism showed this same profound concern for the social good, at least in the editions overseen by and produced by Luther. His concern to produce for his people a household chart (labeled in other translations of the Small Catechism as the Table of Duties) of Bible passages that described the duties of people from the

various arenas of life revealed the centrality of vocation for his theology.[20] Luther called these "*holy* orders and walks of life," another
direct challenge to the medieval division of Christians into secular (those laypersons and priests in the world) and spiritual (those
monks and friars [laypersons and, predominantly, priests] as well as
all bishops, all of whom were under a vow). To call the pastorate,
governing officials, and all members of the household participants
in "holy orders" was to use traditional language in a new and radical
way, combining a critique of monastic spirituality with the creation
of a Christian life arising out of daily life. What Luther stressed
throughout his exposition of the fourth through eighth commandments in the Large Catechism he reduced to a single, devastating
phrase in the Small. Moreover, they were defined as "offices and
duties," indirectly, at least, turning spouses, parents and children,
employees and employers, and widows and youth into positions of
respect.

Additions to the original table in 1540, most likely not approved
by Luther, had the effect of obscuring his intent.[21] In its first incarnation in 1529 and in all subsequent printings until 1540, Luther's
collection of Bible passages "admonished" the three traditional
walks of life. Pastors guided the *ecclesia*, and so Luther provided
what might have been thought of as a job description for "bishops, pastors and preachers."[22] He took the list from 1 Tim. 3:2-4
and 6a, omitting vv. 5 and 6b, which simply contained explanations
of why particular characteristics were important. (The 1540 edition inserted a line from Titus 1:9.) Although Luther here did not
explain why he chose this text, it functioned to empower the congregational leaders to demand excellence. The title of this section
was addressed not simply to bishops but to pastors and preachers
and made it clear that Luther thought in terms of a univocal min-
isterial office. The first line drew an obvious distinction between
Lutheran clergy and late-medieval priests: "A bishop is to be . . .
the husband of one wife." Here scriptural authority trumped papal
tradition. But Luther did not stop there. The pastor was also to
be "temperate, virtuous, moderate, hospitable, an apt teacher, not
a drunkard, not vicious, not greedy for shameless profit [changed
in 1536 to coincide with the Luther Bible's broader construal: not
involved in dishonorable work], but gentle, not quarrelsome, not

stingy, one who manages his own household well, who has obedient and honest children."[23] Luther's concluding comments in the preface to the Small Catechism could be taken as a commentary on and an expansion of this text.

> Therefore, pastors and preachers, take note! Our office has now become a completely different one than it was under the pope. It has now become serious and salutary. Thus, it now involves much toil and work, many dangers and attacks [*Anfechtung*], and in addition little reward or gratitude in the world. But Christ himself will be our reward, so long as we labor faithfully.[24]

Luther's address to the ruling powers in government continued the same theme: instructing the powers that be what their "holy order" was. Similar to the passages regarding obedience to the clergy in the *ecclesia*, the comments directed to the *politeia* were expanded in 1542, following earlier additions to the Latin translation, in order to give lengthy instructions to the subjects. Originally, however, Luther simply quoted portions of Romans 13, namely vv. 1, 2, and 4b. His omission of vv. 3-4a ("For rulers are not a terror to good conduct, but to bad. Do you wish to have no fear of the authority? Then do what is good, and you will receive its approval; for it is God's servant for your good. But if you do what is wrong, you should be afraid") left out the very phrases addressed to subjects, an argument from silence that Luther meant to address those mentioned in the title to the section: "Concerning *Governing* Authorities."[25]

Luther's point was to define *and limit* governmental authority. First, he defined it as directly instituted by God, a major shift from certain medieval models that argued that all authority, spiritual and temporal, was given to the church (with the pope as its head) and then through the papacy was transferred to secular authorities. Luther was writing, after all, only two years after the last papal crowning of a Holy Roman Emperor, Charles V.[26] Against the Platonic argument, favored by Augustine and much of the medieval tradition, that rulers were simply robbers tolerated by God, Luther and other early Lutherans insisted that God had established government to maintain order and justice. Even this definition, however, implied a limit of sorts to governmental authority. It was as if Luther were saying to these officials, "You are not self-appointed but God-appointed. Therefore, you must follow God's will and not your own."

Luther did not simply argue for the God-given authority of government, but by including a portion of Rom. 13:4 he also defined its purpose: to execute punishment against evildoers. This simple definition, of course, implied for him that two things were simultaneously forbidden by this text: punishment of the innocent (including Luther, who had been [in his view] unjustly condemned as a heretic and made an outlaw of the empire) and exculpation of criminals. Thus, in his comments on the seventh commandment in the Large Catechism, he expressed dismay at the way the big shots, who were by far the biggest crooks, often got off scot-free. "Yes, we might well keep quiet here about individual petty thieves since we ought to be attacking the great, powerful archthieves with whom lords and princes consort and who daily plunder not just a city or two, but all of Germany."[27]

Having defined *oeconomia* and *politeia*, Luther turned to the sixteenth-century German household and included biblical admonitions for husbands and wives, parents and children, servants, maids, day-laborers (that is, workers), masters and mistresses, young people, widows, and finally all Christians. These passages, too, bear more careful scrutiny to tease out what Luther may have intended by choosing these particular texts.[28] Luther placed husbands first, not using the passage from Ephesians 5 but rather 1 Peter 3:7 and Col. 3:19. It is not too difficult to discern a pattern here: the prevention of violence in the household![29] Husbands must "live reasonably" with the "weaker vessels" lest their prayers be hindered (not a minor matter in Luther's worldview). Had Luther simply stopped with 1 Peter's admonitions, one might be unsure about his intent, but he added "And do not be harsh with them" from Colossians. The instruction to wives came from 1 Peter 3:1, 6, but not exclusively, since Luther added "as to the Lord" from Ephesians, thus limiting obedience to husbands by comparison to God. What Luther omitted from 1 Peter—complaints about women wearing too much jewelry—is telling, insofar as it avoided criticizing women's dress (Luther did not think such specific commands applied willy-nilly to his own culture). What he included—an exhortation to follow Sarah's example—is more understandable given his high regard for the matriarchs of Genesis.[30] Early versions of the Small Catechism used the 1522 translation and exhorted women not to be "afraid of any terrifying thing," whereas versions from 1536 used the corrected version: "and are not so fearful." A marginal gloss in the Luther Bible indicated the importance of this last line, where Luther stated, "Women are naturally fearful and are easily frightened. They should be firm and, if suffering occurs, they should not become so womanishly afraid."[31] Although such advice must be viewed through the lens of an early modern society where fathers ruled, nevertheless it would seem that Luther was intent here not to demean women but to empower them to be courageous.[32]

Moving to the relation between parents and children, Luther took the text from Eph. 6:4, addressed to fathers, and by changing the caption applied it to fathers and mothers. He would do the same when dealing with the heads of households. Just as he was quick to note that, unlike in Mosaic law, women were not chattel in his society, so here he assumed a kind of equality in the running of the early modern Lutheran household. Of course, as we have seen, the simple fact that he listed parental responsibilities matched his concerns in the preface to the Small Catechism and in the explanation of the fourth commandment in the Large Catechism, which included parents in a commandment that only listed children. Again, violence in the household seemed here to be his chief concern, not surprising for a man who, as a child, had been beaten for stealing nuts.

When turning his eye toward the larger household, Luther shifted the order, addressing the household workers before their employers, following for the first time the biblical sequence of Eph. 6:5-9. He again expanded the scope of the biblical text through the title, "For Male Servants [*Knechte*], Female Servants [*Mägde*], Day Laborers [*Tagelöhner*], Workers [*Arbeiter*], etc." Similarly, the Pauline comment regarding "lords" was reoriented by Luther to include "Hausherren und Hausfrauen," that is, masters and mistresses of the house. Luther's world knew of no bodily slavery, and thus he changed the texts to describe the working relations of indentured servants, apprentices, and the like. Luther was skeptical about the ability of human beings to improve social structures, and so he insisted on a more humane approach within existing social conventions rather than a literalistic application of first-century structures to his age.

Luther's advice to "Young People in General" went back to
1 Peter 5:5-6, "You young people, be subject to your elders and . . .
in this way show humility. For 'God opposes the proud but gives
grace to the humble' [Isaiah 57:15]. Therefore humble yourselves
under the mighty hand of God, so that he may exalt you in his
time." By omitting three words, "all of you," Luther could turn general comments in the epistle exclusively toward the young. Again, a
marginal gloss in the Luther Bible demonstrated how important this
passage was. There, explaining the phrase "hold fast to humility,"
Luther wrote, "So that humility connects each of you to each other
and is interlaced in each other, so that the Devil cannot divide you
with craft or might."[33] At the other end of the spectrum, Luther also
included advice from 1 Tim. 5:5-6 for what might be called "true
widows," that is, women bereft of all family support (v. 5: "a real
widow . . . left all alone"). Such a person's attitude, who "sets her
hope on God and remains in prayer," was the very response of faith
described for all Christians whom God moves from law to gospel to
prayer (that is, from "We are to . . . trust in God" to "I believe that
I cannot believe" to "Give us today our daily bread" and "Deliver us
from evil").

A final set of Bible verses, designated "For All in the Community" (or, less likely, "For All in Common"), revealed Luther's
profound commitment to God's two hands. For this world, among
human beings (*coram hominibus*), there was Rom. 13:9, "Love
your neighbor as yourself." For one's relation to God (*coram Deo*),
Luther returned to prayer and a loose paraphrase of 1 Tim. 2:1: "And
entreat God with prayers for all people." Luther reached the end of
his replacement for monastic rules and vows with a couplet, probably composed by him: "Let all their lessons learn with care, so that
the household well may fare." He had already employed the word
lessons (*Lektion*) in the title to the chart, referring to the Bible passages through which the various walks of life could be admonished,
"as through lessons (*Lektion*) particularly pertinent to their office
and duty."[34] Merit, earning heaven, reducing one's temporal punishment due to sin—all of these motivations for good behavior had
disappeared, and Luther set family relations back in the real world of
church, society, homes, families, and work—truly the holiest walks
of life, where each person learns, first, to define his or her "office

and duty," and second, to assist the household's well-being. Perhaps this couplet most clearly outlined Luther's ethic: Figure out where you stand and love your neighbor by obedience and care. Advice to preachers and governmental leaders and others in authority is not omitted but rests on the commandment "Love your neighbor as yourself."

The catechisms expressed the heart of Luther's ethical revolution. Common work is good and pleasing to God. Believers stand before God free by faith alone in the coming kingdom, free to serve the neighbor. The order in society, when it serves the neighbor, is good and comes from God. When that order is broken on any side, then all hell breaks loose.

Liturgy for the Christian Household

Had Luther just provided the Small Catechism with the Household Chart, one could argue that he had abandoned his principal commitment to justification by faith alone and left his people to fend for themselves in this world. Of course, the very order of the catechism, from commands to promise to prayer and sacraments, refutes that argument. One of the most trenchant proofs for Luther's commitment to daily life as the locus for the Christian life, however, came in the prayers provided for the household.

Elsewhere, I have argued that these prayers constituted one of the most positive contributions of Luther's own monastic experience to his Reformation theology. What Luther had expressed in 1526 in the preface to the *Deutsche Messe* (German Mass) as a vague hope for a place where committed believers could gather became in his Small Catechism a suggestion to reconstitute the ancient house church, where the father and mother of the household would instruct their children and workers, lead them in prayer, and give them a concrete place to practice their Christian life of faith.[35] In this section, we will examine the specific segments of the "house liturgy" and the way his specific liturgies for baptism and marriage explicated his intentions for the Christian household as a reflection of a worshiping community.

The first thing to note is the traditional character of these prayers.[36] The blessing and thanksgiving at meals not only bore traditional

names (*Benedictio mensae* and *Gratias*), but the prayers themselves
had also already been used in the *Booklet for the Laity and Children*
of 1525.[37] Similarly, the morning and evening prayers were taken
from the traditional breviary. The use of the Lord's Prayer, the sign
of the cross, the Apostles' Creed, and the Trinitarian invocation was
also standard. By instructing the heads of the house to teach (*lehren/
lernen*) them to the household members rather than to present
(*vorhalten*) them, Luther intended above all that these sections of the
catechisms be memorized.

In the Large Catechism, Luther reflected upon the difference
between memorized prayers and "true prayer." In the introduction
to the Lord's Prayer, he wrote:

> It is quite true that the kind of babbling and bellowing that used to
> pass for prayers in the church was not really prayer. Such external repe-
> tition, when properly used, may serve as an exercise for young children,
> pupils, and simple folk; while it may be useful in singing or reading, it
> is not actually prayer. To pray, as the Second Commandment teaches,
> is to call upon God in every need.[38]

Thus, Luther understood these set prayers in the Small Catechism
in a similar light: external repetition, an exercise for children, useful in singing and reading. However, they set the framework within
which prayer and worship occurred. This can be seen from the small
changes and additions Luther made to this material.

First, Luther calls this material not prayers but blessings. The
head of the house is to teach household members "to say morning
and evening blessings" (*sich segnen*), literally to bless themselves,
which in the usage of the sixteenth century meant to make the sign
of the cross. At meals persons bless the food before eating and give
thanks after. Morning and evening blessings begin with making the
sign of the cross and blessing oneself with God's name. These, too,
Luther saw as appropriate, simple, and playful methods of teaching children the proper use of God's name. Again in the Large Catechism, he wrote, this time on the second commandment:

> One must urge and encourage children again and again to honor God's
> name and keep it constantly upon their lips in all circumstances and

experiences, for the proper way to honor God's name is to look to it for all consolation and therefore to call upon it. . . . This is also a blessed and useful habit, and very effective against the devil, who is always around us, lying in wait to lure us into sin and shame, calamity and trouble. He hates to hear God's name. . . . For this purpose it also helps to form the habit of commending ourselves each day to God—our soul and body, spouse, children, servants, and all that we have—for his protection against every conceivable need. This is why the *Benedicite*, the *Gratias*, and other evening and morning blessings were also introduced and have been continued among us. From the same source comes the custom learned in childhood of making the sign of the cross when something dreadful or frightening is seen or heard, and saying, "Lord God, save me!" or, "Help, dear Lord Christ!" and the like. Likewise, if someone unexpectedly experiences good fortune—no matter how insignificant—he or she may say, "God be praised and thanked!" "God has bestowed this upon me!" etc. . . . See, with simple and playful methods like this we should bring up young people in the fear and honor of God so that the First and Second Commandments may become familiar and constantly practiced. . . . But this [noncoercive] kind of training takes root in their hearts so that they fear God more than they do rods and clubs. This I say plainly for the sake of the young people, so that it may sink into their minds, for when we preach to children we must talk baby talk.[39]

Thus, the traditional aura of these prayers was not unintended at all but central to Luther's understanding of the nature of the Christian life lived in households. One lives with simple blessings and thanksgivings that arise out of one's need and the playful use of God's name and talking baby talk. The life of the baptized is lived under the constant attack of the devil, who hates to hear God's name said at baptism and repeated each morning and evening, not simply as a formula ("in the name of the Father . . .") but as a true blessing: "God the Father, Son, and Holy Spirit watch over me. Amen." This blessing then was followed by a commendation of one's day to God and everything in it—that is, all of one's needs.

To the morning and evening prayers, Luther added two short comments that revealed his point of view. After the invocation, the sign of the cross, the simple morning prayer, the Apostles' Creed, and the Lord's Prayer, Luther included another part of the catechism, traditionally defined, suggesting that the person sing a hymn, "for example, one on the Ten Commandments." Here again Luther was criticizing the special lifestyle of those under a vow and sending everyone to work (singing) with the Ten Commandments on their lips. Luther had even written two hymned versions of the commandments.[40] Moreover, rather than inventing some special set of rules for Christians to follow, he stuck to the basics: giving guidance for living in this world (what later Lutherans came to call the first use of the law). Moreover, his other comment, "You are to go to your work joyfully," underscored his commitment to daily life as the locus of the Christian life. The same simple Christian who went to work joyfully now went to sleep "quickly and cheerfully," having asked for forgiveness for wrong done during the day and for protection during the night. This encouragement (joy and cheer) marked for Luther the life of the one who lives by faith alone, commending each day to God and living by God's gifts and mercy. Indeed, the only gloss Luther added to these prayers, which comes in the table blessing, explained the phrase from Ps. 145:16, "satisfy all living things with delight." Luther commented, "'Delight' means that all animals receive enough to eat to make them joyful and of good cheer, because worry and greed prevent such delight."[41] Living in this world by faith alone meant receiving everything from God as gifts and enjoying them.

The other part of the household "liturgy" came in the form of the services of marriage and baptism. In the first place, this material, like the preface, was explicitly written for pastor and preacher. Living in rural Saxony or Thuringia and without a true church order, these simple folk needed a great deal of help. In 1523, Luther revised the Latin Mass and in 1526 provided the *Deutsche Messe*, the German celebration of the Lord's Supper. Services of baptism and marriage were also published, but with the printings of the catechisms Luther had a chance to propagate his German revisions of these Latin services much more widely. Although no one can say for sure how often this material was read by literate laypersons, nevertheless Luther's prefatory material to these services further underscored the centrality of living the Christian life in this world.

In the preface to the *Marriage Booklet*,[42] Luther first distinguished the two realms of God's activities, admitting that each land had its own customs regarding marriage and that such things were up to the local authorities. He then argued in favor of the involvement of the church not so much to legalize the marriage but to bless it and pray for the couple. Not surprisingly, Luther compared marriage ceremonies to the big to-do at the consecration of monks and nuns, contrasting such human invention with marriage, which "has God's Word on its side and is not a human invention or institution."[43] A second reason to lift up the importance of marriage and create such a rite as Luther was proposing here, Luther argued, had to do with teaching young people "to take this estate seriously, to hold it in high esteem as a divine work and command, and not to ridicule it in such outrageous ways with laughing, jeering, and similar levity." Marriage, Luther went on to say, was no joke or child's play. He again returned to the theme of blessing, arguing that those who first brought the couple to church "wanted to receive God's blessing and the community's prayers." This was no comedy or pagan farce![44] His concluding words then depicted all the dangers and misery a Christian married couple would be facing. Here, as in all of the other sections discussed in this chapter (and indeed in the entire Small Catechism), the devil made an appearance.

> For all who desire prayer and blessing from the pastor or bishop indicate thereby—whether or not they say so expressly—to what danger and need they are exposing themselves and how much they need God's blessing and the community's prayers for the estate into which they are entering. For we experience every day how much unhappiness the devil causes in the married estate through adultery, unfaithfulness, discord, and all kinds of misery.[45]

The marriage service itself was quite traditional, with the obvious omission of the Eucharist. The marriage vows and declaration of marriage took place at the door of the church, indicating the secular nature of this walk of life. The couple then came before the altar where, in short succession, a series of Bible verses was read over them.[46] The first, Gen. 2:18, 21-24, described the institution of marriage in the Garden of Eden and implied the collaborative nature of marriage. The second, from Eph, 5:25-29, 22-24 (in that order), described what Luther called "the commandment concerning this estate," emphasizing with

Paul's unequal directives the husband's need to love and the wife's need to obey. The third told of "the cross," using Gen. 3:16-19 to describe the toil of the man and the pain in childbirth of the woman. Finally, passages from Gen. 1:27-28, 31 and Prov. 18:22 (paraphrase) were designed to show the couple "your comfort, that you know and believe how your estate is pleasing and blessed in God's eyes." This led to the prayer of thanksgiving and blessing, taken from the nuptial Mass of Luther's day. For all the male-oriented material here (down to Prov. 18:22: "Whoever gets a wife gets a good thing and will obtain delight from the Lord"), there was no explicit mention of the role of the fathers of the bride and groom. Luther's description of these Bible passages betrayed his theological orientation, placing marriage within God's institution, command, cross, and promise. Thus, the marriage service itself illustrated the Christian life described throughout these sections of the catechism.

The preface to the baptismal service showed many of the same concerns.[47] Luther fretted over the lack of solemnity—"to say nothing of out-and-out levity"—in this "holy and comforting" sacrament.[48] He argued that part of the problem stemmed from the fact that the service was in Latin, but he also wanted to make clear just how crucial baptism was. Here the church begged God to free an infant, "possessed by the devil and a child of sin and wrath," and make him or her a child of God. The language Luther employed here made it clear that baptism enacted the victory proclaimed in the second article of the Creed and prayed for in the third, sixth, and seventh petitions of the Lord's Prayer.

> Therefore, you have to realize that it is no joke at all to take action against the devil and not only to drive him away from the little child but also to hang around the child's neck such a mighty, lifelong enemy. Thus it is extremely necessary to stand by the poor child with all your heart and with a strong faith and to plead with great devotion that God, in accordance with these prayers, would not only free the child from the devil's power but also strengthen the child, so that the child might resist him valiantly in life and in death.[49]

Luther also saw himself forced to criticize the very ceremonies that he preserved, especially in the first edition of the baptismal liturgy. These human embellishments were neither necessary nor effective against the devil, who "sneers at even greater things than these!"[50] What Luther would later emphasize in every aspect of the catechism (this preface was written in 1523) was already present here. "See to it that you are present there in true faith, that you listen to God's Word, and that you pray along earnestly."[51] The Word (see the first petition of the Lord's Prayer), faith (see the second petition), and prayer (see the Amen) comprised the heart of the Christian's needy life. Saying "Amen" to prayers read clearly and slowly would result, Luther thought, in the participants being of one mind with the priest, "carrying before God the need of the little child with all earnestness, on the child's behalf setting themselves against the devil with all their strength, and demonstrating that they take seriously what is no joke to the devil."[52] Given the earnestness of opposing the devil, one of the hallmarks of Luther's life and theology,[53] it was not surprising that Luther warned against using drunken priests or good-for-nothing godparents, lest the ceremony become an opportunity for the devil's mockery. Luther concluded with a paean to the benefits of baptism as a sign of God's grace.

> God himself calls [baptism] a "new birth" [John 3:3, 5], through which we, being freed from the devil's tyranny and loosed from sin, death, and hell, become children of life, heirs of all God's possessions, God's own children, and brothers and sisters of Christ. Ah, dear Christians, let us not value or treat this unspeakable gift so half-heartedly. For baptism is our only comfort and the doorway to all of God's possessions and to the communion of all the saints.[54]

The service itself was indeed quite traditional. It emphasized driving out the devil so much (two exorcisms, the sign of the cross, and a renunciation of the devil) that dissension arose later in Lutheran circles over the use of exorcisms, causing this service to be eliminated from many versions of *The Book of Concord* and, thereafter, from printings of the Small Catechism.[55] The celebrant and the people also gathered to pray for God's grace for the child and spiritual rebirth. Luther's so-called "Flood Prayer" emphasized the faith of those who are saved and then prayed for "true faith in the Holy Spirit," the drowning of the old creature, and salvation. It also included, even before the first rebaptisms in Zurich in 1525, the story of Jesus blessing the children. The priest prayed the Lord's Prayer over the head of the child, and after the renunciation of the devil and a short confession of faith in the triune God derived from the Apostles' Creed, the baptism itself (assumed to be an immersion) took place. While the christening robe was being put on the child (the baptismal candle having been eliminated from the second edition), the priest gave a blessing, followed by the Peace.

A Final Comment

From time to time, Wittenberg's printers, other theologians, or perhaps even Martin Luther added other things to the Small Catechism. Thus, in 1529 the German Litany, purged of its invocations of the saints and providing a long list of believers' needs to God, was in some versions.[56] In 1536, 1537, and 1539, the German versions of the *Te Deum* and the *Magnificat* were included.[57] In 1543, *A Prayer against the Turks* was included. All were designed to aid the household or school in praying to and praising God. The same was true of additions made by printers outside Wittenberg. In 1542, for example, Valentine Bapst of Leipzig included Luther's (relatively new) "children's hymn," as he labeled it, "Erhalt uns Herr" ("Lord, keep us steadfast"), a fitting conclusion to any book about the catechisms and proof positive that, in order to understand Luther's precious gift to the church, we truly must remain children of the catechism and, with Luther, "do so gladly."[58]

> Lord, keep us steadfast in your Word;
>   Curb those who by great craft or sword
> Would wrest the kingdom from your Son
>   And set at naught all he has done.
> Lord Jesus Christ, your power make known,
>   For you are Lord of lords alone.
> Defend your lowly church that we
>   May sing your praise eternally.
> O Comforter of priceless worth,
>   Send peace, send unity on earth.
> Support us in our final strife,
>   And lead us out of death to life. Amen.

NOTES

Preface

1. *Concordia. Pia et unanimi consensus repetita Confessio Fidei & doctrinae Electorum, Principum, et Ordinum Imperii, Atque eorundem Tehologorum, qui Augustanam Confessionem amplectuntur* (Leipzig: Georg Defner, 1584), 349–77, passim.

1. Martin Luther's Contributions to Christian Catechesis

1. Portions of this chapter were first published in "Forming the Faith through Catechisms: Moving to Luther and Today," in *Formation in the Faith: Catechesis for Tomorrow*, Concordia Seminary Publications, Symposium Papers, no. 7 (St. Louis, Mo.: Concordia Seminary, 1997), 25–48 (used by permission).

2. Cited in G. H. Gerberding, *The Lutheran Catechist* (Philadelphia: Lutheran Publication Society, 1910), 90.

3. See Henry George Liddell and Robert Scott, eds., *A Greek-English Lexicon . . . with a Supplement 1968* (Oxford: Clarendon, 1968), s.v. "κατηχέω." See also Gerhard Kittel, ed., *Theological Dictionary of the New Testament*, trans. Geoffrey W. Bromiley, 10 vols. (Grand Rapids, Mich.: Eerdmans, 1964–76), 3:638–40.

4. Charlton T. Lewis and Charles Short, eds., *A Latin Dictionary* (Oxford: Clarendon, 1879), s.v. "catechismus," citing Augustine, *De fide et operibus*, 13.

5. Denis Janz, *Three Reformation Catechisms: Catholic, Anabaptist, Lutheran* (New York: Mellen, 1982), 7–12.

6. Ibid., 47.

7. Ibid., 82.

8. LW 43:3–45.

9. Note, however, that in the 1526 preface to the *Deutsche Messe* (German Mass), he refers to the *Betbüchlein* in his description of catechisms. See LW 53:64–66.

10. LW 43:13–14, with slight changes.

11. SC, Holy Baptism, 20 and 29, in BC, 360 and 362.

12. LW 53:64–65.

13. LW 53:66.

14. See, for example, the catechism of Ambrose Moibanus of 1533 in Johann Michael Reu, ed., *Quellen zur Geschichte des Katechismus-Unterrichts*, vol. 2, pt. 2 (Gütersloh: Bertelsmann, 1911), 710–54. Moibanus began with the distinction of the twofold righteousness: before God and in this world.

15. Underneath these questions and this approach lurked a very different hermeneutic for the Scripture, one codified in the so-called *Quadriga*, where *allegoria* defined faith (*credenda*: what must be believed) and *tropologia* defined love (*agenda*: what must be done). Most Luther scholars, to say nothing of Lutheran pastors, have often missed this hermeneutical key to the catechisms, an oversight that leads necessarily to legalism at all levels in the church.

16. See Timothy J. Wengert, "Wittenberg's Earliest Catechism," *Lutheran Quarterly* 7 (1993): 248–49.

17. For an English translation, see *A Booklet for Laity and Children*, in *Sources and Contexts of the Book of Concord*, ed. Robert Kolb and James Nestingen (Minneapolis: Fortress Press, 2001), 1–12.

18. See Gordon Lathrop and Timothy J. Wengert, *The Marks of the Church in a Pluralistic Age* (Minneapolis: Fortress Press, 2004).

19. Christian educators thus need to be wary of another prevalent practice in today's church: demanding faith statements from our children. Apart from the fact that this denigrates the Creed and the testimony of the church and can leave the impression that our faith is up to us and that ultimately it does not matter what you believe as long as

you are sincere, this demand actually continues to reverse Luther's order and return our use of the catechism to the late Middle Ages. If one wants personal faith statements, one must confess to the children in the face of their deepest questions and needs, and not simply demand of them another work. One could teach them Luther's explanation so well that they could paraphrase it for themselves, to make sure they understand what they are saying, but do not confuse that with true faith, which is in the hands of the Holy Spirit, who works through our broken words to bring young and old to faith.

20. SC, preface, 1–3, in BC, 347–48.

21. Timothy J. Wengert, "'Fear and Love' in the Ten Commandments," *Concordia Journal* 21 (1995): 14–27; and Wengert, *Law and Gospel: Philip Melanchthon's Debate with John Agricola of Eisleben over "Poenitentia"* (Grand Rapids, Mich.: Baker, 1997).

22. LW 40:269–320. Melanchthon himself called this booklet a catechism. The title, incorrectly translated in LW 40, has been correctly given above.

23. Translated in Kolb and Nestingen, *Sources and Contexts of the Book of Concord*, 13–30.

24. Kolb and Nestingen, *Sources and Contexts of the Book of Concord*, 15–17, 25.

25. LC, Ten Commandments, 77, in BC, 396.

26. See BC, 351, 354, 356, 359, 362. Only for the household prayers (BC, 363, 364) did Luther use the word *teach* (*lehren*), that is, learn by heart.

27. LW 51:137. See also p. 136, where, in his instruction to parents on the previous day, he went into more detail: "You have been appointed their bishop and pastor; take heed that you do not neglect your office over them."

28. See both the LC, Ten Commandments, 170–78, and the SC, preface, 19–20, in BC, 409–10 and 350, respectively.

29. LC, Ten Commandments, 145–46, in BC, 406.

30. SC, Household Chart, 1, in BC, 365.

31. BC, 367–75.

32. SC, Baptism, 12, in BC, 360.

33. LW 50:302.

34. LC, preface, 5, 7, 8, in BC, 380.

2. Diagnosing with the Ten Commandments

1. The most helpful study is Albrecht Peters, *Kommentar zu Luthers Katechismen*, vol. 1, *Die Zehn Gebote*, ed. Gottfried Seebass (Göttingen: Vandenhoeck & Ruprecht, 1990).

2. LC, Ten Commandments, 326, in BC, 430.

3. LC, Ten Commandments, 2, in BC, 386.

4. For the phrase "fear and love," see Timothy J. Wengert, "'Fear and Love' in the Ten Commandments," *Concordia Journal* 21 (1995): 14–27.

5. See his summary of the dispute in "Sunday, Luth. View of," in *The Lutheran Cyclopedia*, ed. Henry Eyster Jacobs and John A. W. Haas (New York: Scribner's, 1899), 466–67.

6. A third example, the prohibition of graven images, can only be an argument from silence. Nevertheless, one of the reasons Luther did not renumber the Ten Commandments (as did Ulrich Zwingli and other Reformed theologians) is because he understood the prohibition of graven images as simply one way Moses applied the first commandment to his own people.

7. LC, Ten Commandments, 82, in BC, 397, and n. 64, which refers to *Against the Heavenly Prophets* (1525), in LW 40:97–98.

8. LC, Ten Commandments, 87–88, 91, in BC, 398–99.

9. LC, Ten Commandments, 83, in BC, 397.

10. LC, Ten Commandments, 84, in BC, 397.

11. LW 44:54–80, esp. 72.

12. LC, Ten Commandments, 90, 96, in BC, 398–99.

13. LC, Ten Commandments, 293, in BC, 425.

14. LC, Ten Commandments, 294–95, in BC, 425.

15. SC, A Marriage Booklet, 1, in BC, 367.

16. Which looked at how one violated a commandment in "thought, word, and deed" and at the work of the "Devil, the world, and our sinful flesh."

17. S.Theol. II/II, q. 184, a. 1–8 and q. 186, a. 1–10 (see also S. Theol. I/II, q. 108, a. 4).

18. LW 41:61, for example.

19. He made some of the same points the following year in his *Judgment of Martin Luther on Monastic Vows* (e.g., LW 44:256–61).

20. It is also remarkable how many pastors and theologians have remained ignorant of this idol over the years.

21. One complaint about the author's translation of the Small Catechism was that it included magic—something that modern folk have grown out of. Of course, its inclusion arose not only from a desire to reflect more carefully Luther's actual text but also from personal pastoral experience.

22. More on these two positive commandments in the next section.

23. Luther's clever (but inaccurate) rendering of the low German dialect *Stohl*, which actually means "interest" and not "stool."

24. Heiko Oberman, "Immo: Luthers reformatorische Entdeckungen im Spiegel der Rhetorik," in *Lutheriana: Zum 500. Geburtstag Martin Luthers von den Mitarbeitern der Weimarer Ausgabe*, ed. Gerhard Hammer and Karl-Heinz zur Mühlen (Cologne: Böhlau, 1984), 17–38.

25. See chapter 4, on the Lord's Prayer.

26. Melanchthon, of course, wrote in the introduction to his *Loci communes theologici*, "To know Christ is to know his benefits."

27. LC, Ten Commandments, 25–26, in BC, 389.

28. This also resulted in his rejection of the Hebrew ordering of the commandments, where the second commandment was the prohibition of graven images. Not only did he find no reason for theologians, acting on their own, to change the good order of the Western church's tradition, but he also realized that this command was simply a specific form of the first commandment meant particularly for the Hebrew people. His oppo-

nents in the Lord's Supper controversy, such as Ulrich Zwingli, who denied Christ's presence in material bread and wine, actually twisted this "new" commandment to serve their own spiritualizing of Christianity—a trend that continues among some American denominations to this day.

29. LC, Ten Commandments, 284, in BC, 424.

30. See especially Luther's comments in LC, Ten Commandments, 167–78, in BC, 409–10.

31. LC, Ten Commandments, 246–47, in BC, 419.

32. LC, Lord's Prayer, 84, in BC, 452.

33. The same can be said of the other Reformers. See David C. Steinmetz, "Calvin and Melanchthon on Romans 13:1-7," *Ex Auditu: An Annual of the Frederick Neumann Symposium on Theological Interpretation of Scripture* 2 (1986): 67–77.

34. LC, Ten Commandments, 116, in BC, 402.

35. SC, preface, 19–20, in BC, 350. He spent most of the 1520 *Treatise on Good Works* (LW 44:80–100) describing the responsibility of the authorities.

36. LC, Ten Commandments, 170, in BC, 409–10.

37. LC, Ten Commandments, 172, in BC, 410. He went on to say (par. 174): "Therefore let all people know that it is their chief duty—at the risk of losing divine grace—first to bring up their children in the fear and knowledge of God, and, then, if they are so gifted, also to have them engage in formal study and learn so that they may be of service wherever they are needed."

38. The woodcuts for these two commandments do demonstrate the breaking of these commandments: the Israelites and the Golden Calf, and David and Bathsheba.

39. LC, Ten Commandments, 202, in BC, 414.

40. On occasion, such as in his sermon on the wedding at Cana, he railed against certain sourpusses who wanted to forbid people having fun at weddings. If it was not a sin to sit or to walk, then it was not a sin to dance. At this point in the text, a pious editor

noted that, in Luther's day, dances were not as lascivious as they are "now." See *Dr. Martin Luthers sämtliche Schriften*, 2nd ed., ed. Georg Walch, 23 vols. (St. Louis, Mo.: Concordia, 1892–1910), 11:467–68. Clearly, the editor had not seen Bruegel's late-sixteenth-century paintings of peasants dancing at a wedding.

41. See especially his Invocavit Sermons of March 1522. See LW 51:79–80.

42. See Luther's attack on Andreas Karlstadt in *Against the Heavenly Prophets* (1525) (LW 40:84–90).

43. LC, Ten Commandments, 22, in BC, 388–89.

44. LC, Ten Commandments, 54, in BC, 393.

45. See chapter 8 of this book.

46. See SC, A Marriage Booklet, 10–15, in BC, 369–71; and SC, Household Chart, 6–7, in BC, 366.

47. LW 28:1–56.

48. LC, Ten Commandments, 205–8, in BC, 414.

49. LC, Ten Commandments, 219, in BC, 415.

50. LC, Ten Commandments, 212, in BC, 415.

51. LC Ten Commandments, 216, in BC, 415.

52. See Timothy J. Wengert, "Martin Luther on Spousal Abuse," *Lutheran Quarterly* 21 (2007): 337–39; and Hermann Kunst, *Evangelischer Glaube und politische Verantwortung: Martin Luther als politischer Berater* (Stuttgart: Evangelisches Verlagswerk, 1976), 86.

53. See James Estes, "Luther's Attitude toward the Legal Traditions of His Time," *Luther-Jahrbuch* (forthcoming).

54. See Timothy J. Wengert, *Law and Gospel: Philip Melanchthon's Debate with John Agricola of Eisleben over "Poenitentia"* (Grand Rapids, Mich.: Baker, 1997), 148–53.

55. LC, Ten Commandments, 316, in BC, 428. See also LC, Creed, 1–3, in BC, 431, and LC, Lord's Prayer, 2, in BC, 440–41.

3. Luther's Down-to-Earth Confession of Faith

1. LC, Creed, 64–65, in BC, 439–40.

2. See Charles Arand, *That I May Be His Own: An Overview of Luther's Catechisms* (St. Louis, Mo.: Concordia, 2000), 136–41; and Albrecht Peters, *Kommentar zu Luthers Katechismen*, vol. 2, *Der Glaube*, ed. Gottfried Seebaß (Göttingen: Vandenhoeck & Ruprecht, 1991), 36–55.

3. The single book-length treatment of the subject rendered into English is by Regin Prenter, *Spiritus Creator*, trans. John M. Jensen (Philadelphia: Muhlenberg, 1953).

4. WA 28:50–53.

5. Oswald Bayer, *Theology the Lutheran Way*, trans. Jeffrey Silcock and Mark Mattes (Grand Rapids, Mich.: Eerdmans, 2007).

6. It is an irony of the English language that just as the use of the adverbial "-ly" is fading, our children cannot quite, like, use, like, "like" quite enough. Like, you know, like, what I mean?

7. See Rolf Schäfer, "Melanchthon's Interpretation of Romans 5:15: His Departure from the Augustinian Concept of Grace Compared to Luther's," in *Philip Melanchthon (1497–1560) and the Commentary*, ed. Timothy J. Wengert and M. Patrick Graham (Sheffield: Sheffield Academic Press, 1997), 79–104.

8. LC, Creed, 16, in BC, 432.

9. One of the letters concerning this affair in Luther's correspondence was written by him to Baumgartner's wife, Sibylle (nee Tichtel von Tutzing), and dated July 8, 1544 (WA Br 10:604–6, no. 4009).

10. Luther, preaching on December 10, is quoting Matt. 21:5, the gospel for the first Sunday in Advent, which in 1528 had fallen on November 29. For Luther's sermons that day, see WA 27:433–43, esp. 435–36.

11. The text reads "Deus," probably a mistaken reading or writing for "Dominus."

12. WA 30^1:89–90. Cf. LW 51:164–65.

13. LC, Creed, 27, in BC, 434.

14. LC, Creed, 30, in BC, 434.

15. LC, Creed, 31, in BC, 434.

16. Thus, "Deliver us from evil" is "*Erlöse uns von den Bösen.*"

17. With the word *rules*, Luther explained the ascension to God's right hand over against literalists like Zwingli, who, in order to protect his worldview and to prevent Christ from coming to us in bread and wine, had contended that God's right hand was a place. As Luther would argue against him that very year (1529) at the colloquy held in Marburg, God's right hand is a picture in Scripture for God's reign.

18. It is also not clear how much scholarly literature about Christianity would remain either.

19. See Gerhard Forde, *The Captivation of the Will: Luther vs. Erasmus on Freedom and Bondage* (Grand Rapids: Eerdmans, 2005); Robert Kolb, *Bound Choice, Election, and Wittenberg Theological Method: From Martin Luther to the Formula of Concord* (Grand Rapids: Eerdmans, 2005); Timothy J. Wengert, *Human Freedom, Christian Righteousness: Philip Melanchthon's Exegetical Dispute with Erasmus of Rotterdam* (New York: Oxford University Press, 1998).

20. Smalcald Articles, III.8.3–9, in BC, 322–23.

21. Gerhard Forde, *Where God Meets Man: Luther's Down-to-Earth Approach to the Gospel* (Minneapolis: Augsburg, 1972).

22. LC, Creed, 38, in BC, 436 (emphasis added).

23. For a taste of the older debate, see WA 30¹:367, 6 with n. 4.

24. *Veni Creator Spiritus*, which Luther translated as "Kom Gott schepfer heyliger geyst," where this phrase reads as follows (WA 35:446): "Du bist mit gaben siebenfallt der finger an Gotts rechter hand. Des vaters wort gibstu gar bald mit zungen ynn aller land." Luther's translation is more faithful to the Latin and well read in the older English translation of Edward Caswall: "The sev'nfold gifts of grace are Thine, O Finger of the Hand Divine; True Promise of the Father Thou [Latin: Tu rite promissum Patris], Who dost the tongue with speech endow" (*Lutheran Hymnal*, no. 233 [St. Louis, Mo.: Concordia, 1941]).

25. Among Lutherans, this stemmed from two factors. First, in the 1550s, as they strove to counteract the theology of Andreas Osiander, Lutherans insisted that justification is, narrowly conceived, the forgiveness of sins and that sanctification is, properly understood, the fruits of justification in the life of the believer. Second, it later was the medieval insistence on separating the states of sin and grace that influenced how contrition, conversion, justification, and sanctification were understood. As these became more fixed points in an order of salvation (*ordo salutis*), justification became more theory than experience.

26. See Gerhard Forde and James Nestingen, *Free to Be*, 2nd ed. (Minneapolis: Augsburg Fortress, 1993).

27. See Gordon Lathrop and Timothy J. Wengert, *Christian Assembly: The Marks of the Church in a Pluralistic Age* (Minneapolis: Fortress Press, 2004), 27.

28. Luther knew nothing of the modern proposal that "sanctorum" could be taken as a neuter and thus mean "communion of holy things" rather than "communion of holy people [saints]," an interesting proposal, since it comes in the Apostles' Creed exactly where the Nicene Creed mentions baptism and thus meant participation in holy things, that is, in the sacraments.

29. LC, Creed, 51–55, in BC, 437–38.

30. The fact that both here and above Luther used the term *Christenheit* is simply a product of his paraphrastic approach to these explanations, where in common parlance *Christenheit* was the favored translation for *ecclesia*.

31. See Timothy J. Wengert, ed., *Centripetal Worship: The Evangelical Heart of Lutheran Worship* (Minneapolis: Augsburg Fortress, 2007), 9–31.

4. The Lord's Prayer and Believers' Needs

1. Parts of this chapter were first published as "Luther on Prayer in the Large Catechism," *Lutheran Quarterly* 18 (2004): 249–74, used by permission.

2. LC, Lord's Prayer, 32, in BC, 444. For a more traditional understanding of the petition from Luther, see, for example, *Luthers Werke: Kritische Gesamtausgabe: Tischreden*, 6

vols. (Weimar: H. Böhlau, 1912–21), 2:119 (no. 1510, dated May 1–7, 1532 [henceforth WA TR 2:119]), where he contrasted God's will to human desire.

3. For Luther's other treatments of prayer, see especially *A Simple Way to Pray* (1535) (WA 38:351–75; LW 43:187–211), and *A Personal Prayer Book* (1522) (WA 10²:339–406; LW 43:3–45).

4. Bibliography for this topic is endless. Some of the more recent resources include Rudolf Damerau, *Luthers Gebetslehre*, 2 vols. (Marburg: Im Selbstverlag, 1975–77); Martin E. Lehmann, *Luther and Prayer* (Milwaukee: Northwestern, 1985); Gunnar Wertelius, *Oratio continua: Das Verhältnis zwischen Glaube und Gebet in der Theologie Martin Luthers* (Lund: Gleerup, 1970); D. F. Wright, "What Kind of "Bread"? The Fourth Petition of the Lord's Prayer from the Fathers to the Reformers," in *Oratio: das Gebet in patristischer und reformatorischer Sicht*, ed. Emidio Campi et al. (Göttingen: Vandenhoeck & Ruprecht, 1999), 151–61; Martin Brecht, "'Und willst das Beten von uns han': Zum Gebet und seiner Praxis bei Martin Luther," in *Frühe Reformation in Deutschland als Umbruch*, ed. Bernd Moeller (Gütersloh: Gütersloher Verlagshaus, 1998), 268–88; Mark Sander, "Cyprian's 'On the Lord's Prayer': A Patristic Signpost in Luther's Penitential Theology," *Logia* 7 (Epiphany 1998): 13–18; George Tavard, "Luther's Teaching on Prayer," *Lutheran Theological Seminary Bulletin* 67 (Winter 1987): 3–22; Friedemann Hebart, "The Role of the Lord's Prayer in Luther's Theology of Prayer," *Lutheran Theological Journal* 18 (May 1984): 6–17; David P. Scaer, "Luther on Prayer," *Concordia Theological Quarterly* 47 (1983): 305–15; Vilmos Vajta, "Luther als Beter," in *Leben und Werk Martin Luthers von 1526 bis 1546*, ed. Helmar Junghans (Göttingen: Vandenhoeck & Ruprecht, 1983), 279–95; Gerhard Ebeling, "Beten als Wahrnehmen der Wirklichkeit des Menschen, wie Luther es lehrte und lebte," *Luther-Jahrbuch* 66 (1999): 151–66; Albrecht Peters, *Kommentar zu Luthers Katechismen*, vol. 3, *Das Vaterunser*, ed. Gottfried Seebaß (Göttingen: Vandenhoeck & Ruprecht, 1992).

5. *A Simple Way to Pray for a Good Friend* (1535).

6. *Melanchthons Briefwechsel: Kritische und kommentierte Gesamtausgabe: Regesten*, ed. Heinz Scheible, 10+ vols. (Stuttgart-Bad Cannstatt: Frommann-Holzboog, 1977–), no. 949 (henceforth MBW 949). The text is in *Corpus Reformatorum: Philippi Melanchthonis opera quae supersunt omnia*, ed. Karl Bretschneider and Heinrich Bindseil, 28 vols. (Halle: A. Schwetschke & Sons, 1834–60), 2:159 (henceforth CR 2:159), dated June 30, 1530. See also Julius Köstlin and Gustav Kawerau, *Martin Luthe: Sein Leben und Schriften*, 5th ed. (Berlin: Duncker, 1903), 2:219, translated in H. G. Haile, *Luther: An Experiment in Biography* (Garden City, N.Y.: Doubleday, 1980), 278; also quoted in Ebeling, "Beten," 154.

7. For a dramatic reconstruction of these events, see Haile, *Luther*, 277–80. See also Martin Brecht, *Martin Luther: The Preservation of the Church, 1532–1546*, trans. James Schaaf (Minneapolis: Fortress Press, 1993), 209–10.

8. WA TR 5:129 (no. 5407), dated Spring 1542: "Wir habe drey todt wiederumb lebendig gebethen, mich, meyne Kethe vnd Philippum, welchem zu Weinbeer schon die augen gebrochen waren." See also the much more detailed description by the physician Matthäus Ratzeberger in CR 28:67–70 (see also Matthäus Ratzeberger, *Die handschriftliche Geschichte Ratzeberger's über Luther und seine Zeit / mit literarischen, kritischen und historischen Anmerkungen*, ed. Christian Gotthold Neudecker [Jena: Mauke, 1850]). "Denn die Augen waren ihm gleich gebrochen, aller Verstand gewichen, die Sprache entfallen, das Gehör vergangen, und das Angesicht schlaff und eingefallen, und, wie Lutherus sagte, 'facies erat Hippocratica' [in need of a physician?]. Dazu kannte er niemand, aß und trank nichts."

9. CR 28:69–70 (the italicized portion in Latin). See also Haile, *Luther*, 278–79. Luther had already begun to pray before leaving Wittenberg. See WA TR 5:95 (no. 5364), dated June 1540.

10. CR 28:69–70 (the italicized word is Greek: *organon*, a sense organ).

11. A plot of land recently purchased by Luther from his brother-in-law, Hans von Bora.

12. *Luthers Werke: Kritische Gesamtausgabe: Briefwechsel,* 18 vols. (Weimar: H. Böhlau, 1930–85), 9:168 [henceforth WA Br 9:168], dated July 2, 1540. Justus Jonas's account to Johannes Bugenhagen (CR 3:1060, dated July 7, 1540, from Eisenach, where they had brought their still weakened colleague) also mentioned answered prayer of the church: "Quod attinet ad D. Philip. Melan. certe hic e media morte, in qua profecto Wimariae luctabatur, oratione Ecclesiae et piorum revocatus est ad vitam." He also noted the encouragement of Luther, himself, and the other brothers (including Paul Eber, later pastor in Wittenberg, and Melanchthon's son Philip Jr.). See Gustav Kawerau, ed., *Der Briefwechsel des Justus Jonas,* 2 vols. (Halle: O. Hendel, 1884–85; repr., Hildesheim: G. Olms, 1964), 1:398, no. 504. Melanchthon, in a letter to Bugenhagen written the next day in a still shaky hand, underscored this belief (MBW 2459 [CR 3:1061]): "Si vixero, vere praedicare potero, me divinitus ex ipsa morte in vitam revocatum esse. Id omnes, qui una fuerunt, testantur. Utinam igitur possim deo gratias agere et ad laudem ipsius vivere."

13. WA TR 2:628 (no. 2742a). The context is clear from WA TR 2:629 (no. 2742b), where before saying this, Luther described his experience ministering to a woman dying in childbirth. "Si enim semper nostris votis respondere deberet, so were er vnser gefangener, vnd hette mir dies weib auch mussen wieder geben, aber er wuste es besser."

14. WA TR 6:162 (no. 6751, only in Aurifaber's collection).

15. See also WA TR 5:437–38 (no. 6013). Speaking about the Lord's Prayer, Luther noted that outside of temptation [*Anfechtung*] there is no true prayer, only blabbering: "Dorinne [in the Lord's Prayer] begrieffen omnem necessitatem in omnibus tentationibus, nam extra tentationem non potest vere orari. Ideo Dauid dicit [Ps. 50:15]: Invoca me in die tribulationis etc. Alioqui ista βαττολογια friget." This pas-

sage from Psalm 50 also figured in his exposition in the LC.

16. For details of the illness and her later move to Lichtenburg, see Brecht, *Martin Luther,* 239.

17. According to the Grimms' *Deutsches Wörterbuch,* 15:856, this refers to the custom of a widow, who, when she cannot pay her deceased husband's debts, places the house keys either at the foot of the grave or on the bier, to show that she is no longer beholden to him and thus free of her debts. Thus, it means something akin to "washing one's hands of the whole affair." However, another possible source might be 2 Baruch 9:18, where the text describes the priests' reaction to the destruction of Solomon's Temple: "Moreover, you priests, take you the keys of the sanctuary, and cast them into the height of heaven, and give them to the Lord and say: 'Guard Your house Yourself, For lo! We are found false stewards.'" Luther could scarcely have known this particular book of the pseudepigrapha, but the parallel is striking. See Rivka Nir, *The Destruction of Jerusalem and the Idea of Redemption in the "Syriac Apocalypse of Baruch"* (Atlanta: Society of Biblical Literature, 2003), 83–100, where references in the Talmud are also discussed. I am grateful to Matthias Henze of Rice University for this reference.

18. German: *Zinsgutter* (literally, the tax owed a lord on a piece of property).

19. WA TR 5:438 (no. 6015). For Luther's prayers in English, see Andrew Kosten, ed., *Devotions and Prayers: Martin Luther* (Grand Rapids, Mich.: Baker, 1956).

20. WA TR 5:438–39 (no. 6015). Luther uttered a similarly direct prayer on June 9, 1532, in the face of a drought (WA TR 2:157f. [no. 1636]), where he again cited Ps. 145:18f. He also said that if God was not going to give rain, he would give something even better: peace and tranquility. He also warned God that if the prayer was not answered, ungodly people would say that God and God's Son were liars, concluding with these words: "Ich weis, das wir von hertzen zu dir schreien vnd bitten mit senlichem seufftzen; warum wiltu vns den nicht

erhörn?" See also WA TR 4:99 (no. 4046), dated October 10, 1538, where Luther encouraged people to pray for daily bread against an outbreak of mice. The inflation of grain prices came also because of greedy farmers and merchants: "Let us pray for the godly paupers, who have to bear this the most, so that they may have daily bread and God's blessing. Amen."

21. WA TR 3:447 (no. 3605).

22. See CR 24:830, where Melanchthon attributed the saying to Pseudo-Dionysius.

23. WA TR 3:447–48 (no. 3605). He concluded on a personal note that at home he did not pray as well as in the local church, where prayers are "from the heart and penetrating." For another discussion of the contrast of true prayer and works that pass for prayer, see WA TR 5:228 (no. 5545), dated late February/early March 1543.

24. See his itinerary in MBW 10:483–85.

25. WA TR 4:450 (no. 4722), on January 6, 1539 (in worship service for the Feast of the Epiphany), praying for the conversion of Charles V; WA TR 4:464–65 (no. 4744), March 2, 1539 (in Sunday service), prayer for peace; WA TR 4:293 (no. 4396; LW 54:335–36), March 15, 1539 (at Saturday Vespers?), a prayer for peace against the papal raging, and so forth; WA TR 4:466 (no. 4758), May 11, 1539 (in worship service), a prayer of thanks for God's continued protection and for peace (and the miraculous death of Duke George of Saxony).

26. See WA TR 4:308f. (no. 4430, dated March 23, 1539), upon the receipt of a letter from Melanchthon (MBW 2160 [WA Br 8:392–94], written from Frankfurt/Main on March 14, 1539; Luther's answer, MBW 2168 [WA Br 8:397–98], written on March 26, 1539), Luther prayed for peace. See also his comments on December 25, 1538, in WA TR 4:196–97 (no. 4200) and his public prayers against the "bloodthirsty papists" and encouragement to pray: "Ergo vos pii orate, poenitentiam agite, non tantum audite verbum sed secundum illud etiam vivite. Das wir doch vnserm Hergott eine trutzischk [from the Latin, *trochiscus*: a sweet perfume

or breath freshener] oder weirach anlegten." Regarding prayers against the Turks, in WA TR 5:152 (no. 5437, dated Summer/Fall 1542), he recalled the legend of Jacob of Nisibis (see also Gennadius, *De viris illustribus*, 1), who was said to have prayed against Persian invaders in the fourth century. "So God can take away the heart of the Turk, if we pray constantly and in faith."

27. WA TR 2:659 (no. 2786), dated Fall 1532.

28. WA TR 4:374–75 (no. 4555), dated May 1, 1539. "Oratio piorum fuit arma contra ipsos, ut illorum fraudes sint revelatae."

29. For this section, see Peters, *Das Vaterunser*, 13–41, especially the literature cited on pp. 39–41.

30. WA 30^1:95–98 (sermon on December 14, 1528) and CR 26:13–15, 54–56. The Latin version of 1527, written by Melanchthon, had a separate section on the prayer, including a very brief exposition of the petitions of the Lord's Prayer. The 1528 German version, worked on by Luther, Melanchthon, Bugenhagen, and even John Agricola, dropped material on the Lord's Prayer and subsumed a general discussion of prayer under the second commandment, reducing Melanchthon's four admonitions (command, promise, specific needs, persistence) to three by subsuming the fourth under the third. This corrects Peters, *Das Vaterunser*, 15–16.

31. LC, Lord's Supper, 39–84, in BC, 470–75.

32. Werner Krusche, "Zur Struktur des Kleinen Katechismus," *Lutherische Monatshefte* 4 (1965): 316–31.

33. See *A Simple Way to Pray*, LW 43:193–95 (WA 38:358–59) and WA TR 5:209–10 (no. 5517), dated Winter 1542–43, where Luther spoke of praying the Ten Commandments, the Lord's Prayer, and one or two passages from the Bible at night: "Thus, I fall asleep."

34. LC, Lord's Prayer, 1–2, in BC, 440–41.

35. LC, Ten Commandments, 316, in BC, 428.

36. LC, Lord's Prayer, 2, in BC, 440.

37. See Peters, *Das Vaterunser*, 28–29

38. LC, Lord's Prayer, 2, in BC, 440.

39. LC, Lord's Prayer, 2, in BC, 440–41.

40. WA 36:183, 20–21, cited in Fred Meuser, *Luther the Preacher* (Minneapolis: Augsburg, 1983), 50n26. The original, a comment from a sermon on the gospel for Pentecost Monday 1532, reads: "Quando facio praedicationem, accipio Antithesin, ut hic Christus facit." Regarding the commandments, this was hardly Luther's invention, since it was related to sins of omission and commission.

41. In the SC, the two exceptions are the first commandment, spoken of only in its positive side (demanding faith in God), and the sixth commandment, where Luther (perhaps for cultural reasons) refused to list sexual sins.

42. SC, Ten Commandments, 4, in BC, 352. See also LC, Ten Commandments, 324–29, in BC, 429–30.

43. In German, scholars now assume that there was always a difference between *bitten* and *beten*. However, each petition of the Lord's Prayer is called not *Gebete* but, as in English, *Bitte*.

44. LC, Ten Commandments, 70–77, in BC, 395–96.

45. LC, Ten Commandments, 70, in BC, 395.

46. Luther was thinking here of the daily prayers in the SC, Blessings, 1–11, in BC, 363–64.

47. LC, Ten Commandments, 74, in BC, 396.

48. LC, Lord's Prayer, 4–6, in BC, 441.

49. Luther also thought in antitheses when it came to the petitions of the Lord's Prayer. Thus, his comments in *A Simple Way to Pray* included both prayers and curses. Similarly, he even could imagine that praying to hallow God's name implied a curse on such teachers as Erasmus. See WA TR 3:147 (no. 3128), March 13–28, 1533: "Omnes, qui orant, maledicunt; velut cum dico: Sanctificetur nomen tuum, maledico Erasmo et omnibus contra verbum sentientibus."

50. Similarly, see Luther's comments in LC, Lord's Supper, 45–54, in BC, 471–72,

where he clobbered the "cold and indifferent" with the law.

51. LC, Lord's Supper, 42, in BC, 471.

52. LC, Lord's Prayer, 7, in BC, 441.

53. WA TR 3:485–86 (no. 3651), dated December 21–25, 1537, where practices included locking himself in his cell and trying to catch up on his prayers. Von Amsdorff and others finally got him to stop by laughing at him. See also WA TR 2:11 (no. 1253, December 14, 1531), where Luther dated this event to 1520. For another reflection on monastic praying, see WA TR 4:654 (no. 5094), dated June 11–19, 1540.

54. SC, Lord's Prayer, 2, in BC, 356. See also Birgit Stolt, "Martin Luther's Concept of God as a Father," *Lutheran Quarterly* 8 (1994): 383–94.

55. LC, Lord's Prayer, 11, in BC, 442, revised by the author.

56. LC, Lord's Prayer, 13, in BC, 442.

57. WA 38:364, 25, cited in Peters, *Vaterunser*, 36.

58. WA TR 5:123 (no. 5392), dated Spring 1542. For a different translation, see Haile, *Luther*, 278.

59. Peters, *Das Vaterunser*, 32–34. His unconsidered comment about the "melanchthonische Richtung" of article eleven of the Formula of Concord misses completely the fact that, except when dealing with "an unbeliever" like Erasmus, Luther always grounded comments about predestination in God's promise, especially when dealing with the conscience under attack.

60. LC, Lord's Prayer, 21, in BC, 443. This same combination as an introduction to confident prayer occurs in *A Simple Way to Pray* (LW 43:194–95; WA 38:359–60) and in the explanation of "Amen" in the SC, Lord's Prayer, 21, in BC, 358.

61. LC, Lord's Prayer, 22, in BC, 443. The Latin translator, too, understood that the singular German ("Über das") implied the first two sections and translated with the plural ("Praeter haec").

62. LC, Lord's Prayer, 22, in BC, 443: "In this way we see how deeply concerned he is about our needs, and we should never

doubt that such prayer pleases him and will assuredly be heard."

63. Scott Hendrix, "Martin Luther's Reformation of Spirituality," now in Timothy J. Wengert, ed., *Harvesting Martin Luther's Reflections on Theology, Ethics, and the Church* (Grand Rapids, Mich.: Eerdmans, 2004), 240–60.

64. LC, Lord's Supper, 20–37, in BC, 468–70. See also WA TR 1:183 (no. 421, dated Christmas 1532), where Luther compared the Lord's Prayer and the Psalms but finally admitted that he prayed the Lord's Prayer more avidly [German: *lieber*] than any psalm.

65. Peters, *Das Vaterunser*, 28–31.

66. LC, Lord's Prayer, 25, in BC, 443.

67. LC, Lord's Prayer, 26, in BC, 444.

68. See WA TR 3:79 (no. 2918, January 26–29, 1533): "Christianus semper orat, sive dormiat sive vigilet. Cor enim eius orat semper, et suspirium est magna et fortis oratio. Sic enim dicit: Propter gemitum pauperum nunc exurgam, Esa[iae] 11 [actually Ps. 12:6]. Sic christianus semper fert crucem, licet non semper eam sentiat." For Luther's early use of this phrase and its importance in his theology, see Heiko Oberman, "'Simul gemitus et raptus': Luther and Mysticism," in *The Reformation in Medieval Perspective*, ed. Steven Ozment (Chicago: Quadrangle, 1971), 219–51.

69. SC, Lord's Prayer, 3–20, in BC, 356–58. See also WA TR 5:57 (nos. 5317–18, dated October 19–November 5, 1540) for an explanation of the grammar of the Lord's Prayer.

70. LC, Lord's Prayer, 27, in BC, 444.

71. Here, the German word *Mantel* designated the common cloak worn by either sex.

72. For a fine summary of this point, see Peters, *Das Vaterunser*, 37–39. See also WA TR 1:340 (no. 700, from the first half of the 1530s), where Luther linked the Lord's Prayer especially to this common praying. See also WA 6:237, 33—239, 19 (LW 44:64–66) and WA 2:114, 3–31 (LW 42:60). I am indebted to my student Gary Steeves for this reference.

73. See especially Heiko Oberman, *Luther: Man Between God and the Devil* (New Haven, Conn.: Yale University Press, 1989).

74. SC, Creed, 4, in BC, 355. See Peters, *Das Vaterunser*, 28–34.

75. LC, Lord's Prayer, 33, in BC, 444–45.

76. For an analysis of his exposition, see Peters, *Das Vaterunser*, 42–188, and, in English, Charles P. Arand, "Battle Cry of Faith: The Catechism's Exposition of the Lord's Prayer," *Concordia Journal* 21 (1995): 42–65.

77. SC, Lord's Prayer, 21, in BC, 358.

78. Birgit Stolt, "Martin Luther's Concept of God as Father," *Lutheran Quarterly* 8 (1994): 383–94.

79. SC, Lord's Prayer, 2, in BC, 356.

80. SC, Lord's Prayer, 4, 7, 10.

81. Ibid.

82. SC, Lord's Prayer, 5, in BC, 356.

83. The word *sanctification* is one of the most unfortunate in the theological vocabulary. It immediately assumes a distinction from justification and, hence, from faith and then forces believers to depend on their own devices. Here, Luther made it all depend on the Word and, as the following petitions make clear, on the Holy Spirit, faith, and the work of Christ defeating the old and bringing in the new.

84. It is too bad that Lutheran congregations are not in the habit of jumping up just before the preacher opens his or her mouth on Sunday morning and shouting, "Father, hallowed be your name! Amen."

85. SC, Lord's Prayer, 8, in BC, 357.

86. The LC, Lord's Prayer, 67, in BC, 449, even offers this paraphrase: "Dear Father, your will be done and not the will of the devil or of our enemies, nor of those who would persecute and suppress your holy Word or prevent your kingdom from coming; and grant that we may bear patiently and overcome whatever we must suffer on its account, so that our poor flesh may not yield or fall away through weakness or sloth."

87. I am indebted to my student Pastor Kim Kemmerling for this insight.

88. SC, Lord's Prayer, 13, in BC, 357.

89. LC, Lord's Prayer, 73–74, in BC, 450.

90. LC, Lord's Prayer, 82–83, in BC, 451.

91. See, for example, LC, Lord's Prayer, 85, in BC, 452: "This petition has to do with our poor miserable life."

92. SC, Baptismal Booklet, 3, in BC, 372.

93. SC, Lord's Prayer, 16, in BC, 358.

94. What Luther here and elsewhere did not notice was that the "as we forgive" is not so much "I must forgive everyone or else" but, rather, as indeed Luther intimates in the LC, a sign of what forgiveness by God must really be like.

95. LC, Lord's Prayer, 96, in BC, 453.

96. LC, Lord's Prayer, 98, in BC, 453.

97. For this insight, I am indebted to Gerhard Forde and James Nestingen, *Free to Be*, 2nd ed. (Minneapolis: Augsburg, 1993).

98. LC, Lord's Prayer, 113, in BC, 455.

5. Luther, Children, and Baptism

1. A portion of this chapter first appeared in a condensed version as "Luther on Children: Baptism and the Fourth Commandment," *dialog* 37 (1998): 185–89 (reprinted by permission).

2. Martin Manlius, *Locorum communium collectanea a Iohanne Manlio*, 3 vols. (Basel: J. Oporinus, 1562–63), 2:53.

3. See Konrad von Rabenau, "Reformatorische Themen in Bildern des 16. Jahrhunderts" (Dresden: Kirchlicher Kunstverlag, 1982); and Christoph Weimer, "Luther and Cranach on Justification in Word and Image," *Lutheran Quarterly* 18 (2004): 387–405. The dust jacket of Stephen Ozment's *Protestants: The Birth of a Revolution* (New York: Doubleday, 1992) features an example of the painting described here.

4. For a succinct discussion in English of Luther's view of baptism, see Mark Tranvik, "Luther on Baptism," in *Harvesting Martin Luther's Reflections on Theology, Ethics, and the Church*, ed. Timothy J. Wengert (Grand Rapids, Mich.: Eerdmans, 2004), 23–37.

5. LW 36:57.

6. For Gabriel Biel, see Heiko Oberman, *Harvest of Medieval Theology*, 2nd ed. (Durham, N.C.: Labyrinth, 1983), 134–35. Baptism offered first grace dependent on the disposition of the godparents. Discussion of the Sacrament of Penance completely overshadowed baptism.

7. LW 36:67–68.

8. LW 36:63.

9. LW 36:68. "This death and resurrection we call the new creation, regeneration, and spiritual birth. This should not be understood only allegorically as the death of sin and the life of grace, as many understand it, but as actual death and resurrection."

10. *To the Christian Nobility of the German Nation concerning the Reform of the Christian Estate* (1520), LW 44:129.

11. LW 36:58, 61. See also LC, Holy Baptism, 80–82, in BC, 466.

12. Letter to Philip Melanchthon dated January 13, 1522 (LW 48:371).

13. LW 40:229–62.

14. LW 53:98–99, 108. This text may also have been a part of the late-medieval service adapted by Luther for use in Wittenberg. Unfortunately, while reinserting a version of Luther's flood prayer into the baptismal liturgy (something also featured in both German and English versions of the colonial baptismal service used by Henry Melchior Muhlenberg and the Pennsylvania Ministerium), the *Lutheran Book of Worship* and, *Evangelical Lutheran Worship* omit the reading of this story. Perhaps in the future, Lutherans could revive the practice of reading a passage from the Bible at a baptism, including this one for infant and children baptisms.

15. LC, Baptism, 47–63, in BC, 462–64.

16. LC, Baptism, 52, in BC, 463.

17. LC, Baptism, 53, in BC, 463.

18. LC, Baptism, 58, in BC, 464.

19. LC, Baptism, 59, in BC, 464.

20. Indeed, "believers' baptism" could be termed, using Luther's vantage point, "unbelievers' baptism," because it rejected God's ability to work through external means with the Word and left everything to depend on the work or decision of faith.

21. Criticisms of monasticism abounded before Luther. The Brethren of the Common Life, which espoused a monastic life without vows (thought to foster spiritual pride), and caricatures of evil monks from Chaucer to Erasmus are only two examples. For Anabaptists' relation to monasticism and medieval theology, see George H. Williams, *The Radical Reformation*, 3rd ed. (Kirksville, Mo.: Sixteenth Century Journal Press, 1992); and David C. Steinmetz, "Scholasticism and Radical Reform: Nominalist Motifs in the Theology of Balthasar Hubmaier," *Mennonite Quarterly Review* 45 (1971): 123–44.

22. Still the best essay on this topic is Gustaf Wingren, *Luther on Vocation*, trans. Carl C. Rasmussen (Philadelphia: Muhlenberg, 1957).

23. LW 45:81–129.

24. SC, Household Chart, 1, in BC, 365. See chapter 8 of this book.

25. Especially Gerald Strauss, *Luther's House of Learning: Indoctrination of the Young in the German Reformation* (Baltimore: Johns Hopkins University Press, 1978).

26. See Klaus Petzold, *Die Grundlagen der Erziehungslehre im Spätmittelalter und bei Luther* (Heidelberg: Quelle & Meyer, 1969). It is noteworthy that the term *justification* occurs in the Small Catechism only once, as part of the third question on baptism.

27. For the former, see WA 7:204–29; for the latter, LW 43:11–45.

28. See Albrecht Peters, *Kommentar zu Luthers Katechismen*, vol. 1, *Die Zehn Gebote* (Göttingen: Vandenhoeck & Ruprecht, 1990), 180–208.

29. LW 44:85.

30. LW 44:86.

31. LW 44:86–87. In the tract, he goes on to make similar comments about spiritual and secular authorities, emphasizing their responsibility and the right of Christian disobedience when the first three commandments are violated.

32. LW 51:146. This is from the third sermon preached in November and December 1528.

33. LW 51:146.

34. LW 51:150–51, slightly revised.

35. LC, Ten Commandments, 145–47, in BC, 406.

36. In the preface to his baptismal service (SC, 3, in BC, 372), Luther stated: "Therefore you have to realize that it is no joke at all to take action against the devil and not only drive him away from the little child but also hang around the child's neck a mighty, lifelong enemy."

37. This broadening of a text associated with obedience to authority also occurred in the Reformers' interpretations of Romans 13. See David C. Steinmetz, "Calvin and Melanchthon on Romans 13:1–7," *Ex Auditu: An Annual of the Frederick Neumann Symposium on Theological Interpretation of Scripture* 2 (1986): 76–87.

38. LW 51:136.

39. SC, preface, 19–20, in BC, 350. This was also the theme in his *To the Councilmen of All Cities in Germany That They Establish and Maintain Christian Schools*, of 1524 (LW 45:347–78), and in *A Sermon on Keeping Children in School*, of 1530 (LW 46:213–58).

40. LC, Ten Commandments, 174, in BC, 410.

41. LW 46:217. See also LW 45:348–49.

42. For the latter, see Philip Melanchthon, *Apology of the Augsburg Confession* 13.3, in BC, 219, with n. 379.

43. SC, Baptism, 1–2, in BC, 359.

44. Here, the irony of so-called remembrances of baptism that focus solely on the water and downplay or ignore the promise of God to forgive sin is that such ceremonies actually substantiate Anabaptist claims. Without the Word of promise, all the officiant is doing is getting people wet.

45. See Albrecht Peters, *Kommentar zu Luthers Katechismen*, vol. 4, *Die Taufe, Das Abendmahl*, ed. Gottfried Seebaß (Göttingen: Vandenhoeck & Ruprecht, 1993), 28–31. The notion of sacraments as visible words goes back to Augustine.

46. LC, Baptism, 6, in BC, 457.

47. LC, Baptism, 10, in BC, 457.

48. LC, Baptism, 11–13, in BC, 458.

49. LC, Baptism, 17, in BC, 458.

50. LC, Baptism, 18, in BC, 458, quoting Augustine, *Tractates on John*, 80.

51. LC, Baptism, 19, in BC, 459.

52. LC, Baptism, 23, in BC, 459.

53. SC, Baptism, 5–6, in BC, 359.

54. LC, Baptism, 30, in BC, 460. In paragraph 29, he stated: "Faith must have something to believe—something to which it may cling and upon which it may stand."

55. SC, Baptism, 9–10, in BC, 359.

56. SC, Baptism, 10, in BC, 359.

57. SC, Baptism, 10, in BC, 359.

58. LC, Baptism, 34, in BC, 460.

59. LC, Baptism, 35–37, in BC, 460–61.

60. There is a certain irony that in contemporary North American Christianity, churches that have "Baptist" in their name or that practice "believers' baptism," as they call it, have little or no place for baptism itself as the center of the Christian life. If any church *should* be called "Baptist," it would be the Lutheran Church, where baptism could arguably be seen as the very center of the entire Christian life.

61. LC, 41–46, in BC, 461–62.

6. The Daily Sacrament of Baptismal Absolution

1. WA 2:489, 11–12, translated by the author. For another translation, see LW 27:219. We are examining here simply the printed examples of the phrase, which also occurred in Luther's lectures, especially his lectures on Romans from 1515–16. This and the following references were found using *Luthers Werke im WWW* (Proquest-CSA, 2000–2007).

2. WA 2:497, 13, translated by the author. For another translation, see LW 27:231. There are similar statements in the *Operationes in Psalmos*, published around the same time. See WA 5:164, 23.

3. WA 7:137, 18–19, translated by the author.

4. WA 8:67–68 (LW 32:172–73).

5. WA 31¹:379, 9–10, translated by the author.

6. WA 40¹:368, 26–27, translated by the author. For another translation, see LW 26:232. The manuscript of the lectures themselves states (368, 8–9): "So the Christian is

at the same time sinner and saint [*sanctus*], enemy and son of God."

7. Martin Luther, *Luthers Werke: Kritische Gesamtausgabe: Bibel*, 12 vols. (Weimar: H. Böhlau, 1906–61), 7:22, 3–13, accessed through Proquest, *Luthers Werke im WWW*, and translated by the author. For another translation, see LW 35:377.

8. For a more complete listing of the various parts of the Small Catechism in these early printings, see Charles P. Arand, *That I May Be His Own: An Overview of Luther's Catechisms* (St. Louis, Mo.: Concordia, 2000), 189–92.

9. LC, Baptism, 74–75, in BC, 465–66.

10. LC, Baptism, 84, in BC, 466.

11. LC, Baptism, 86, in BC, 467.

12. Translated by the author from WA 30¹:343–45. For another translation, see LW 53:116–18.

13. This second form found its way into other catechisms mentioned above.

14. See Timothy J. Wengert, *Law and Gospel: Philip Melanchthon's Debate with John Agricola of Eisleben over "Poenitentia"* (Grand Rapids, Mich.: Baker, 1997).

15. For these articles, *Instruction by the Visitors for the Parish Pastors in Germany*, see LW 40:261–320, noting the mistranslated title.

16. See SC, Baptism, 15–29, in BC, 360–62.

17. See Heiko Oberman, *Harvest of Medieval Theology*, 3rd ed. (Durham, N.C.: Labyrinth, 1983).

18. SC, Baptism, 18, in BC, 360.

19. SC, Baptism, 24, in BC, 361.

20. SC, Baptism, 20, in BC, 360.

21. SC, Baptism, 26, in BC, 361.

22. SC, Baptism, 29, in BC, 362.

23. See *Martin Luther's Sermons from Holy Week and Easter, 1529*, trans. Irving Sandberg (St. Louis, Mo.: Concordia, 1999).

24. LC, Confession, 1–3, in BC, 476.

25. LC, Confession, 5, in BC, 476. He discussed the problem of failure to receive the Lord's Supper in similar terms but with more nuance. See chapter 7 in this book.

26. LC, Confession, 6, in BC, 477.

27. LC, Confession, 7, in BC, 477.

28. See Timothy J. Wengert, *Law and Gospel* (Grand Rapids, Mich.: Baker, 1997), for the details of this debate.

29. LC, Confession, 9, in BC, 477.

30. LC, Confession, 13, in BC, 477.

31. LC, Confession, 14, in BC, 477.

32. LC, Confession, 16–17, in BC, 478.

33. LC, Confession, 18 and 22, in BC, 478.

34. LC, Confession, 23, in BC, 478.

35. LC, Confession, 26–27, in BC, 479.

36. LW 54:476 (no. 5677).

37. SC, preface, 23, in BC, 350–51.

38. LC, Confession, 32, in BC, 479.

39. LC, Confession, 33–34, in BC, 479–80.

40. For the early history of this sacrament among Lutherans, see Ronald Rittgers, *The Reformation of the Keys: Confession, Conscience and Authority in Sixteenth-Century Germany* (Cambridge, Mass.: Harvard University Press, 2004). I have titled this section playing off a book title by psychologist Karl Menninger, *What Ever Became of Sin?* (New York: Hawthorn, 1973).

41. The alternative thanksgiving for baptism in the *Evangelical Lutheran Worship*, while trying to make baptism more central, has two weaknesses. First, it imagines that remembrance of baptism is simply thanking God that one had at one time been baptized rather than actually using baptism's gifts in the present through a similar declaration of grace (for example, absolution), and second, it does not actually proclaim any unconditional promise to the assembly, leaving them with a "bathkeeper's remembrance" and little else. As with the absolution itself, where the jussive ("God forgive you") or the subjunctive ("May God forgive you") finally leaves the sinner wondering ("Does God or doesn't God forgive?"), so a remembrance of baptism can arise never from a command ("Remember your baptism" or "May you remember your baptism") but only from a declaration ("I baptize you" or "You are forgiven").

42. Gerhard Forde and James Nestingen, *Free to Be*, 2nd ed. (Minneapolis: Augsburg, 1993), 200.

7. Treasuring the Lord's Supper

1. Portions of this chapter first appeared as "Luther's Catechisms and the Lord's Supper," *Word and World* 17 (1997): 54–60.

2. See *Martin Luther's Sermons from Holy Week and Easter, 1529*, trans. Irving Sandberg (St. Louis, Mo.: Concordia, 1999).

3. See Helmar Junghans, "Luther on the Reform of Liturgy," now in *Harvesting Martin Luther's Reflections on Theology, Ethics, and the Church*, ed. Timothy J. Wengert (Grand Rapids, Mich.: Eerdmans, 2004), 213.

4. See Reinhard Schwarz, "The Last Supper: The Testament of Jesus," *Lutheran Quarterly* 9 (1995): 391–403.

5. Zwingli and the Reformed tradition quickly adopted the discovery that the Hebrew Scriptures numbered the commandments differently, consolidating the Latin version's ninth and tenth commandments into one and creating a second commandment from the prohibition of images. Luther, who saw no reason for unnecessary innovation, argued that the command regarding graven images (like the literal meaning of the third commandment) applied only to the Israelites as a special case of the first commandment.

6. In his later writings, Zwingli used the Greek term ἀλλοίωσις (*alloeosis* in Latin), which in grammar means replacing one term with another. This technique also affected his Christology. For later Lutheran debates over the Lord's Supper, see Timothy J. Wengert, *A Formula for Parish Practice: Using the Formula of Concord in the Parish* (Grand Rapids, Mich.: Eerdmans, 2006).

7. Luther's use of the preposition *under* came close to the Roman view of transubstantiation, a doctrine approved in 1215 by the Lateran IV council that the substance (the quiddity of a thing as opposed to its accidents or qualities) of the bread was transformed into the body of Christ presented under the form of bread and wine. Later, in the Wittenberg Concord of 1536 (an agreement between Luther and some former adherents to Zwingli's point of view, notably the Strasbourg pastor Martin Bucer), Luther and the Lutherans agreed to use the phrase

"with the bread." Only in later centuries did the three prepositions come (incorrectly) to denote the Lutheran position that Christ is present "in, with, and under" the bread and wine.

8. For a lengthy refutation of the notion of the sacrament effectiveness by the mere performance of the rite (*ex opere operato*), see Philip Melanchthon, *The Apology of the Augsburg Confession*, 24, in BC, 258–77.

9. LC, Lord's Supper, 6, in BC, 467.

10. SC, Lord's Supper, 2, in BC, 362.

11. In LC, Lord's Supper, 8, in BC, 467, he even wrote, "in and under the bread and wine."

12. LC, Lord's Supper, 9, in BC, 467.

13. LC, Lord's Supper, 12–14, in BC, 468.

14. LC, Lord's Supper, 16–18, in BC, 468.

15. Cf. 1 Cor. 11:27. Luther realized that this passage had to do with the appalling way some in Corinth were treating the poor. However, even for him, the danger of unworthy eating went far beyond this and, for his followers at least, also included not discerning Christ's presence in the sacrament itself. For Luther, questioning Christ's presence according to some human criterion (here: worthiness) completely undermined Christ's promise and left participants with a recipe for complete uncertainty.

16. Philip Melanchthon addressed this issue in the Augsburg Confession, 13, in BC, 46–47.

17. LC, Lord's Supper, 20, in BC, 468–69. For a broader discussion of this aspect of Luther's catechesis, see chapter 5.

18. It occurs ten times in LC, Lord's Supper, 20–37, in BC, 468–70.

19. LC, Lord's Supper, 22, in BC, 469.

20. LC, Lord's Supper, 23–27, in BC, 469.

21. SC, preface, 23, in BC, 351.

22. LC, Lord's Supper, 30, in BC, 469. The use here and throughout the catechisms of the phrase "set within" is an attempt to capture more literally Luther's use of the German *fassen*, which some translations overintellectualize with Latin terms, such as *com-*

prehend. This is, literally, the language used to describe a jewel set within a ring.

23. LC, Lord's Supper, 31, in BC, 469.

24. LC, Lord's Supper, 31, in BC, 470.

25. LC, Lord's Supper, 33, in BC, 470.

26. LC, Lord's Supper, 35, in BC, 470. Earlier printings of the BC read, "It is also your responsibility," a misreading of the German phrase "es gehört aber dazu."

27. SC, Lord's Supper, 10, in BC, 363.

28. See *Martin Luther's Sermons from Holy Week and Easter, 1529*, 71–79.

29. LC, Lord's Supper, 39–84, in BC, 470–75.

30. LC, Lord's Supper, 40, in BC, 471.

31. LC, Lord's Supper, 42, in BC, 471.

32. Luther dealt with the three in LC, Lord's Supper, 45–54, 55–74, and 75–84, respectively.

33. LC, Lord's Supper, 45, in BC, 471.

34. SC, preface, 22, in BC, 350.

35. LC, Lord's Supper, 45, in BC, 471. In paragraphs 46–47, Luther remarked that the words "as often as you do it" (1 Cor. 11:25) implied that "we should do it frequently." Christ added them not to restrict the sacrament to a particular time of year, like the Passover, but to allow it to be celebrated frequently.

36. LC, Lord's Supper, 49, in BC, 472.

37. LC, Lord's Supper, 52, in BC, 472.

38. LC, Lord's Supper, 53, in BC, 472. For the same reason, he changed his paraphrastic explanations of the Decalogue from "*you* are to fear and love God" to "*we*."

39. LC, Lord's Supper, 55, in BC, 472.

40. Here is where the modern distinction, popularized by Paul Tillich, that Luther was searching for a gracious God while modern people are simply searching for God needs to be reconsidered. Luther's experience was motivated less by guilt (like Paul, Luther could have said, "As to the law: blameless") and more by a theology of glory ("Where is God?"), and contemporary experience shows that guilt is still alive and well as a tool to cause religious paralysis.

41. LC, Lord's Supper, 58–60, in BC, 473. This passage clearly indicates that distinguishing different types of motivation for

the same outward behavior was a conscious part of Luther's approach to pastoral care. "For this reason we must make a distinction here among people," he wrote (par. 58). The "impudent and unruly" (quite frankly, a fairly small group in American "free" churches) need to be told to stay away. The unworthy, however, must not be broken further by more law.

42. LC, Lord's Supper, 61 and 62, in BC, 473. This is the same argument Luther employs for those who do not think they can pray to God. See chapter 4.

43. LC, Lord's Supper, 64–65, in BC, 473.

44. LC, Lord's Supper, 66–67, in BC, 473–74.

45. LC, Lord, Supper, 71, in BC, 474.

46. SC, preface, 23, in BC, 350.

47. LC, Lord's Supper, 75, in BC, 474.

48. LC, Lord's Supper, 76, in BC, 474.

49. LC, Lord's Supper, 78, in BC, 475.

50. LC, Lord's Supper, 79, in BC, 475.

51. In a tract published the following year, he also mentioned death itself.

52. See Heiko Oberman, *Luther: Man between God and the Devil* (New Haven, Conn.: Yale University Press, 1989).

53. LC, Lord's Supper, 81, in BC, 475.

54. LC, Lord's Supper, 82, in BC, 475. I have often given the advice to young pastors, eager to increase the celebration of the Lord's Supper in their new congregations, simply to preach about these "daggers, spears and arrows" and the marvelous benefits in the Supper each week without suggesting any change in practice. If, after five years, no one in the congregation brings up on his or her own a suggestion to increase the celebration, then look for a new call, because the people are either not listening or not believing what they hear.

55. LC, Lord's Supper, 82, in BC, 475.

56. LC, Lord's Supper, 83, in BC, 475.

8. The Catechisms as a Vocational School

1. Stephen Ozment, *The Reformation in the Cities* (New Haven, Conn.: Yale University Press, 1975), 47–120; *When Fathers Ruled* (Cambridge, Mass.: Harvard University Press, 1983); *Protestantism: The Birth of Revolution* (New York: Doubleday, 1992), 28–31, 151–68. Criticisms of Ozment's work tend to judge Luther's approach to sixteenth-century social issues using twenty-first century sensibilities.

2. See especially George H. Williams, *The Radical Reformation*, 3rd ed. (Kirksville, Mo.: Sixteenth Century Journal Publishers, 1992).

3. LW 44:251–355.

4. LW 28:1–56.

5. Translated in Martin Luther, *Sermons*, trans. John Lenker, 8 vols. (repr., Grand Rapids, Mich.: Baker, 1989), 1:240–43.

6. See chapter 12 of Timothy J. Wengert, *A Formula for Parish Practice: Using the Formula of Concord in the Congregation* (Grand Rapids, Mich.: Eerdmans, 2006).

7. It is better to say that life is sanctified than that the person is "sanctified" or moves from justification to sanctification. Rather, faith that God is not wrathful and arbitrary but merciful and creating, which comes through justification by faith alone, opens up creation as gift and not threat.

8. For this distinction, see Gerhard Forde, *Where God Meets Man: Luther's Down-to-Earth Approach to the Gospel* (Minneapolis: Augsburg, 1972), 89–115.

9. See, for example, his 1523 tract *On Secular Authority*, LW 45:75–129.

10. LC, Ten Commandments, 158, in BC, 408.

11. SC, Ten Commandments, 1, in BC, 351. Here as elsewhere the phrase literally read "Father of the house," and the household included the servants, day workers, apprentices, and other kith and kin who lived and worked in the household. This was not a private sphere, as the word *family* is often construed today. As we saw in chapter 1, in the sermons he termed men and women "bishops and bishopesses" of the household.

12. LC, Ten Commandments, 172, in BC, 410.

13. LC, Ten Commandments, 145–48, in BC, 406–7.

14. LC, Ten Commandments, 116, in BC, 402 (emphasis added).

15. LC, Ten Commandments, 170, in BC, 409–10. He gave similar advice in the preface to the Small Catechism, 19–20, in BC, 350.

16. LC, Ten Commandments, 284, in BC, 424.

17. LC, Ten Commandments, 274, in BC, 422–23.

18. See LC, Lord's Prayer, 75, in BC, 450–51.

19. LC, Lord's Prayer, 80–81, in BC, 451.

20. See chapter 1 for a further discussion of the title. The notion of assembling such Bible verses goes back at least to Jean Gerson.

21. Not surprisingly, Martin Bucer's catechism published in Strasbourg in the 1530s included additions admonishing congregational members and citizens to obedience.

22. SC, Household Chart, 2, in BC, 365.

23. SC, Household Chart, 2, in BC, 365. For Luther's own commentary on this text from lectures delivered at nearly the same time (1528), see LW 28:281–95.

24. SC, preface, 26–27, in BC, 351.

25. SC, Household Table, 4, in BC, 365 (emphasis added).

26. For Philip Melanchthon's equally adamant arguments in favor of governmental authority, see Timothy J. Wengert, *Human Freedom, Christian Righteousness: Philip Melanchthon's Exegetical Dispute with Erasmus of Rotterdam* (New York: Oxford University Press, 1998), 110–36.

27. LC, Ten Commandments, 230, in BC, 417. The phrase "with whom lords and princes consort" was considered so volatile that the printer took it out of later editions. It was not reinserted into the text until the printing of *The Book of Concord* in 1580.

28. The following are all in SC, Household Chart, 6–14, in BC, 366–67.

29. For Luther's arguments in favor of a woman being granted a divorce from an abusive husband, see Timothy J. Wengert, "Martin Luther on Spousal Abuse," *Lutheran Quarterly* 21 (2007): 337–39.

30. See Mickey Mattox, *"Defender of the Most Holy Matriarchs": Martin Luther's Interpretation of the Women of Genesis in the "Enar-*

rationes in Genesin," 1535–1545 (Leiden: Brill, 2003).

31. Martin Luther, *Luthers Werke: Kritische Gesamtausgabe: Bibel*, 12 vols. (Weimar: H. Böhlau, 1906–61), 7:307, accessed through Proquest, *Luthers Werke im WWW* [hereafter WA DB 7:307].

32. For the mixed messages of Luther's comments on women, see Mickey Mattox, "Luther on Eve, Women and the Church," *Lutheran Quarterly* 17 (2003): 456–74; and Susan Karant–Nunn and Merry Wiesner, eds., *Luther on Women: A Sourcebook* (Cambridge and New York: Cambridge University Press, 2003).

33. WA DB 7:313. The association of the devil with craft and might (*List* and *Kraft*) was echoed in the first verse of "A Mighty Fortress": "Mit Kraft und viel List, sein grausam Rüstung ist" (With craft and great might, he arms himself for fight).

34. SC, Household Chart, 15 and 1, respectively, in BC, 367 and 365.

35. Timothy J. Wengert, "'Per mutuum colloquium et consolationem fratrum': Monastische Züge in Luthers ökumenischer Theologie," in Christoph Bultmann et al., eds., *Luther und das monastische Erbe* (Tübingen: Mohr Siebeck, 2007), 243–68.

36. SC, Prayers, 1–11, in BC, 363–64.

37. See *Sources and Contexts of the Book of Concord*, ed. Robert Kolb and James Nestingen (Minneapolis: Fortress, 2001), 7–8.

38. LC, Lord's Prayer, 7–8, in BC, 441.

39. LC, Ten Commandments, 70–71, 73–75, 77, in BC, 395–96.

40. LW 53:277–81.

41. SC, Prayers, 8, in BC, 364.

42. SC, Marriage Booklet, in BC, 367–71.

43. SC, Marriage Booklet, 3, in BC, 368.

44. SC, Marriage Booklet, 4, in BC, 368.

45. SC, Marriage Booklet, 5, in BC, 369.

46. SC, Marriage Booklet, 11–15, in BC, 370–71.

47. SC, Baptismal Booklet, in BC, 371–75.

48. SC, Baptismal Booklet, 1, in BC, 371.

49. SC, Baptismal Booklet, 3, in BC, 372.

50. SC, Baptismal Booklet, 5, in BC, 372.

51. SC, Baptismal Booklet, 6, in BC, 372.

52. SC, Baptismal Booklet, 7, in BC, 373. The "Amen" may be found in Luther's explanation to the articles of the Creed ("This is most certainly true"), the Amen of the Lord's Prayer, and the third question in baptism, as well as here.

53. See Heiko Oberman, *Luther: Man between God and the Devil* (New Haven, Conn.: Yale University Press, 1989).

54. SC, Baptismal Booklet, 8–9, in BC, 373.

55. See Mark Tranvik, "Luther on Baptism," in *Harvesting Martin Luther's Reflec-*tions on Theology, Ethics, and the Church, ed. Timothy J. Wengert (Grand Rapids, Mich.: Eerdmans, 2004), 23–37; and Philip D. W. Krey and Timothy J. Wengert, "A June 1546 Exorcism in Wittenberg as a Pastoral Act," *Archive for Reformation History* 98 (2007): 71–83, and the literature on Lutheran exorcisms cited there.

56. See LW 53:163–69.

57. See LW 53:171–79.

58. The translation here is by Catherine Winkworth, with slight changes by the author.

A SELECT BIBLIOGRAPHY
ON LUTHER'S CATECHISMS

Arand, Charles P. "Battle Cry of Faith: The Catechism's Exposition of the Lord's Prayer." *Concordia Journal* 21 (1995): 42–65.

Arand, Charles P., and David P. Daniel, comps. *A Bibliography of the Lutheran Confessions*. St. Louis, Mo.: Center for Reformation Research, 1988, 111–35.

————. "Luther's Catechisms: Maps for the Study of Scripture." *Issues in Christian Education* (Summer 1990).

————. *That I May Be His Own: An Overview of Luther's Catechisms*. St. Louis, Mo.: Concordia, 2000.

Asendorf, Ulrich. "Luther's Small Catechism and the Heidelberg Catechism." In *Luther's Catechisms—450 Years*, edited by David P. Scaer and Robert D. Preus, 1–7. Fort Wayne, Ind.: Concordia Theological Seminary, 1979.

Bachmann, E. Theodore. "The Small Catechism and the 'Two-Thirds World.'" *Lutheran Forum* (Advent, 1979): 9–11.

Bayer, Oswald. "I Believe That God Has Created Me with All That Exists: An Example of Catechetical-Systematics." *Lutheran Quarterly* 8 (1994): 129–61.

Bedouelle, Guy. "The Birth of the Catechism." *Communio (US)* 10 (1983): 35–52.

Bodensieck, Julius. "Luthers kleiner Katechismus in Amerika." In *Ich glaube eine heilige Kirche: Festschrift für D. Hans Asmussen zum 65. Geburtstag zum 21. August 1963*, edited by Walter Bauer et al., 141–49. Stuttgart: Evangelisches Verlagswerk, 1963.

Bruno, Jordahn. "Katechismus-Gottesdienst im Reformationsjahrhundert." *Luther: Mitteilungen der Luthergesellschaft* 30 (1959): 64–77.

Buchwald, Georg. *Die Entstehung der Katechismen Luthers und die Grundlage des Grossen Katechismus*. Leipzig: Georg Wigand, 1894.

Cohrs, Ferdinand. *Die Evangelische Katechismusversuche vor Luthers Enchiridion*. 4 vols. Monumenta Germaniae Paedagogica, 20–23. Berlin: A. Hofmann, 1900–1902.

Collijn, Isak. "The Swedish-Indian Catechism: Some Notes." *Lutheran Quarterly* 2 (1988): 89–98.

Denef, Lawrence. "Praying the Catechism: Spirituality as Luther Envisioned It." *Lutheran Forum* 19 (1985): 17–19.

Drevlow, Arthur H. "How Luther Wanted the Catechism Used." *Concordia Journal* 4 (1981): 152–57.

Drickamer, John M. "The Religion of the Large Catechism." *Concordia Journal* 8 (1982): 139–42.

Fredrich, Edward C. "The Evangelical Character of Luther's Catechism." In *Luther's Catechisms—450 Years*, edited by David P. Scaer and Robert D. Preus, 8–15. Fort Wayne, Ind.: Concordia Theological Seminary, 1979.

Frenzel, Otto. "Luthers Katechismus und das Zeitalter der Aufklärung." *Allgemeine Evangelisch-Lutherische Kirchenzeitung* 62 (1929): 511–14, 535–39, 558–62, 583–89.

Gerberding, G. H. *The Lutheran Catechist*. Philadelphia: Lutheran Publication Society, 1910.

Graebner, Theodore. *The Story of the Catechism*. St. Louis, Mo.: Concordia, 1928.

Green, Lowell C. "Introduction and Index to the Quellen of J. M. Reu." *Bulletin of the Library Foundation for Reformation Research* 6 (1971): 9–11, 17–32; 7 (1972): 1–7.

Gritsch, Eric W. "Luther's Catechisms of 1529: Whetstones of the Church." *Lutheran Theological Seminary Bulletin* 60 (1980): 3–17.

Grueneisen, Ernst. "Grundlegendes für die Bilder in Luthers Katechismen." *Luther-Jahrbuch* 20 (1938): 1–44.

Haemig, Mary Jane. "Preaching the Catechism: A Transformational Enterprise." *Dialog* 36 (1997): 100–104.

Hoffmann, Georg. "Der Kleine Katechismus als Abriß der Theologie Martin Luthers." *Luther: Mitteilungen der Luthergesellschaft* 30 (1959): 49–63.

Janetzki, Elvin W. "Teaching Luther's Small Catechism as Law and Gospel." *Lutheran Theological Journal* 14 (1980): 73–79.

Johnston, A. G. "Lutheranism in Disguise: The *Corte Instruccye* of Cornelis Vander Heyden." *Nederlands Archief voor Kerkgeschiedenis* 68 (1988): 23–29.

Johnston, Paul I. "Reu's Understanding of the Small Catechism." *Lutheran Quarterly* 7 (1993): 425–50.

Klein, Leonard, ed. "The Small Catechism and the Formation of Piety." *Lutheran Forum* 22 (1988): 4–5, 8–34. Includes articles by Klein, Hinlicky, Bretscher, S. Bouman, Yeago, and Almen.

Kohls, Ernst-Wilhelm, ed. *Evangelische Katechismen der Reformationszeit vor und neben Martin Luthers Kleinem Katechismus.* Gütersloh: Gerd Mohn, 1971.

Kolb, Robert. "The Layman's Bible: The Use of Luther's Catechisms in the German Late Reformation." In *Luther's Catechisms—450 Years,* edited by David P. Scaer and Robert D. Preus, 16–26. Fort Wayne, Ind.: Concordia Theological Seminary Press, 1979.

———. *Teaching God's Children His Teaching.* Mankato, MN: Crown, 1992.

———. "'That I May Be His Own': The Anthropology of Luther's Explanation of the Creed." *Concordia Journal* 21 (1995): 28–41.

Krodel, Gottfried G. "Luther's Work on the Catechism in the Context of Late Medieval Catechetical Literature." *Concordia Journal* 25 (1999): 364–404.

Krusche, Werner. "Zur Struktur des Kleinen Katechismus." *Lutherische Monatshefte* 4 (1965): 316–31.

Krych, Margaret A. "The Catechism in Christian Education." *Word and World* 10 (1990): 43–47.

Laetsch, Theodore. "The Catechism in Public Worship." *Concordia Theological Monthly* 5 (1934): 234–41.

Leaver, Robin. "Luther's Catechism Hymns: 1. 'Lord Keep Us Steadfast in Your Word.'" *Lutheran Quarterly*, n.s., 11 (1997): 397–410.

———. "Luther's Catechism Hymns: 2. Ten Commandments." *Lutheran Quarterly*, n.s., 11 (1997): 411–22.

———. "Luther's Catechism Hymns: 3. Creed." *Lutheran Quarterly*, n.s., 12 (1998): 79–88.

———. "Luther's Catechism Hymns: 4. Lord's Prayer." *Lutheran Quarterly*, n.s., 12 (1998): 89–98.

———. "Luther's Catechism Hymns: 5. Baptism." *Lutheran Quarterly*, n.s., 12 (1998): 161–170.

———. "Luther's Catechism Hymns: 6. Confession." *Lutheran Quarterly*, n.s., 12 (1998): 171–80.

Loewenich, Walther von. "Die Selbstkritik der Reformation in Luthers Grossem Katechismus." In *Von Augustin zu Luther: Beitraege zur Kirchengeschichte,* 269–93. Witten: Luther-Verlag, 1959.

———. *Wahrheit und Bekenntnis im Glauben Luthers dargestellt im Anschluß an Luthers Grossen Katechismus.* Wiesbaden: Franz Steiner Verlag, 1974.

Ludwig, Alan. "Preaching and Teaching the Creed: The Structures of the Small Catechism's Explanations as Guides." *Logia: A Journal of Lutheran Theology* 3, no. 4 (October 1994): 11–24.

Luther, Martin. *The Large and Small Catechisms. D. Martin Luthers Werke: Kritische Gesamtausgabe*, vol. 30, pt. 1. Weimar: Hermann Böhlaus Nachfolger, 1910.

Luther's Small Catechism: A New English Translation Prepared by an Intersynodical Committee [With an Historical Introduction]: A Jubilee Offering, 1529–1929. Columbus, Ohio: Lutheran Book Concern, 1929.

Marshall, Ronald F. "Luther the Lumberjack." *Lutheran Quarterly*, n.s., 10 (1996): 107–10.

Mattes, John C. "The English Translation of Luther's Small Catechism by Thomas Cranmer." *Lutheran Church Review* 46 (1927): 60–90.

———, ed. *Luther's Small Catechism in the English Translation of Thomas Cranmer MDXLVIII.* Philadelphia: United Lutheran Publishing House, n.d. [1948?].

Nestingen, James A. "Preaching the Catechism." *Word and World* 10 (1990): 33–42.

Peters, Albrecht. "Die Theologie der Katechismen Luthers anhand der Zuordnung ihrer Hauptstücke." *Luther-Jahrbuch* 43 (1976): 2–35.

———. *Kommentar zu Luthers Katechismen.* 5 vols. Göttingen: Vandenhoeck & Ruprecht, 1990–1994.

Pless, John T. "Catechesis for Life in the Royal Priesthood." *Logia: A Journal of Lutheran Theology* 3, no. 4 (October 1994): 3–10.

Raabe, Paul R. "Children's Sermons and Luther's Small Catechism." *Concordia Journal* 15 (1989): 100–102.

Reed, Stephen D. "The Decalogue in Luther's Large Catechism." *Dialog* 22 (1983): 264–69.

Repp, Arthur C., Sr. *Luther's Catechism Comes to America.* Metuchen, N.J.: Scarecrow Press, 1982.

Reu, Michael. "Luthers Katechismus in Zeitalter der Orthodoxie," *Allgemeine Evangelisch-Lutherische Kirchenzeitung* 62 (1929): 462–66, 485–92.

———. *Luther's Small Catechism.* Chicago: Wartburg Publishing House, 1929.

———. *Quellen zur Geschichte des Katechismus Unterrichts.* 10 vols. Guetersloh: Bertelsmann, 1904–1932.

———. "Religious Instruction of the Young in the 16th Century." *Lutheran Church Review* 34 (1915): 566–85.

Rietschel, G. "Die erste Ausgabe des kleinen Katechismus in Tafelform." *Theologische Studien und Kritiken* 71 (1898): 522–27.

Roschke, Ronald W. "A Catechism on Luther's Catechisms." *Currents in Theology and Mission* 4 (1977): 68–75.

Saarnivaara, Uuras. "Baptism and Faith according to Luther's Catechisms and Other Teachings," in *Luther's Catechisms—450 Years*, edited by David P. Scaer and Robert D. Preus, 27–31. Fort Wayne, Ind.: Concordia Theological Seminary Press, 1979.

Scaer, David P. "The New Translation of Luther's Small Catechism: Is It Faithful to Luther's Spirit?," in *Luther's Catechisms—450 Years.* Edited by David P. Scaer and Robert D. Preus. Fort Wayne, Indiana: Concordia Theological Seminary Press, 1979, pp. 32–40.

Schaaf, James L. "The Large Catechism: A Pastoral Tool." In *Luther's Catechisms—450 Years*, edited by David P. Scaer and Robert D. Preus, 41–46. Fort Wayne, Ind.: Concordia Theological Seminary Press, 1979.

Scharffenorth, Gerta. "The Ecumenicity of Luther's Catechism." *Mid-Stream* 23 (1984): 162–75.

Schmidt, Martin. "August Hermann Franckes Katechismuspredigten." *Luther-Jahrbuch* 33 (1966): 88–117.

Schroeder, Edward H. "Baptism and Confession." *Trinity Seminary Review* 6 (1984): 13–21.

Schultz, Robert. "The Theological Significance of the Order of the Chief Parts in Luther's Catechism." In *Teaching the Faith*, edited by Carl Volz. River Forest, Ill.: Lutheran Education Association, 1967.

Seeger, Ulrich. "Die eschatologische Grundhaltung in Luthers grossem Katechismus." *Evangelische Theologie* 2 (1935): 67–95.

Skarsten, Trygve. "Johan Campanius, Pastor in New Sweden." *Lutheran Quarterly*, n.s., 2 (1988): 47–87.

Strauss, Gerald. *Luther's House of Learning: Indoctrination of the Young in the German Reformation*. Baltimore: Johns Hopkins University Press, 1978.

Tjernagel, N. S. "Forerunners of the Catechism: A View of Catechetical Instruction at the Dawn of the Reformation." in *Luther's Catechisms—450 Years*, edited by David P. Scaer and Robert D. Preus, 47–54. Fort Wayne, Ind.: Concordia Theological Seminary Press, 1979.

Vinay, Valdo. "Die italienischen Übersetzungen von Luthers Kleinem Katechismus." In *Vierhundertfuenfzig Jahre lutherische Reformation 1517–1967: Festschrift fuer Franz Lau zum 60. Geburtstag*, 384–94. Göttingen: Vandenhoeck & Ruprecht.

Voelz, James W. "Luther's Use of Scripture in the Small Catechism." In *Luther's Catechisms—450 Years*, edited by David P. Scaer and Robert D. Preus, 55–63. Fort Wayne, Ind.: Concordia Theological Seminary Press, 1979.

Weidenhiller, Egino. *Untersuchungen zur deutschsprachigen katechetischen Literatur des späten Mittelalters*. Munich, 1965.

Weinrich, William C. "Early Christian Catechetics: An Historical and Theological Construction." In *Luther's Catechisms—450 Years*, edited by David P. Scaer and Robert D. Preus, 64–73. Fort Wayne, Ind.: Concordia Theological Seminary Press, 1979.

Wengert, Timothy J. "'Fear and Love' in the Ten Commandments." *Concordia Journal* 21 (1995): 14–27.

———. "Forming the Faith Today through Luther's Catechisms." *Lutheran Quarterly*, n.s., 11 (1997): 379–96.

———, ed. *Harvesting Martin Luther's Reflections on Theology, Ethics, and the Church*. Grand Rapids: Eerdmans, 2003.

———. *Law and Gospel: Philip Melanchthon's Debate with John Agricola of Eisleben over "Poenitentia."* Grand Rapids, Mich.: Baker, 1997.

———. "Luther on Children: Baptism and the Fourth Commandment." *Dialog* 37 (1998): 185–89.

———. "Luther on Prayer in the Large Catechism." *Lutheran Quarterly* 18 (2004): 249–74.

———. "Luther's Catechisms and the Lord's Supper." *Word and World* 17 (1997): 54–60.

———. "Martin Luther and the Ten Commandments in the Large Catechism." *Currents in Theology and Mission* 31 (2004): 104–14.

———. "Wittenberg's Earliest Catechism." *Lutheran Quarterly*, n.s., 7 (1993): 247–60.

Wingren, Gustav. *Luther on Vocation*. Translated by Carl C. Rasmussen. Philadelphia: Muhlenberg Press, 1957.

INDEX

absolution, 122–23, 126–29. *See also* forgiveness

Absolution, Sacrament of, 114, 118–19, 126, 128, 183

adiaphora ("external matter"), 28, 109

Agricola, John, 9, 14–16, 40, 121–22, 172, 173, 178, 183

antinomianism, 16, 20, 40, 77, 122, 141

Anabaptists, 102–3, 108, 133, 150, 171, 182, 183

Apostles' Creed, 74, 75, 170, 175

Aquinas, Thomas, 104, 149

Arand, Charles, 174, 180, 183

Aristotle, 60, 110

attributes of God, 52

Augustine, 3, 110, 132, 134, 159, 171, 183

authorities, governmental, 33, 37, 78, 85, 107, 110, 156, 159, 167, 173, 182, 187. *See also* government

Bapst, Valentine, 170

Baptism, 6–7, 10, 18–19, 20–21, 40, 47, 63–64, 67, 83, 87, 95, 99–115, 117, 119–20, 129, 134, 136, 137, 145, 147, 163, 166, 168, 181–82, 188

"believers' baptism," 103, 150, 182–83

benefits of, 111–12, 114, 169, 184

and children, 99–108, 169–70

and faith, 102–3, 112–13

and grace, 112–13, 169, 184

infant baptism, 101–4, 108, 113–14, 168, 182

liturgy, 168–70

and promises, 100, 102, 108, 111, 183–84

"sacrament of justification," 101, 105, 113

vocation, 18, 103, 135, 153

Word and command, 102–3, 108

and Word of God, 112, 182, 183

Baumgartner, Jerome, 55

Bayer, Oswald, 45, 174

Beskendorff, Master Peter, 69, 80

Betbüchlein. *See* Luther, Martin, writings, *Personal Prayer Book*

Biel, Gabriel, 122, 181

Book of Concord, ix, 19, 27, 38, 169, 187

Booklet for the Laity and Children, 9, 13, 19, 21, 111, 164, 171, 164

Brecht, Martin, 176–77

Brenz, John, 9

Brethren of the Common Life, 149, 182

Bucer, Martin, 185, 187

Bugenhagen, John, 14, 177–78

catechism

catechetical sermons, 14, 17, 44–45, 50, 55–56, 73, 106–7, 131, 133

Christian instruction, viii, 3–4, 6, 9, 13

evangelical purpose, 21

history of, 3–20, 118–19, 171

ordering of topics, 6–8, 20–21, 163, 172

origin, 3–4

"What is this?" 11–12, 16

Charles V, 159, 178

children, viii, 3, 12, 16–18, 30, 34–35, 37–38, 44, 51–53, 66, 76, 78, 80, 87, 90, 92, 99–108, 112, 139, 151, 153–55, 158–61, 163–65, 169–70, 171–72, 173, 174, 182

and baptism, 99–108

Christian calling in the world. *See* Christian life

Christian life, viii, 7, 11, 18, 20–22, 33, 63, 64–66, 74, 96, 114, 123, 125, 127, 145, 149–70, 183

medieval division, 158

three arenas of, 153, 158

and household, 153, 158, 162

and love of neighbor, 152, 155–57, 162–63

See also vocation

church, 10, 63–66, 102, 147, 152–53, 167, 170

"communio sanctorum," 64–65, 175

commandments (commands), 6–7, 10, 12, 16, 85, 87, 157, 173, 179, 184.

See also law; Ten Commandments

confession (of sin), viii, 4–5, 7, 9, 14, 40, 74, 118–29, 131, 140, 184

and baptism, 124

command to confess, 125–26

and forgiveness, 118–23

and Lord's Supper, 124

private confession, 119, 122, 124–25, 129.

See also penance; absolution

confession (of faith), 6, 8, 12–13, 22, 45, 48, 50, 52–54, 64–65, 92, 170, 172

confession and absolution, 7, 127,128

conscience, 8, 37, 65–66, 72, 84, 94, 114, 120–21, 123–26, 134–35, 140, 154, 180

consolation, 76

counsels, 30, 40, 75, 104, 149, 156

Cranach Sr., Lucas, 99, 102

creation, 54

Creed, 3–4, 6–8, 43–44, 47, 50, 56, 59, 63–64, 66, 94, 137, 171, 188

First Article (*see also* Father), 47–54, 56, 59, 91–93, 157

Creation, 48–49, 54, 56

"God created me," 48, 53

Creator, 54, 59

193

Schroeder, Edward H. "Baptism and Confession." *Trinity Seminary Review* 6 (1984): 13–21.

Schultz, Robert. "The Theological Significance of the Order of the Chief Parts in Luther's Catechism." In *Teaching the Faith*, edited by Carl Volz. River Forest, Ill.: Lutheran Education Association, 1967.

Seeger, Ulrich. "Die eschatologische Grundhaltung in Luthers grossem Katechismus." *Evangelische Theologie* 2 (1935): 67–95.

Skarsten, Trygve. "Johan Campanius, Pastor in New Sweden." *Lutheran Quarterly*, n.s., 2 (1988): 47–87.

Strauss, Gerald. *Luther's House of Learning: Indoctrination of the Young in the German Reformation*. Baltimore: Johns Hopkins University Press, 1978.

Tjernagel, N. S. "Forerunners of the Catechism: A View of Catechetical Instruction at the Dawn of the Reformation." in *Luther's Catechisms—450 Years*, edited by David P. Scaer and Robert D. Preus, 47–54. Fort Wayne, Ind.: Concordia Theological Seminary Press, 1979.

Vinay, Valdo. "Die italienischen Übersetzungen von Luthers Kleinem Katechismus." In *Vierhundertfuenfzig Jahre lutherische Reformation 1517–1967: Festschrift fuer Franz Lau zum 60. Geburtstag*, 384–94. Göttingen: Vandenhoeck & Ruprecht.

Voelz, James W. "Luther's Use of Scripture in the Small Catechism." In *Luther's Catechisms—450 Years*, edited by David P. Scaer and Robert D. Preus, 55–63. Fort Wayne, Ind.: Concordia Theological Seminary Press, 1979.

Weidenhiller, Egino. *Untersuchungen zur deutschsprachigen katechetischen Literatur des späten Mittelalters*. Munich, 1965.

Weinrich, William C. "Early Christian Catechetics: An Historical and Theological Construction." In *Luther's Catechisms—450 Years*, edited by David P. Scaer and Robert D. Preus, 64–73. Fort Wayne, Ind.: Concordia Theological Seminary Press, 1979.

Wengert, Timothy J. "'Fear and Love' in the Ten Commandments." *Concordia Journal* 21 (1995): 14–27.

———. "Forming the Faith Today through Luther's Catechisms." *Lutheran Quarterly*, n.s., 11 (1997): 379–96.

———, ed. *Harvesting Martin Luther's Reflections on Theology, Ethics, and the Church*. Grand Rapids: Eerdmans, 2003.

———. *Law and Gospel: Philip Melanchthon's Debate with John Agricola of Eisleben over "Poenitentia."* Grand Rapids, Mich.: Baker, 1997.

———. "Luther on Children: Baptism and the Fourth Commandment." *Dialog* 37 (1998): 185–89.

———. "Luther on Prayer in the Large Catechism." *Lutheran Quarterly* 18 (2004): 249–74.

———. "Luther's Catechisms and the Lord's Supper." *Word and World* 17 (1997): 54–60.

———. "Martin Luther and the Ten Commandments in the Large Catechism." *Currents in Theology and Mission* 31 (2004): 104–14.

———. "Wittenberg's Earliest Catechism." *Lutheran Quarterly*, n.s., 7 (1993): 247–60.

Wingren, Gustav. *Luther on Vocation*. Translated by Carl C. Rasmussen. Philadelphia: Muhlenberg Press, 1957.

Ludwig, Alan. "Preaching and Teaching the Creed: The Structures of the Small Catechism's Explanations as Guides." *Logia: A Journal of Lutheran Theology* 3, no. 4 (October 1994): 11–24.

Luther, Martin. *The Large and Small Catechisms. D. Martin Luthers Werke: Kritische Gesamtausgabe*, vol. 30, pt. 1. Weimar: Hermann Böhlaus Nachfolger, 1910.

Luther's Small Catechism: A New English Translation Prepared by an Intersynodical Committee [With an Historical Introduction]: A Jubilee Offering, 1529–1929. Columbus, Ohio: Lutheran Book Concern, 1929.

Marshall, Ronald F. "Luther the Lumberjack." *Lutheran Quarterly*, n.s., 10 (1996): 107–10.

Mattes, John C. "The English Translation of Luther's Small Catechism by Thomas Cranmer." *Lutheran Church Review* 46 (1927): 60–90.

———, ed. *Luther's Small Catechism in the English Translation of Thomas Cranmer MDXLVIII*. Philadelphia: United Lutheran Publishing House, n.d. [1948?].

Nestingen, James A. "Preaching the Catechism." *Word and World* 10 (1990): 33–42.

Peters, Albrecht. "Die Theologie der Katechismen Luthers anhand der Zuordnung ihrer Hauptstücke." *Luther-Jahrbuch* 43 (1976): 2–35.

———. *Kommentar zu Luthers Katechismen*. 5 vols. Göttingen: Vandenhoeck & Ruprecht, 1990–1994.

Pless, John T. "Catechesis for Life in the Royal Priesthood." *Logia: A Journal of Lutheran Theology* 3, no. 4 (October 1994): 3–10.

Raabe, Paul R. "Children's Sermons and Luther's Small Catechism." *Concordia Journal* 15 (1989): 100–102.

Reed, Stephen D. "The Decalogue in Luther's Large Catechism." *Dialog* 22 (1983): 264–69.

Repp, Arthur C., Sr. *Luther's Catechism Comes to America*. Metuchen, N.J.: Scarecrow Press, 1982.

Reu, Michael. "Luthers Katechismus in Zeitalter der Orthodoxie," *Allgemeine Evangelisch-Lutherische Kirchenzeitung* 62 (1929): 462–66, 485–92.

———. *Luther's Small Catechism*. Chicago: Wartburg Publishing House, 1929.

———. *Quellen zur Geschichte des Katechismus Unterrichts*. 10 vols. Guetersloh: Bertelsmann, 1904–1932.

———. "Religious Instruction of the Young in the 16th Century." *Lutheran Church Review* 34 (1915): 566–85.

Rietschel, G. "Die erste Ausgabe des kleinen Katechismus in Tafelform." *Theologische Studien und Kritiken* 71 (1898): 522–27.

Roschke, Ronald W. "A Catechism on Luther's Catechisms." *Currents in Theology and Mission* 4 (1977): 68–75.

Saarnivaara, Uuras. "Baptism and Faith according to Luther's Catechisms and Other Teachings," in *Luther's Catechisms—450 Years*, edited by David P. Scaer and Robert D. Preus, 27–31. Fort Wayne, Ind.: Concordia Theological Seminary Press, 1979.

Scaer, David P. "The New Translation of Luther's Small Catechism: Is It Faithful to Luther's Spirit?," in *Luther's Catechisms—450 Years*. Edited by David P. Scaer and Robert D. Preus. Fort Wayne, Indiana: Concordia Theological Seminary Press, 1979, pp. 32–40.

Schaaf, James L. "The Large Catechism: A Pastoral Tool." In *Luther's Catechisms—450 Years*, edited by David P. Scaer and Robert D. Preus, 41–46. Fort Wayne, Ind.: Concordia Theological Seminary Press, 1979.

Scharffenorth, Gerta. "The Ecumenicity of Luther's Catechism." *Mid-Stream* 23 (1984): 162–75.

Schmidt, Martin. "August Hermann Franckes Katechismuspredigten." *Luther-Jahrbuch* 33 (1966): 88–117.